FEMINISM AND BLACK ACTIVISM IN CONTEMPORARY AMERICA

Recent Titles in
Contributions in Women's Studies

Feminism and Black Activism in Contemporary America

AN IDEOLOGICAL ASSESSMENT

Irvin D. Solomon

CONTRIBUTIONS IN WOMEN'S STUDIES, NUMBER 106

GREENWOOD PRESS
New York • Westport, Connecticut • London

Library of Congress Cataloging-in-Publication Data

Solomon, Irvin D.
  Feminism and Black activism in contemporary America : an
ideological assessment / Irvin D. Solomon.
    p. cm.—(Contributions in women's studies, ISSN 0147–104X ;
no. 106)
  Bibliography: p.
  Includes index.
  ISBN 0–313–26204–7 (lib. bdg. : alk. paper)
    1. Social movements—United States. 2. Civil rights movements—
United States. 3. Afro-Americans—Civil rights. 4. Afro-
Americans—Social conditions. 5. Black nationalism—United States.
6. Feminism—United States. 7. Women—United States—Social
conditions. 6. Women's rights—United States. I. Title.
II. Series.
  HN65.S583   1989
  303.4′84—dc19   89–1980

British Library Cataloguing in Publication Data is available.

Library of Congress Catalog Card Number: 89–1980
ISBN: 0–313–26204–7
ISSN: 0147–104X

First published in 1989

Greenwood Press, Inc.
88 Post Road West, Westport, Connecticut 06881

Printed in the United States of America

The paper used in this book complies with the
Permanent Paper Standard issued by the National
Information Standards Organization (Z39.48–1984).

10 9 8 7 6 5 4 3 2 1

Copyright Acknowledgment

Grateful acknowledgment is given for permission to quote
from Robin Morgan, ''Letter to a Sister Underground,'' from
Monster: Poems by Robin Morgan © 1972, published by
Random House, Inc.

To Betsy L. Winsboro,
my inspiration

Contents

Preface

In the following pages readers will find an analysis of the analogy between recent black activism and modern feminism, two major historical and contemporary social movements. In addressing this issue I have proposed a three-part methodology that focuses on the legal, cultural and economic phases of race and sex protest, past and present. I have concluded that although the women's movement developed from a number of sources, including civil rights activity, it was primarily women's own protest history and commitment that led to the contemporary so-called third wave of feminism.

I believe this type of study is significant in a number of ways. As this book goes to press, no study as yet links the two movements under review in a systematic way.[1] Also, this work can be of immense value to readers, including students and advanced scholars of the movements, because it brings together a critical corpus of materials on race and gender protest movements. In this regard, the reader is especially encouraged to review the Notes and the Selected Bibliography, and thus use this volume as a sourcebook as well as a focused study.

Throughout the preparation of this study I have endeavored to err on the side of readability over jargon in the hopes of broadening its popular appeal. I feel it is valuable to capture the movements in this sort of insightful study, but I believe that such scholarship should appeal equally to the academic and nonacademic communities. If historians should teach meaningful lessons regarding how we as a people might better understand the historical inter-relatedness of events, the society in which we live and the possibility for bettering that society, then we must move away from the arcane toward creating new works on the common ground of understanding. As a trained and active historian, I see our profession as serving its greatest usefulness by reaching out to all disciplines and to all levels of readers, not solely to others who happen to hold advanced degrees in history. If historians have berated the late-nineteenth-century artists of the Western world for "creating art only for other artists," our profession should beware of making precisely the same mistake—turning out scholarship solely for other historians.

Despite the amount of time spent in preparing such a study, one inevitably encounters criticism of the methodology and analysis or the overuse or underuse of certain sources. There will be those who suggest that I should have explored and used this particular source or probed and developed that significant line of inquiry. Yet by their focusing on such concerns, I will have, in effect, done my job by forcing them to conceptualize in perhaps new and meaningful ways about this subject matter. On the other hand, I will refer persistent critics to the groundbreaking fourteenth-century Arab historian Ibn Khaldûn, who once prophetically stated about his ambitious synthesis of history *The Muqaddimah*, "I confess my inability to penetrate so difficult a subject. I wish that men of scholarly competence and wide knowledge would look at the book with a critical, rather than a complacent eye, and silently correct and overlook the mistakes they come upon. The capital of knowledge that an individual scholar has to offer is small. Admission (of one's short-comings) saves from censure. Kindness from colleagues is hoped for."[2]

NOTES

1. Sara Evans's *Personal Politics: The Roots of Women's Liberation in the Civil Rights Movement and the New Left* (New York: Vintage, 1979), perhaps comes closest to fulfilling this mission, although it is primarily a study of the personal rather than the ideological linkages of the two movements under review.

2. Ibn Khaldûn, *The Muqaddimah: An Introduction to History*, trans. Franz Rosenthal (New York: Pantheon, 1958), Vol. 1, 14.

Acknowledgments

Many individuals contributed time and energy to this project, but none offered more scholarly assistance and personal encouragement than Robert L. Zangrando, Sheldon B. Liss and Betsy L. Winsboro. James F. Richardson, Daniel Nelson, Robert H. Jones and the late Warren F. Kuehl offered constructive criticism and support on early drafts, and David B. Mock, F. P. Cremonese and Anne M. Marcus tendered especially felicitous comments on later revisions. Additionally, I would like to thank Greenwood editors Jackie Remlinger and Arlene Belzer, the latter of whom especially helped me bring a manuscript into conformity with a publisher's rigorous standards and priorities.

I am grateful also for the assistance of the research staffs at the University of Akron, the University of Wisconsin, the State Historical Society of Wisconsin, the University of Pittsburgh, Case Western Reserve University, Howard University, Radcliffe University, The University of Washington Libraries, the KNOW, Inc. Library, the Library of Congress and the National Archives. Those persons who shared personal collections with me or allowed me to interview them for this study were almost uniformly supportive and gracious with their time; especially helpful was the late Pauli Murray, who prodded me into asking not just questions but the right kinds of questions about the two movements. Others too numerous to mention helped me discover facts about the movements and give them meaning. The author, however, accepts sole responsibility for the interpretation and presentation of those facts.

Abbreviations

A-APRP	All-Afrikan People's Revolutionary Party
AFL-CIO	American Federation of Labor and Congress of Industrial Organizations
AWSA	American Woman Suffrage Association
CACSW	Citizens' Advisory Council on the Status of Women
CLUW	Coalition of Labor Union Women
COFO	Council of Federated Organizations
CORE	Congress of Racial Equality
CP-USA	Communist Party of the United States of America
CR	consciousness raising
EEOC	Equal Employment Opportunity Commission
ERA	Equal Rights Amendment (federal)
IDCSW	Interdepartmental Committee on the Status of Women
Inc. Fund	Legal Defense and Education Fund
KNOW	Pittsburgh Area Feminist Work and Publishing Collective
LDF	Legal Defense Fund (NOW)
LDF	Legal Defense Fund (WEAL)
MCP	male chauvinist pig
MFDP	Mississippi Freedom Democratic Party
MIA	Montgomery Improvement Association
MOWM	March on Washington Movement
NAACP	National Association for the Advancement of Colored People

NAWSA	National American Woman Suffrage Association
NBFO	National Black Feminist Organization
NCNP	National Conference for a New Politics
NOW	National Organization for Women
NUL	National Urban League
NWP	National Woman's Party
NWPC	National Women's Political Caucus
NWSA	National Woman Suffrage Association
NWSA	National Women's Studies Association
NYRF	New York Radical Feminists
NYRW	New York Radical Women
OFCC	Office of Federal Contract Compliance
RNA	Republic of New Africa
RW	Seattle Radical Women
SCLC	Southern Christian Leadership Conference
SCUM	Society for Cutting Up Men
SDS	Students for a Democratic Society
SNCC	Student Nonviolent Coordinating Committee
SPA	Socialist Party of America
SWP	Socialist Workers Party
SWP/YSA	Socialist Workers Party/Young Socialist Alliance
UNIA	Universal Negro Improvement Association
VWLM	*Voice of the Women's Liberation Movement*
WEAL	Women's Equity Action League
WITCH	Women's International Terrorist Conspiracy from Hell

Introduction: Perspective and Methodology

This study is designed to place into historical perspective certain ideological relationships between recent black activism and contemporary feminism by assessing their roots, mutual goals, parallel strategies, common obstacles and shared ranges of responses. Although relevant background discussions will be presented as necessary, investigation will focus primarily on the mid-twentieth-century years when massive direct actions on both national and grass-roots levels dominated race and sex protest theory and lent them definable characteristics. By the 1960s and 1970s public protest forced many issues to the top of the national agenda: race, sex, peace, student rights, education, environmental protection, implications of advanced technology, youth and counterculture movements, and consumer protection. Yet in terms of social policy, it was primarily the civil rights and the women's movements which led to a fundamental and lasting reappraisal of American attitudes and values. Consequently, the ultimate purpose of this book is to highlight ideological interconnections between race and sex protests, two of the most significant movements of contemporary times, and to discuss how they evolved from being groups *in* themselves to groups *for* themselves.

It is useful to note that in the 1960s and 1970s blacks and women were often set apart from white male protesters in the other protest movements. Frequently these men found no impediments to their re-entry into the dominant social currents after their protest commitment had run its course. Blacks and women, on the other hand, suffered collective discriminations that impeded their entry (let alone re-entry) into those mainstream currents. This fact both physically and psychologically distinguished their activism from the other groups that challenged the nation's moral and social fabric during this time. There tended to be relatively little sustained interaction with other contemporary movements: blacks and women were, after all, challenging historical patterns of discrimination grounded in negative perceptions of biological differences rather than simply assaulting contemporary philosophical, political and ideological targets.

Race and sex protests are not exclusively twentieth-century phenomena. Indeed, such protests have occurred in America since the earliest colonial days. The second chapter will establish this trend, while developing the theme that race and sex protests have appeared historically as personal and organizational challenges to elitist notions that there are inferior beings in society who must be relegated to their proper place and proper role. This chapter will present a thematic basis for contemporary race and gender protest in theory and in practice. Subsequent chapters will expand on an understanding of the roots and development of contemporary feminism as it becomes our primary focus. It will therefore be necessary to recapitulate only peripherally the experiences of the organizationally older black movement. By following such a methodological approach, it is the author's hope that the contemporary women's movement will come to be understood as a social protest movement of indigenous origin. It is, however, one not totally inconsistent with the goals, strategies and experiences of past and parallel protest movements, for example, black civil rights. A further, and perhaps more important, desire is that the reader will use this work as a heuristic tool by which to discover and explore uncharted and potentially significant lines of inquiry into these two singularly important social protests.

A protest movement is defined as a form of collective behavior with theoretical and organizational contours, definable rules and traditions, and stability and continuity over time. The goals of such movements, as Ralph H. Turner and Lewis M. Killian pointed out, include the reformation of society, the realignment of power and economic relationships favorable to the movement and the promotion of various schemes designed to result in group empowerment.[1] In studying contemporary struggles, researchers such as Doug McAdam and Jo Freeman suggested that race and gender protest movements are comprised largely of groups perceiving themselves as locked out of society's policy-making framework.[2] Those who feel relatively powerless seek to mobilize impact. The movement thus becomes the vehicle by which the powerless or the marginally powerful seek to gain wider entry into the policy-making arena of any given society.

Such powerless groups, as English scholar E. P. Thompson concluded some years ago, have suffered historically from a minority status within the larger society.[3] American race and ethnic scholar Louis Wirth discussed minority-group status in similar terms:

We may define a minority as a group of people who, because of their physical or cultural characteristics, are singled out from the others in the society in which they live for differential and unequal treatment, and who therefore regard themselves as objects of collective discrimination. The existence of a minority in a society implies the existence of a corresponding dominant group enjoying higher social status and greater privileges. Minority status carries with it the exclusion from full participation in the life of the society.[4]

Given the treatment accorded them and the discrimination they suffered, women, despite their recent standing as a numerical majority, still suffer a rather unique status in terms of their historical, systematic exclusion from power within the American institutional framework. For women, like blacks, the relationship between dominant group and minority status rests on ranking and privilege, not numbers.

In the past most sociological and historical treatments of race and sex protests as manifestations of minority group responses to collective discrimination have, as historian William H. Chafe noted, focused on the experience of blacks or women as the "other half."[5] The "other half," of course, referred to the fact that blacks and women commonly have been defined by social scientists as analogous powerless groups. Because of immutable facts of nature (i.e., race and sex), they are said to have qualities different from the privileged group (i.e., white males), which most often sets the standards for acceptable attitudes, roles and behavior in society. It is a commonplace that such cross-group awareness of injustice has led to similar patterns of protest. The question now becomes: if so, then to what extent did older black protest ideologically nurture feminism? Surely this is a complicated and controversial query, and one that has been heretofore only partially explored.

Although the literature on the two movements is indeed voluminous, scholars have seldom endeavored to build a conceptual framework with which to assess the possible parallels or the dynamic interplay between race and sex protests. It seemed instructive when undertaking this work to develop a theory of ideological interaction as an interconnection between the two groups in order to assess the parallels and the extent of shared protest experiences. The adopted theoretical framework involves a threefold model that deals primarily with the similar obstacles, strategies, tactics and goals of historical race and sex protests that have led to presumed typological relationships between those two movements.

At first it seemed feasible to approach the question of such ideological relationships between contemporary black activism and feminism from two directions: that of black and female assimilationists (i.e., the elimination of a social stigma through legal-traditional reform), and that of black and female separatists (i.e., the militant repudiation of an unjust society through various nontraditional demands for cultural autonomy). But it soon became apparent that a third empirical mode of personal and organizational protest profoundly characterized race and sex protests. This was the economic-determinist perspective (i.e., the concept that no capitalist society can ever be free of social ranking). It is important to note that numerous crosscurrents of allegiance existed among protesters themselves, and it was therefore difficult to establish the exact level of participation each of the three models commanded in terms of numbers, longevity and intensity. Moreover, even though some protesters' enthusiasms shifted from one approach to another in a rather fluid fashion, the transition itself was not necessarily sequential, as categories tended to connect or overlap in particular ways over time and space.

We have, then, three major ideological paradigms by which to identify and examine possible intersections of contemporary black activism and feminism. The first of our three categories, the legal approach, assumes that a large number of protesters have sought primarily to create a more egalitarian society with full social integration. This group does not seek to overturn society, but rather to reform it through traditional legal measures so that blacks and women may participate on more equitable terms.

Unlike the legalists, the cultural-nationalists see little possibility for meaningful reconciliation with the targets of their protests. Cultural-oriented women reject legal assimilation in favor of radical unorthodox alternative arrangements that stress self-definition and intragroup strength practiced apart from the dominant group. The practitioners of this, the radical phase, and usually the most kinetic phase of protest, argue that the powerful exhibit such a high degree of control that they will accept only those reforms that diffuse protest and co-opt minority members. But it must be understood that this typology frequently did not involve the kind of clear, systematic arguments indicative of neatly defined contextual categories. For example, the women of Seneca Falls in the nineteenth century were both reformist and radical in nature since they sought legal change while simultaneously challenging deeply rooted cultural norms like the concept of the "cult of domesticity." Accordingly, this category in particular must be seen in light of efforts to understand the developments of contemporary black activism and feminism, not to lock each into rigid ideological barriers.

The third protest phase relies on Marxist/socialist economic precepts. Indicative of anticapitalist approaches, these protesters assume that minority-status emancipation lies in social revolution and significant alterations in the traditional mode of production and distribution. The proponents of this line, the economic phase of protest, argue that all hierarchical social systems are based historically in private property ownership and have a distinct relationship to production and market values in capitalist society. What has occurred in recent years, however, is the rise of neo-Marxists who find the older orthodox Marxist critique guilty of economic myopia. Its analysis, they claim, has failed to recognize social, political and psychological oppressions derived not solely from modes of production. What has evolved from this approach is a contemporary radical Marxist/minority-status paradigm based on a social liberation deemed impossible under capitalism and improbable under communism. What is needed, the new Marxists argue, is a truly wrenching social upheaval that will change the very cultural fiber of society as well as its economic institutions.

To recapitulate briefly, this work represents an effort to explore the common ground of ideological and behavioral relationships between contemporary black activism and feminism. The framework within which we shall examine the roots, development and nature of race and sex protests involves a three-pronged approach: (1) legal-oriented protest; (2) cultural-oriented protest; and (3) economic-oriented protest. While it is not argued that these are original methodologies, it is my contention that the three paradigms offer useful ideological and conceptual frameworks to this project by addressing systematically the three major underlying currents of past and modern race and sex protests. But the reader is cautioned that these are not rigid protest models, and over time and space there have been numerous points of intersection and divergence from them by groups and individuals alike. Looking to the past, then, one realizes that twentieth-century civil rights and feminist activists who adopted these models were the heirs of a long and vigorous protest history. Looking toward the future, one hopes that this study will contribute in sound and useful ways to the growing body of scholarship on race and sex protest.

NOTES

1. Ralph H. Turner and Lewis M. Killian, "Social Movements: Character and Processes," in Ralph H. Turner and Lewis M. Killian, eds., *Collective Behavior* (Englewood Cliffs, NJ: Prentice-Hall, 1972), 245–56.

2. Doug McAdam, *Political Process and the Development of Black Insurgency, 1930–1970* (Chicago: University of Chicago Press, 1982), 1–19; Jo Freeman, *The Politics of Women's Liberation: A Case Study of an Emerging Social Movement and Its Relation to the Policy Process* (New York: David McKay, 1975), 4, see 1–11.

3. E. P. Thompson, *The Making of the English Working Class* (New York: Pantheon, 1964), 9–10.

4. Louis Wirth, "The Problem of Minority Groups," in Ralph Linton, ed., *The Science of Man in the World Crisis* (New York: Columbia University Press, 1945), 347.

5. William H. Chafe, *Women and Equality: Changing Patterns in American Culture* (New York: Oxford University Press, 1977), vii–viii.

The Long March Forward: Modern Black Activism and Contemporary Feminism Come of Age

In this chapter we shall analyze and put into historical perspective the roots of contemporary black and female protests through three ideological approaches: the traditional or legal/reform approach; the radical or cultural/ nationalistic approach; and the economic or Marxist/socialist approach. These models are designed to focus attention on three particular strains of protest ideology whose backgrounds may reflect either shared or unique lessons for the two movements under study.

ORIGINS AND DEVELOPMENT OF CONTEMPORARY BLACK PROTEST

The Legal/Lobbying Approach: The NAACP and the NUL as Models

In 1910 literary figure H. L. Mencken wrote that the

Negro of today is a failure, not because he meets insuperable difficulties in life, but because he is a Negro. His brain is not fitted for the higher forms of mental effort; his ideals, no matter how laboriously he is trained and sheltered, remain those of a clown. He is, in brief, a low-caste man, to the manner [sic] born, and he will remain inert and inefficient until fifty generations of him have lived in civilization. And even then, the superior white race will be fifty generations ahead of him.[1]

Many whites growing up in the years prior to World War I shared Mencken's views. For black America these attitudes often were translated into strict codes that governed the conduct of race relations and served to circumscribe black life and opportunity within the confines of what whites thought to be "proper place." It is against this backdrop that interracial liberals of the Progressive era banded together to form the National Association for the Advancement of Colored People (NAACP) and the National Urban League (NUL). One cannot understand the nature and thrust of contemporary civil rights without exploring the background and program of these two organizations.

Since its creation in 1909 the National Association for the Advancement of Colored People's program has demanded immediate and full integration of black America into the mainstream of society. Like other mass membership reform organizations, the NAACP operated through a national leadership body working in concert with state and local branches.[2] As the NAACP grew over the years to become the largest civil rights organization, it remained loyal to its initial program of working for change within the system through legal maneuvers, especially those of lobbying and litigation.[3]

The impetus for the National Urban League came as much from whites as from blacks. The NUL organized shortly after the NAACP and in its early years shared many of the latter's characteristics.[4] Initially, the League sought guarantees of employment opportunities for blacks from organized labor and the business community; by the outset of World War II the NUL had established a more conservative and less confrontational image than the NAACP.[5] As Executive Director Lester B. Granger recalled, by 1940 the League functioned primarily as a "professional social welfare agency for urban Negroes."[6]

From the outset the NAACP and the NUL shared an interracial character based on the premise that meaningful change for black Americans could be gained by working within the American democratic framework rather than against it. Such goals and strategies were stated in the NAACP's journal, *The Crisis*, and in the NUL's journal, *Opportunity*. Both publications have educated the black community by disseminating information and by setting and reflecting a wide range of civil rights priorities. In this respect the programs of the NAACP and the NUL have provided guidelines for many subsequent social crusades, although certainly the NAACP offered the stronger model over the years.

The Cultural/Nationalistic Approach: Marcus Garvey as Model

Compared to the fledgling NAACP and NUL, Marcus Garvey's more militant movement in the 1920s symbolized a resurrected sense of historical black pride and activism. While all blacks did not agree with Garvey's radical theories, few could deny that his program greatly altered black consciousness. His brand of nationalism and his program for self-definition and for total emancipation from white domination were worldwide in scope and attracted adherents from as far away as Africa. Moreover, by virtue of its vast membership and financial backing, Garvey's Universal Negro Improvement Association ranked as one of America's historically noteworthy social protests.[7]

The UNIA found its roots in the advocacy of anti-integrationist black cultural nationalism—what many have termed Negritude or Pan-Africanism—and the dignity and beauty of blackness; its concept of indigenous power and pride explained its phenomenal appeal to the black masses. As Garvey stated, "let us not waste time in breathless appeals to the strong while we are weak."[8] In particular, the UNIA sought to develop race pride, to create an independent black nation in Africa and to gain the allegiance of "oppressed" black communities in the United States. Garvey's movement crystalized into a new militancy and thus eclipsed older Pan-African movements like that of Dr. W.E.B. DuBois.[9] Garvey's worldview lived on after his demise and in this sense continued a long scenario of black nationalism encouraged by such earlier individuals as Martin R. Delany, Bishop Henry M. Turner, Benjamin "Pap" Singleton and Professor Edward W. Blyden.[10]

Nationalism itself is a complex structure which may incorporate political, cultural, economic, religious, ideological and sometimes territorial themes. Separatism is a subcategory of nationalism that can be practiced both territorially and, as Robert L. Zangrando has demonstrated, psychologically.[11] Within this framework, it becomes apparent that separation could be practiced at the local or community level, or by the nation-within-a-nation concept, or through Pan-Africanism as an ultimate, worldwide expression (e.g., reunification of the African Diaspora). Another view of Pan-Africanism is that black people everywhere should practice an African cultural unity—a cultural nationalism.

Indeed, Garvey's particular brand of cultural nationalism presented a bold vision to disenchanted black Americans. Employing the strident rhetoric of self-determination and separation, Garvey developed institutions to meet the particular needs of black people, such as his Black Star Line, Black Cross Navigation and Trading Company, Negro Factories Corporation, African Legion, and Black Cross Nurses—all of which offered structural alternatives to white-controlled institutions. But Garveyism itself floundered after its leader was jailed in 1925 for mail fraud. Following President Coolidge's commutation of his sentence in 1927, Garvey moved back to his native Jamaica and later relocated to London, where he remained until his death in 1940.

The legacy of Garveyism is singularly important because it has offered working models of black nationalistic mass movements, especially those of a separatist nature, to more recent militants. Later black nationalists would be strongly influenced by the memories of Garveyism. The Black Muslims, Stokely Carmichael and the Republic of New Africa traced the origin of their emphasis on nationalism back to Garvey. Malcolm X, whose father was a Garveyite, and Dr. Martin Luther King, Jr., also recognized the UNIA's founder as a moving force behind modern Black Power ideologies.[12]

After the demise of Garveyism, the Depression and New Deal years starkly revealed how white America viewed its black citizens. The lean years of the 1930s also demonstrated an important analogy between blacks and women in that both were considered expendable components of the labor market.[13] Not only did these two groups suffer the most visible aspects of a "last hired, first fired" practice, but similar wage discrimination patterns characterized those who did find work. For example, the median earning in 1939 for white males was $1,112 and for white women was $672, while that for black males was $460 and for black women was $246.[14] It may be true then that New Deal programs had a positive psychological effect on Afro-Americans, yet they had almost negligible practical economic effects.[15] Even the NAACP, which had seen the 1930s as an especially propitious time to steer a long-desired antilynching bill through Congress, stated flatly: "On the subject of the Negro, the Roosevelt record [is] spotty."[16] Out of this sea of despair, Afro-Americans increasingly gravitated toward radical economic solutions. The Communist Party (CP-USA) especially became a visible champion of black justice during this period.

The Marxist/Socialist Approach: The CP-USA as Model

The mid–1930s marked an important turning point in the communist courtship of black Americans. In earlier decades the CP-USA argued for the creation of a separate state, the so-called Black Republic, to guarantee true black self-determination. Possibly the Party adopted the separatist-nationalist position as a result of Garveyism. However, evidence indicates that the CP-USA attracted mostly intellectuals and never established a true base of solidarity among the black masses as Garvey and the UNIA had done.[17] A survey published by *Opportunity* in May 1932, for example, showed that only 51 black Americans out of 3,973 polled supported the Communist presidential nominee.[18]

A few articulate black males did rise to positions of prominence within Communist Party circles, including George Padmore (the foremost black figure in the Communist International); James W. Ford (The CP-USA's candidate for vice-president of the United States in 1932); Benjamin Davis, Jr. (the second black member of the New York City Council); Claude M. Lightfoot (the CP-USA delegate to the Seventh World Congress of the Communist International in Moscow, 1935); and Angelo Herndon (who, in the 1930s, gained widespread support around the country after he was charged with a violation of an 1869 Georgia insurrection statute).[19] On balance, nonetheless, the CP-USA had little effect on Afro-Americans, who in most cases saw its civil rights statements as shallow and vacillating. Furthermore, the CP-USA's policies challenged the American democratic ideal, which many blacks, despite the racism scarring it, were reluctant to repudiate.[20] Still the CP-USA, unlike the American Socialist Party, did make special overtures to blacks and over the years continued to speak to race concerns.

The Marxist appeal largely dissolved with the advent of World War II, not to arise again for decades as a major protest ideology. That blacks remained

only peripherally concerned with the Marxists and that the Communists themselves remained only peripherally concerned with the race question, remained a salient factor characterizing the nature of black/Marxist allegiances
until a new synthesis of race and Marxism would appear in the 1960s.

World War II and Its Aftermath

World War II itself fostered a reborn spirit of legal protest designed to
bring race concepts into conformity with America's democratic creed, much
as had been the experience of World War I. At the outset of the war many
industries refused to drop their color line against the hiring of nonwhite
males, while the Army, Army Air Corps, Navy and Marines continued to restrict
nonwhites to "mess duty" or to "general service" units (a euphemism for
segregated corps).[21] A wide range of black leaders immediately voiced concerns.[22] As black sociologist E. Franklin Frazier noted in 1942:

The present war has brought to the surface the changes that have taken place in the
Negro's attitude toward his status in America during the past quarter of a century.
Although the first World War was a struggle for democracy, the most radical leaders
expressed the faith that the Negro's status would be improved after the war and
advocated the "closing of ranks" and forgetting of wrongs and injustices. During the
last twenty-five years the isolation of the Negro has been broken down, and he has
been brought into contact with a larger world of ideas. The traditional relationship
of loyalty to whites has been destroyed, and race consciousness and loyalty to his
race have taken its place.[23]

The NAACP's *The Crisis* spoke more directly to the domestic issue of World
War II: "This is no fight merely to wear a uniform. This is a struggle for status,
a struggle to take democracy off of parchment and give it life."[24]

Against this backdrop A. Philip Randolph, long-time socialist and head of
the largely black Brotherhood of Sleeping Car Porters, called on blacks to
unite in a mass march on the nation's capital.[25] To coordinate the effort,
reminiscent of Garveyism, Randolph formed the March on Washington Movement (MOWM), an all-black effort whose goal was to create "faith and confidence of the Negro people in their own power for self-liberation."[26]

The MOWM's goals, imaginative tactics and broad-based orientation struck
a responsive chord among the legion of wartime unemployed and disenchanted blacks. Reacting to Randolph's assertion that he could march "100,000
strong" on Washington, moderate civil rights leaders from the NAACP and
other groups moved to dissuade him from his scheme. Randolph remained
adamant until President Roosevelt promised him an executive order with
"teeth in it." Roosevelt soon delivered Executive Order 8802 which established a Committee on Fair Employment Practice in the Office of Production
Management. Only then did Randolph cancel the march.[27] Both the NAACP
and NUL, which had initially opposed Randolph's new "radical" tactic, reacted

optimistically to the announcement of a new federal commitment to their cause,[28] demonstrating that the term "radical" itself could undergo swift and dramatic alteration of perception based on changing protest milieus. In retrospect, Randolph's MOWM presaged what would become the symbol of major social protest in the late 1950s and 1960s, namely mass, nonviolent demonstrations of unity and power designed to push the federal government to new levels of awareness and commitment. Moreover, the moderate/radical dichotomy engendered by Randolph's strident rhetoric presaged later conflicts in both movements under review in this study.

The complex issues of war and domestic policy that had spawned the MOWM led to the creation of the nation's third major civil rights organization, the Congress of Racial Equality (CORE), which would come to represent another example of the moderate/radical metamorphosis. In many respects, as August Meier and Elliott Rudwick have demonstrated, CORE, like the MOWM, foreshadowed the goals, tactics and strategies of mid-twentieth-century black masses, and economic matters pertinent to the quality of black life in America.[29]

First organized in 1942 as an outgrowth of the Fellowship of Reconciliation, a pacifist group of some 12,000 members, the new organization proposed to attack the racial problems of Chicago at a time when the issues of global racism and human rights loomed in the American mind.[30] The group combined the 1930's union sit-down techniques with the direct-action techniques of Gandhian satyagraha to introduce what would later become the radical tactic of the nonviolent sit-in.[31] Within a year this tactic had prompted a number of Chicago restaurants to drop their "color line."[32]

During the 1940s the NAACP eschewed such tactics and continued to seek reform solely through legal and judicial means. It underwrote numerous amicus briefs and initiated or backed a number of important court cases, including the precedent-setting *Mitchell* v. *U.S.* (1941), which stated that blacks in possession of first-class passenger tickets had to be provided accommodations equal in comfort and convenience to those provided whites, and *Smith* v. *Allwright* (1944), which declared all-white primary elections unconstitutional.[33] The NAACP also shifted its substantial judicial program to the newly tax-exempt Legal Defense and Education Fund, later known as the Inc. Fund, which has been widely emulated by other organizations. The brilliant black lawyer Thurgood Marshall, who had served as both assistant special counsel and special counsel to the NAACP, molded it into one of the nation's most respected legal machines. Through the 1950s the Inc. Fund had participated directly in more than twenty important Supreme Court civil rights decisions and helped move a reluctant Congress toward the weak Civil Rights Act of 1957.[34] As constitutional scholar Alfred H. Kelly noted, the NAACP's judicial thrusts remained the real "cutting edge" of the civil rights movement until the dramatic actions of the mid–1950s,[35] after which the judicial thrust paled somewhat in comparison to other tactics, as we shall see, but nevertheless remained a singularly important strategy of contemporary protest.

It was in the mid–1950s, too, that the Supreme Court dealt with the paramount issue of segregation itself in *Brown* v. *Board of Education*, a landmark ruling striking down the "separate-but-equal" principle in public education.[36] Because President Eisenhower declined to support the decision actively, most states of the Deep South either ignored the decision or, sensing the weak enforcement measures forthcoming from Washington, openly disavowed legal integration.[37] In many ways the unanimous *Brown* decision and its aftermath embodied the theme of promise and betrayal which had underwritten the civil rights struggle for so many years. Against this backdrop of rising expectations and continuing disillusionmnent emerged a new and unprecedented era of black protest.

A Quarter Century of Fervent Activism, 1955–1980: A Confluence of Models

The civil rights movement underwent dramatic alterations in structure and style in the mid–1950s. The period of black political and social impotency in the United States, which noted researcher Gunnar Myrdal identified with great foresight in 1944 as an "interregnum," seemed destined by the late 1950s to crumble under its own weight.[38] Certainly, as we have noted, the events and the people that brought about these changes benefited from an important and varied black protest legacy; equally important, nevertheless, was the altered political and social context in which these changes occurred. The result was two and a half decades of accelerated civil rights protests, in which many streams of ideology burst forth to unleash one of the greatest social and cultural upheavals this nation has witnessed.

The unlikely catalyst for this event was a black seamstress, Rosa Parks, who on December 1, 1955, ignored a Montgomery, Alabama, segregation code by refusing to give up her seat on a city bus to a white man. Parks later recalled that on that day she "was especially tired and acted spontaneously, although [she] had always found the rule distasteful anyway."[39] The arrest of the widely respected Parks triggered a long-simmering reaction, eventually resulting in her becoming the symbol of the spontaneous moral repudiation of unjust laws and practices. Almost overnight 17,500 black commuters instituted an effective transit boycott; black church leaders quickly formed the Montgomery Improvement Association (MIA) to coordinate its activities under the direction of Dr. Martin Luther King, Jr., a young inspirational Baptist minister from Atlanta, Georgia.[40]

The Montgomery protest represented a true watershed in the historical civil rights movement. Through the late 1950s and early 1960s the movement increased with such fervor and velocity that terms like *Negro revolution* and *black revolt* came to characterize both its demands and intensity. The branch of the movement led by King expanded quickly, notably in the form of the Southern Christian Leadership Conference (SCLC), created in 1957 to coordinate the new spate of nonviolent protest activities throughout the South.[41] Initially, King and other apostles of nonviolence became the most visible leaders of the new social activism; however, by the mid–1960s a restated militant nationalism much along the Garvey lines appeared, resulting in a profound alteration of black protest goals and tactics.

On February 1, 1960, four black students of North Carolina Agricultural and Technical College in Greensboro staged a sit-in that set off a protest train of events dramatically transfiguring the movement. The students' arrest and removal from the white-only lunch counter at Woolworth's galvanized others into action throughout the South; in a little over a year 74,000 student protesters had staged sit-ins in eleven southern states.[42] The successes of their actions soon challenged the pre-eminence of the legal-oriented wing of the movement, especially the NAACP and King factions: the idea of changing hearts and laws gave way to a surging ideology of changing actual attitudes and practices.

The Student Nonviolent Coordinating Committee (SNCC, pronounced *snik*), which began under SCLC and King sponsorship in 1960, especially underwent sweeping transformation.[43] It quickly came to specialize in the new "eyeball-to-eyeball" or "putting your body on the line" tactics of confrontation and possible (probable!) arrest. In 1961 CORE added more momentum to the movement by resurrecting the concept of Freedom Rides, a tactic it had used with varying degrees of success in the 1940s.[44] By 1966 both CORE and SNCC had undergone a radical ideological evolution from demands for integration to an emphasis on black nationalism. The reason for such a transition can be traced largely to the "field" experiences of the two groups— SNCC in the rural South and CORE in the urban North. It was the protest experience itself, then, that led organizations like SNCC and CORE away from the established NAACP legal model, which had long stressed assimilation within the framework of traditional American goals and concepts, to new models of activism and rejection.

The bloody events of Birmingham, perhaps more than any other single event, pushed both protesters and observers into new modes of consciousness. In the spring of 1963 shocked television viewers throughout the nation witnessed the disturbing events in Birmingham: the safety forces under the command of Eugene "Bull" Connor brutally and repeatedly attacked passive civil rights protesters, including women and children engaged in innocent prayer vigils. The police terrorism in Birmingham helped focus Washington's and the nation's attention on the southern movement and lent a new sense of energy and urgency to civil rights.[45] In response to movement pressures and experiences like those of Birmingham and the 1963 March on Washington, in which King led over a quarter of a million blacks and whites on the largest mass action civil rights protest in American history, and additional moral and political pressure exerted by President Lyndon B. Johnson, America finally acted on the civil rights issue.[46] For in 1963 the entire nation came to realize as never before just how profound a gap existed between the noble words of the Constitution and the vicious reality of American racism, a reality that led black novelist James Baldwin to write in that very same year in *The Fire Next Time*, that the black "no longer believes in the good faith of white Americans."[47] Soon events would prove Baldwin's words prophetic in a manner he might not have envisioned.

In January 1964 the states ratified the Twenty-fourth Amendment outlawing the poll tax in federal elections. In July Congress enacted the Civil Rights Act of 1964, the most comprehensive piece of civil rights legislation ever passed. The Act prohibited discrimination in the use of federal funds and in places of public accommodation and gave additional powers to the ineffective Civil Rights Commission. It also established an Equal Employment Opportunity Commission (EEOC) to "endeavor to eliminate . . . alleged unlawful employment practice."[48] Significantly, the Act contributed to the optimism of women as well as blacks, since Title VII included a precedent-setting ban on job discrimination on the basis of gender. The sex provision had been suggested as a ploy by Congressman Howard Smith (D-VA) to galvanize conservative opposition to the bill. But Smith's stratagem failed, and Title VII subsequently backfired on him and other conservatives by becoming an important rallying point and legal weapon for contemporary protesters.

Attempts to gain increased civil rights for blacks were not confined to Capitol Hill. During that summer civil rights workers dramatically expanded their grass-roots voter registration drive in Mississippi, the closed society, in which NAACP leader Medgar Evers had been killed in 1963. Freedom Summer itself represented an attempt by civil rights workers to escalate political activity in the South and reflected the combined efforts of various grass-roots organizations to combat racism wherever and at whatever levels it existed. What happened in the Mississippi Delta communities that summer sent shock waves throughout the South and North and helped thereby to focus new attention on the vicious nature of southern racism.[49]

Significantly, the summer project and subsequent actions created a link to another social movement of the era, contemporary feminism. Historian Sara Evans established that females comprised over one-half of the northern whites participating in Freedom Summer. As Evans and others argued, these experiences reawakened a sense of sex oppression, because many women faced the embarrassment of being expected by the male leadership to provide clerical and support services rather than to contribute fundamentally to the policy-making process. The effects of this sense of common oppression awakened a new feminist consciousness, or "sisterhood," which contributed directly to the 1960's feminist surge, as will be discussed in greater depth in a later chapter.[50]

As a result of Freedom Summer, too, one of the most forceful models of black female leadership, Fannie Lou Hamer, captured the nation's attention and admiration. Indeed, throughout the history of the Afro-American experience, black women have played a critical role in setting the agenda for elevating their race and sex. In that respect Fannie Lou Hamer's name will be enshrined next to those of such notables as the abolitionist Harriet Tubman, known to her people as the "black Moses," and the abolitionist and masterful feminist orator Sojourner Truth, to name but two.[51] Hamer, who had been shot at, arrested and beaten, became one of the most respected and durable civil rights leaders as a result of her founding the Mississippi Freedom Democratic Party (MFDP), which eventually numbered nearly 60,000 disenfranchised blacks. Despite Hamer's thunderous grass-roots leadership, the MFDP suffered a number of setbacks, including rejection of its alternative delegates to the all-white Mississippi representation at the 1964 Democratic Convention in Atlantic City.[52]

In a broader sense, the perception of white liberal betrayal of the MFDP served to solidify an important new faction in the movement. In early 1965 SNCC's Jack Minnis reiterated this sense of black outrage: "To sum up, then, the MFDP experience has shown that access to the national political structure ... is closed to grass-roots movements which seek basic and fundamental change in the society."[53] Minnis further stated, somewhat presciently, that if the political leadership of this country continued to disregard or co-opt black political challenges, "it will, in effect, be closing the last avenue for basic political change within the institutional structure of American politics. It will be telling the American people that Mississippi is not a southern phenomenon, but that it begins at the Canadian border and runs south to the Gulf and east and west to the Atlantic and the Pacific."[54]

On the heels of realities that stretched from Greensboro to Atlantic City, some blacks, especially northern youths, became increasingly militant and dedicated to the concept of total self-determination by any and all means necessary. They had indeed, as Baldwin had prophesied earlier, simply lost faith in white America. Thus by the mid–1960s new angry voices of protest were pressing for strategies far removed from the traditional integrationist approach of such organizations as the NAACP and SCLC. The disillusionment with legal goals, the recognition of unique problems of the black masses, and the consequences of indignation and frustration born from ghetto life had set the stage for the dramatic reassertion by black Americans of belligerent alternative protest ideologies like militant nationalism and Marxism. The new protest concept was reflected most dramatically in new "Black Power," self-defense and retaliatory violence credos reminiscent of Garvey's earlier nationalistic rhetoric. Stokely Carmichael, who was credited with initiating the slogan in 1966, has commented that the Black Power era was "the greatest revolution ever of rising expectations among black people."[55] He might have added that Black Power actually translated to Black *Male* Power, since black women were seen as being essentially peripheral to the direction and dynamics of the movement. Black Power detractors, on the other hand, interpreted the slogan as representing violence, anarchy, revenge and communism as they came to view the new radicals as enfants terribles. In this regard, the volatile cry aggravated an already growing breach between black moderates and militants.[56] The Black Power movement itself drew much of its inspiration from earlier protagonists, notably Marcus Garvey, the Nation of Islam under Elijah Muhammad, and Malcolm X, the onetime Muslim leader and the founder of the Organization of Afro-American Unity before his assassination in February 1965. Even after his death Malcolm continued to exert great influence upon the nationalistic thought of radical blacks through his stirring *Autobiography*.[57]

Black Power dramatically changed the protest agenda by demanding that the black community mobilize its strengths to counter white power. Moderates like King and the NAACP's Roy Wilkins openly feared that the term would produce a negative image of the movement. New Black Power advocates, such as those of SNCC and CORE, to the contrary, actually sought to create restated positive images of blacks in all areas of life by resurrecting the old themes of self-sufficiency and self-determination. Many Black Power practitioners defined themselves further as an oppressed class and as such part of the Third World wave of neonationalism predicted by Frantz Fanon in his widely read *The Wretched of the Earth*.[58] As Stokely Carmichael and Charles V. Hamilton declared in their broadside *Black Power*:

Many blacks are now calling themselves African-Americans, Afro-Americans or black people because that is *our* image of ourselves. When we begin to define our own image, the stereotypes—that is, lies—that our oppressor has developed will begin in the white community and end there

Only when black people fully develop this sense of community, of themselves, can they begin to deal effectively with the problems of racism in *this* country. This is what we mean by a new consciousness [Black Pride]; this is the vital first step.[59]

Black Pride became the most visible symbol of rejection of nonblack cultural standards. Singer James Brown, the acknowledged "Godfather of Soul," emotionally caught the spirit of this statement in his million-seller single, "Say It Loud—I'm Black and I'm Proud." Yet by the late 1960s and early 1970s the ideology of Black Power and Pride had shifted noticeably in form, character and purpose. The revolutionary Black Panther Party in particular symbolized this ideological swing toward a more militantly economic-determinist point of view.

Huey Newton and Bobby Seale founded the Black Panther Party in October 1966 in the revolutionary spirit of Malcolm X.[60] Initially, the Panthers strove to protect black communities from police brutality and to institute local self-help programs (e.g., black "observer" teams following white police officers and hot breakfasts for ghetto school children). But by 1967 the organization had taken on a markedly revolutionary all-black character firmly grounded in the teachings of Malcolm X, Frantz Fanon and Latin American revolutionary

Che Guevara. In *Revolutionary Suicide*, Newton crystalized the Panther ideology:

Mao and Fanon and Guevara all saw clearly that the people had been stripped of their birthright and their dignity, not by any philosophy or mere words, but at gunpoint.... At bottom, this is a form of self-defense. Although that defense might at times take on characteristics of aggression, in the final analysis the people do not initiate; they simply respond to what has been inflicted upon them.... Though it may mean death, these men will fight, because death with dignity is preferable to ignominy.[61]

By the late 1960s militants like the Panthers came to adopt stridently Pan-African nationalistic views, though the new dedication took on broader cultural connotations than its ideological forebears. Often this new nationalism supported the concept of a separate African personality, countercommunities, or parallel institutions. The objective of this, as Black Power advocate Solomon P. Gethers stated, was to "throw off white oppression by whatever means are necessary, and proceed with the building of...[our] own society separate and apart from that of white America."[62]

Hence, by the second half of the 1960s many revolutionary nationalists were calling for black autonomy based upon an ideology of psychological and cultural identity and antiassimilationist views.[63] This concept, while widely shared by a younger generation of black militants, nonetheless proved odious to older legalists like members of the NAACP, who had worked for over a half century to lay the constitutional and intellectual foundation for complete legal assimilation.

The 1970s saw the belief in racial autonomy spread throughout the United States. While schemes like the Republic of New Africa (RNA) stridently demanded "a separate, independent nation with our own government" within the geographic jurisdiction of the United States, another trend toward black nationalism grew out of a new protest-borne sociopsychological awareness.[64] Organizations such as the Congress of Racial Equality, whose ideology formerly had been oriented toward the goal of integration, clearly began to manifest new separatist thoughts. CORE espoused the new nationalism/separatism when Roy Innis, who accepted Garveyism as a guiding philosophy, became its national director in 1968.[65]

While groups like CORE opted for the nationalistic line, others like the Panthers continued to gravitate toward a more militant Marxist-based ideology. Socialists like the black intellectual Bayard Rustin had long endorsed a mild form of Marxism, but now younger militants began to enunciate a more revolutionary Marxist line that totally overshadowed the Socialist and CP-USA programs.[66] SNCC theoretician James Forman spoke of this new commitment to Marxist solutions: "Our fight is against racism, capitalism and imperialism, and we are dedicated to building a socialist society inside the United States where the total means of production and distribution are in the hands of the State, and that must be led by black people."[67]

Forman's position embraced both Marxism-Leninism and the ideology of class struggle. This notion that racist betrayals would not automatically be addressed by the class struggle increasingly surfaced in black neo-Marxist thought. Many neo-Marxists held the view that capitalism and communism were "the left and right arms of the same white body."[68] We can conclude, therefore, that by the late 1960s the civil rights movement itself demonstrated deep division, ranging from the moderate legal-oriented wing to the cultural-nationalists to the radical Marxist wing.

The teachings of Kwame Nkrumah, founder of independent Ghana and foremost African exponent of the Marxist race/class strategy, lent new ideological dynamism to the situation by preaching a pioneering black-based scientific socialism. American practitioners of Nkrumahism added their own unique character to the argument that racism and capitalism were inexorably linked. As convert Stokely Carmichael stated:

Studying in this framework allows Nkrumahism to correctly analyze the forces of history utilizing the method of dialectics. Nkrumahism having studied its history correctly now dissects it with the principles of Marxism-Leninism, which it accepts as universal truths. Thus Nkrumahism uses these principles.... Consequently, Nkrumahism merely sees Marxism-Leninism as an instrument, thus avoiding dogmatism.[69]

The All-Afrikan People's Revolutionary Party grew from such Nkrumah-based scientific socialism. The A-APRP called for "an independent, socialist, mass, revolutionary political party" and "world socialist revolution," and as such represented a serious attempt to build a contemporary revolutionary Pan-African movement based on the principles of socialism.[70] In this respect Stokely Carmichael, former SNCC official, early Black Power advocate and now spokesperson for radical black scientific socialism, uniquely represented the way in which some protesters had shifted from legal to cultural and finally to economic solutions, all these in themselves both historical and contemporary waves of black protest.

In order to determine if an ideological relationship exists with the three black protest paradigms under review, we shall now review the development and characteristics of another landmark social movement—contemporary feminism. Accordingly, our methodology will utilize the legal, cultural and economic models to examine key aspects of this movement. We are, therefore, entering a new dialogue about the influence of black activism on the contemporary women's movement in the United States in order to determine if there is a common ground where ideological influence or shared protest characteristics can be mutually illuminating and instructive. Clearly, there is no method of assessing the entire range of possible influences and no particular typology can speak for them. The premise is that ideological models, like the social movements from which they spring, are often emulated by similar social protest groups, in the same way that personal models are chosen

and copied by individuals. Therefore we must explore the women's movement in depth in order to establish the degree to which similar experiences
within the black rights movement have been deliberately emulated and the
degree to which they have been results of accidentally shared circumstances.

Inquiry into causal factors at variance with our legal, cultural and economic
models will be limited, by necessity. Because both movements were extraordinarily complex phenomena, many of these factors lie beyond the realistic
parameters of this study. Connections between the two movements will be
alluded to regularly, but the implications of such will not be fully drawn until
the final chapter.

THE ORIGINS AND DEVELOPMENT OF AMERICAN FEMINISM THROUGH 1960

It is often theorized that women's actions in the cause of feminism have
resembled black actions in the cause of civil rights. For example, the anti-
slavery movement preceded the first wave of the women's movement; black
male suffrage presaged women's suffrage; and contemporary civil rights appeared before contemporary feminism. But it would be naive to conclude
that the feminist impulse derived entirely from civil rights because of seem-
ingly interconnected protest actions and ideological stances over time and
space. Accordingly, it is instructive to trace briefly the origins and history of
the feminist "waves," which first appeared in an organizational sense during
the nineteenth century.

The Legal/Reform Approach: Women's Suffrage as Model

In recalling the trials of the antislavery crusade, onetime fugitive slave
Frederick Douglass commented:

When the true history of the Anti-Slavery cause shall be written, women will occupy
a large space in its pages; for the cause of the slave has been peculiarly woman's
cause. Her heart and her conscience have supplied in large degree its motive and
mainspring. . . . Not only did her feet run on "willing errands," and her fingers do the
work which in large degree supplied the sinews of war, but her deep *moral convictions*, and her tender *human sensibilities*, found convincing and persuasive expression
by her pen and her voice.[71]

By stressing the "moral" and "human" qualities of women rather than describing the total scope of energy lent to abolitionism, Douglass betrayed a
prevailing male perception among both races of women's "proper spheres"
in society, a notion that Douglass himself failed to equate with the white
concept of "proper place" for black Americans. Perhaps more than any other
single issue, such attitudes convinced antebellum female activists that the

restrictive notion of females confined to domestic and social circles was as legitimate an issue for protest as was the treatment of humans as chattel.

In many respects, as historian Ellen Carol DuBois has argued, women's participation in the sometimes violent abolitionist movement moved them toward and prepared them for their own struggle. As abolitionists, women observed firsthand the ideological and tactical maneuvers of protest, a "sphere" long considered well beyond women's proper place. Women's role in the antislavery crusade affected them profoundly; not only did they decide to adopt the extant protest model for their own cause, but in the process they challenged the notion of appropriate female spheres, which had become the chief determinant of women's circumscribed domestic role in the first half of the nineteenth century. Barbara Welter and Sheila M. Rothman have found that the notion of women's appropriate worlds, what Welter termed the "Cult of True Womanhood" and Rothman called the "proper place," generally had been defined by the prevailing climate of opinion reinforced by patriarchal control of social institutions. That opinion and that control were seldom so firmly entrenched in the American ethos as at the time of women's entrance into the antislavery cause.[72]

In *History of Woman Suffrage*, the massive six-volume witness account of the suffrage movement, women's rights leaders Elizabeth Cady Stanton, Susan B. Anthony and Matilda Joslyn Gage identified women's discriminatory treatment at the London World Anti-Slavery Convention of 1840 as the first great female awakening to patriarchal concepts:

As Lucretia Mott and Elizabeth Cady Stanton wended their way arm in arm down Great Queen Street that night, reviewing the exciting scenes of the day, they agreed to hold a woman's rights convention on their return to America, as the men to whom they had just listened had manifested their great need of some education on that question. Thus a missionary work for the emancipation of women in "the land of the free and the home of the brave" was then and there inaugurated. As the ladies were not allowed to speak in the Convention, they kept up a brisk fire morning, noon, and night.[73]

Stanton and Mott subsequently orchestrated the first women's rights convention in Seneca Falls, New York, in 1848, from which an organized women's movement gradually evolved. Several well-known abolitionists joined the three hundred participants, who agreed on the need for a statement of intent, a women's creed.[74] "The Declaration of Sentiments and Resolutions," which equated female status with chattel slavery and urged women to pursue with all dispatch their own legal and political rights, thus was drafted and has endured as one of the most important documents of organized feminism. The manifesto included a call for suffrage, a plea that would become the central issue for feminists until ratification of the Nineteenth, or "Suffrage," Amendment some seventy-two years later.[75] It was, consequently, well into the nineteenth century and well after the advent of organized abolitionism when women organized at a national level, coordinated appeals, signed petitions and demanded on a systematic basis their fundamental rights as human beings and American citizens. And by doing so women also demonstrated how nominally legal-oriented protests can become radical challenges to deeply rooted cultural norms, depending on the nature and manifestation of those challenges over time and space.

Almost in unison feminists dropped their challenges during the Civil War and refocused their energies on the paramount issues of slavery and preservation of the Union, only to realize later that their own cause would be sacrificed after the fall of the Confederacy to the goal of black *male* suffrage. Even so, Eleanor Flexner has noted that woman's role in support of the black cause during the Civil War had important consequences for feminists in convincing them further of the value of organization as a functional protest tool. Indeed, through the twentieth century women's suffrage organizations would be the hallmark of conventional feminism, although by no means would they be the only engines of protest.[76]

During Reconstruction new female protests surfaced as women leaders strenuously objected to the inclusion of the word *male* in the section of the Fourteenth Amendment that extended the franchise to the "Freed*man*" (italics added).[77] Women's leaders rose to the issue by organizing and campaigning for specific suffrage amendments to the Kansas and New York Constitutions. They not only failed in both attempts, but in the process drew the opprobrium of white and black liberals alike for "selfishly" espousing their own cause during the so-called "Negro's Hour."[78] Presaging a general and persistent lack of male concern for feminist goals—a problem that would drive an ideological wedge between black and women's struggles in contemporary times as well—Frederick Douglass expressed the sentiment of untold numbers of male reformers: "When women, because they are women, are dragged from their houses and hung upon lamp-posts; when their children are torn from their arms, and their brains dashed upon the pavement; when they are objects of insults and outrage at every turn; when they are in danger of having their homes burnt down over their heads; when their children are not allowed to enter schools; then they will have an urgency to obtain the ballot equal to our own."[79]

Douglass's rebuff to women—of both races—stemmed in large part from his fear that another social crusade might pirate energy away from the cause he had so forcefully espoused. This male belittlement and denial of women's self-defined goals clearly helped direct female activism away from male coalitions toward a more women-centered and women-run movement. The authors of *History of Woman Suffrage* noted:

Our liberal men counseled us to silence during the war, and we were silent on our own wrongs; they counseled us again to silence in Kansas and New York, lest we should defeat "negro suffrage," and threatened if we were not, we might fight the battle alone. We chose the latter, and were defeated. But standing alone we learned our power; we repudiated man's counsels forevermore; and solemnly vowed that there should never be another season of silence until woman had the same rights everywhere on this green earth, as man.[80]

Women organizationally reinforced their legal-oriented commitment in 1869 through the creation of both the National Woman Suffrage Association (NWSA) and the more moderate American Woman Suffrage Association (AWSA). In February 1890 the two merged to form the National American Woman Suffrage Association (NAWSA), which campaigned vigorously for the vote until ratification of the Nineteenth Amendment in 1920. Feminist tactics continued to be legalistic in nature as organized women eschewed broader social issues in favor of policies focused on capturing the national franchise.

Not all women supported organized feminism's commitment to work within the boundaries of traditional protest.[81] In fact, there were those who viewed the feminist cause from perspectives other than the suffrage thrust, women who challenged the very core of prevailing concepts of place and who manifested what can be identified clearly as a women's cultural-oriented approach to protest.

The Cultural-Nationalistic Approach: Woodhull, Gilman and Goldman as Models

Women who protested cultural oppression became more critical of tradition than mainstream reformers. Cultural-oriented females promoted concepts holding that women's domestic sphere worked insidiously to deny one-half of humanity its individual prerogatives. They also argued that there were underlying economic and social restraints in society working to convince the public that woman's paramount concern should remain homemaking. Obtaining the vote was not a panacea. Rather, to acquire true freedom the basic structure of society must be changed to accommodate antitraditional feminist goals. These concerns differed radically from the legal and political emphasis that had come to dominate the women's movement, and the public's general perception of domesticity, and in this sense led to recurring criticism through contemporary times that legal feminism has been conservative and irrelevant to women's true concerns.

In the 1870s Victoria Woodhull, one such radical nontraditionalist, espoused the controversial concept of free love (i.e., the right of any unmarried man or woman to engage in sexual relations) and claimed herself a leading "freethinker" who would help institute new feminist freedoms. She earned a small fortune on Wall Street, pursued a number of goals in opposition to prevailing sex norms, and not only demanded the vote, but shocked the nation by actually seeking the presidency in 1872.[82]

Along with her sister, Tennessee Claflin, Woodhull particularly sought to attack staid suffrage-oriented feminism in her newspaper, *Woodhull and Claflin's Weekly*. The journal quickly became a forum for radical ideas, and in 1871 published the first full-length English translation of *The Communist Manifesto*. It articulated the notion that suffragists were really eccentric advocates of utopian goals. What actually needed reforming, in Woodhull's opinion, was society's unwillingness to discuss such female concerns as prostitution, venereal diseases and abortion—all truly radical propositions for the time period. Woodhull thus resembled in no way the middle-class–oriented reformers of the suffrage movement; she disavowed their values and offered in their place nontraditional discussions that would not be widely accepted as female vehicles of protest until nearly a century later. Although she incurred the enmity of women's organizational leaders as well as that of society at large for "disturbing" the peace of her times, Victoria Woodhull nonetheless must be considered one of feminism's most forceful and revolutionary advocates.

Charlotte Perkins Gilman, whom authors Carol Hymowitz and Michaele Weissman called "the most influential feminist thinker of the early twentieth century,"[83] also represented the ideological core of cultural-oriented feminist protest. Gilman, a distant relative of the famous Beecher literary and religious clan, eschewed conventional domestic life for an independent career as author and lecturer. Though twice married, Gilman never resigned herself to the confinement of traditional household chores, a position she once likened to human bondage. She gravitated instead toward such alternative ideologies as Bellamyite utopianism and unorthodox socialism.[84]

In *Women and Economics*, published in 1898, Gilman advocated options that challenged long-standing gender norms considered by many to be the very bedrock of society. In this work she stated that divisions along sex lines had given "to woman the home and to man the world," and proposed "radical" alternatives to domestic drudgery by suggesting the creation of centralized nurseries and cooperative kitchens run by trained personnel.[85] Essentially an argument for unprecedented feminist prerogatives, Gilman's eclectic work appeared in an industrial age when increasing numbers of women were forced to seek economic solutions outside the home. In practice, Gilman repudiated mainstream feminism as concerned with symbolic changes rather than with concrete self-expression for women. Designed specifically to ensure female social and economic freedom, hers was one of early feminism's most powerful frontal attacks on the cult of domesticity. The notion shocked many traditional women reformers who, although they supported vocational training for women, nevertheless expected the majority of women to remain inside the home.

Emma Goldman also represented the antitraditional protest approach of Woodhull and Gilman. Born in Russia in 1869, Goldman at seventeen migrated to the United States where she adopted anarchism as a solution to the economic and sexual exploitations of her world. During her extraordinarily active life, she excelled as a lecturer, publicist, agitator for free speech, feminist and (along with Margaret Sanger) pioneer advocate of birth control.[86] Although Goldman never received great acclaim among women, her theories, like those of Woodhull and Gilman, were advanced for her time in that they presaged many later radical ideologies, especially with reference to contemporary radical feminism's cultural thrust and attacks on domesticity. On this subject, Goldman claimed:

The right to vote, or equal civil rights, may be good demands, but true emancipation begins neither at the polls nor in courts. It begins in woman's soul. History tells us that every oppressed class gained true liberation from its masters through its own efforts. It is necessary that woman learn that lesson, that she realize that her freedom will reach as far as her power to achieve her freedom reaches.

Marriage is often an economic arrangement purely, furnishing the woman with a life-long life insurance policy and the man with a perpetuator of his kind or a pretty toy. That is, marriage, or the training thereto, prepares the woman for the life of a parasite, a dependent, helpless servant, while it furnishes the man the right of a chattel mortgage over a human life.[87]

Later feminist voices would echo Goldman's call for a forcefully self-directed woman's movement free from what she felt were the corrupting influences of American patriarchal standards. Voltairine de Cleyre, whom Goldman respected as "one of America's great Anarchists,"[88] clarified the thesis and unknowingly identified a large segment of modern feminism when she stated that in the final analysis the female sex must free itself by "recognizing the complete individuality of women" and by "making rebels whenever we can. By ourselves living our beliefs."[89]

The legacy of women like Woodhull, Gilman and Goldman continued in protest ideology through the twentieth century. These feminists in particular offered strong models to women who wished to champion alternative cultural patterns and greater opportunities for human advancement through nontraditional means. The three, in addition, were progenitors of those latter-day feminists who would discount legal-oriented organizational dissent in favor of individual or loosely confederated modes of cultural-oriented protest. Certainly Woodhull, Gilman and Goldman do not represent the entire ideological range of such women, just as the aforementioned black crusaders did not represent the entire scope of their movement; but their views and actions are illustrative of those cultural-oriented feminists who differed markedly from their more numerous legal-oriented sisters.

While many legal-oriented reformers continued to issue conciliatory and respectable rhetoric in regard to traditional sex roles, and the cultural-oriented camp continued to envision a revolutionary line in which society would alter its customary relationships and values in favor of both male and female prerogatives, a third class of feminists arose. Highly kinetic, like those in the cultural-oriented camp, these women began to revamp normative values along socialist lines. In a fundamental sense, by championing nontraditional economic answers to the feminist question, this class of thinkers and doers represented an even more direct challenge to mainstream feminism than radicals like those already mentioned. Thus arises the ideology of the third protest paradigm used as the basis of this study.

The Marxist/Socialist Approach: Socialist and Communist Women as Models

Most socialist women in the late nineteenth and early twentieth centuries eschewed the reforming middle class in favor of working class values. Convinced that feminist goals would be realized fully and finally in the new order, they opted for economic solutions. Early socialist women recognized the root of sexual oppression in the ownership of private property and the gross maldistribution of wealth, while they envisioned a radically transformed society of neither male nor female exploitation. The ideological justification for this position was prepared by Karl Marx and articulated as the "Woman Question" by two of his disciples, August Bebel in *Woman Under Socialism* (1883) and Frederick Engels in *The Origin of the Family, Private Property and the State* (1884).[90] Later in this study we shall further address the seminal works and the divergent approaches to the Woman Question by feminists who sought social justice solely under Marxist banners and by less doctrinaire women who sought total liberation through a number of radical/cultural solutions, only one of which was Marxist. For our present purposes, let it suffice to say that both groups have a common thread, as Olive M. Johnson perceptively noted in 1919, in a belief that "the economic relations . . . determine the social relations."[91]

Socialist women themselves argued continuously over which oppression was greater: the oppression of class or of sex. Yet in one respect they spoke as one; they believed that women could never neutralize the evils of sexism in a capitalist America. In many cases these labor-oriented women identified more with the problems of class than with those of sex. The feminist class/sex argument rested upon the radical perception that all females were affected by stultifying cultural patterns and thus that all societies expected classes of women to behave in socially approved ways. Kate Richards O'Hare, who ran for Congress on the Socialist Party ticket in 1910, expressed her thoughts on this subject: "I, as a Socialist, most emphatically state that I demand Equal Suffrage, not merely as a *Sex Right* but also as a *Class Right*. I demand not only better laws for MY SEX, but more particularly, for MY CLASS."[92] O'Hare and others took such socially explosive stands on the issues of labor and feminism in an attempt to convince all women that true self-expression could come about only in an economically egalitarian society.

Elizabeth Gurley Flynn, the daughter of parents who were active in working-class politics and who herself, as labor historian Alice Kessler-Harris noted, represented long-festering tensions between independent-minded women and the male working class, verbalized one of the strongest defenses of the feminist-socialist line. As recorded in her autobiography *Rebel Girl,* Gurley Flynn delivered her first speech, "What Socialism Will Do for Women," in New York City at the age of fifteen.

The possibility, at least under socialism, [is] of industrializing all the domestic tasks by collective kitchens and dining places, nurseries, laundries, and the like.

I referred to August Bebel's views of a socialist society.... He foresaw ... the right of every woman ... to be a wife, mother, worker and citizen.... I was fired with determination to fight for all this.[93]

In 1906 Gurley Flynn expounded on the question of woman's domestic role: "The State should provide for the maintenance of every child, so that the individual woman shall not be compelled to depend for support upon the individual man while bearing children. The barter and sale that go under the name of love are highly obnoxious."[94]

Gurley Flynn stands out as a woman who rejected conventional sex norms by taking the worker's cause as her own. In her own words she was a woman for whom "domestic life and possibly a large family had no attraction."[95] In later life, Elizabeth Gurley Flynn, like so many other economic-determinist women, discontinued her flirtation with the Socialist Party of America (SPA) and embraced doctrinaire communism as the only viable solution to sex oppression.

The CP-USA itself both won and lost adherents because of its international stand on the feminist issue. When in the 1920s the CP-USA actively began to seek more women for its cause, some veteran socialists like Freda Kirchwey, publisher and editor of *The Nation* and a self-described "left-wing feminist," openly disapproved because of the Party's Moscow ties.[96] Still others saw communism as the only realistic solution to America's social and economic injustices. For example, socialist orator Rose Pastor Stokes helped organize the American Communists in 1919 based on her belief that class and sex were inseparable; she remained an active Party member until her death in June 1933.[97] Long-time labor organizer Gurley Flynn moved, on the other hand, toward the communist camp during the 1920s because "my interest grew out of my friendship with so many of their leaders and my cooperation with them as 'left wingers' of the Socialist Party."[98] Until her death in the 1960s, Gurley Flynn continued to advocate the party's thesis that capitalism relegated groups like blacks and women to an inferior status. During the Cold War she faced prosecution under the Smith Act for conspiring to teach the violent overthrow of the United States government; in January 1955 this outspoken Marxist was remanded to the federal reformatory at Alderson, West Virginia, where she spent the next twenty-eight months. In 1961 Gurley Flynn became head of the National Board of the CP-USA, the top position in the party.[99] The long and active career of Elizabeth Gurley Flynn, perhaps better than that of any other, represented the dedication with which some American feminists sought to address the Woman Question ideologically through orthodox Marxism.

While women like Gurley Flynn rose to positions of importance within Marxist protest, the majority of twentieth-century female advocates have held solidly to their faith in the American capitalist structure and have only sought to adjust the system into more fully accommodating the wide range of women's desires. Throughout the first half of this century there remained a general reluctance to assault conventional social patterns like that of the mother and homemaker role in the family unit, even though nontraditional feminists like Gilman and Goldman had so articulately done this. Indeed, in the decade prior to World War I mainstream feminism often sought to bring women's domestically centered moral and spiritual qualities to bear upon government.[100] Thus, from the Seneca Falls Convention of 1848 to the Progressive period in the opening decades of this century, women's campaign for the vote evolved from an ideologically radical to a morally acceptable crusade. As Jane Addams stated, the franchise would become a means for women to better the quality of the traditional family life, to "take care of those affairs which naturally and historically belong to women."[101] Down to the passage of the "Anthony" Amendment in 1920, Addams personified the majority sentiments of women's partisans, and thus provided at least a partial ideological foundation for future generations of legal-oriented feminists.

Feminism lost much of its public momentum and fervor following the ratification of the Nineteenth Amendment. For many, suffragist dreams finally seemed a reality. From the 1920s through the 1960s the legacy of feminism lived on primarily in two ways: by groups like the National League of Women Voters (formed after 1920 from earlier suffrage organizations), the National Federation of Business and Professional Women's Clubs (created in 1919), and a growing number of similar women's organizations on the one hand; and by a small cadre of women demanding support for an Equal Rights Amendment (ERA) to the United States Constitution on the other. Both approaches held allegiance to the legal reform philosophy; however, the ERA became the one issue that openly symbolized divisiveness within the movement.[102] A gulf resulted between the organizational reformers in one corner, and the fiery Alice Paul and her militant National Woman's Party (NWP) in the other. Thus feminism entered the interwar years characterized by researcher June Sochen as a time of "the hope deferred."[103]

Organization and Militancy, 1920–1960: Feminism at Low Ebb

By the end of World War I the National Woman's Party had become physically and psychologically separated from the larger movement because of its perceived radical nature and tactics. Models of direct action patterned after Englishwomen Emmeline and Christabel Pankhurst especially influenced Alice Paul and the NWP. Beginning in 1923 the NWP directed its energies toward championing a federal ERA in order to realize the full "power of American women." By its strong support of the amendment and pioneering feminist agenda, the NWP alienated many traditional reformers and their working women allies, who feared the amendment would invalidate women's special "protective legislation" at the work site.[104]

The appearance of the National Woman's Party marked an important turning point in twentieth-century American feminism, because its radical tactics and goals forced the issue of complete women's rights into the public arena. Further, the unrelenting militancy of Paul and her followers throughout the interwar years offered new protest models based on focused, direct-action tactics, which established new women's protest standards for morals and manners that would be invoked by feminists during and after the 1960s. In that respect Sochen's characterization of these times as the "hope deferred" seems much more apt than the "hope buried," as some researchers have suggested.

Dorothy Johnson, among others, has pointed out that mainstream feminism lived on as well from the 1920s to the 1960s, primarily through women's professional organizations, which channeled women's drive toward economic and sociological issues and toward the issue of world peace. The National League of Women Voters, the General Federation of Women's Clubs, the National Women's Trade Union League, the National Federation of Business and Professional Women's Clubs and the American Association of University Women emerged as the organizations most actively working for legal-oriented goals. These so-called Special Five continued to press their interests until they were forced to shift priorities with the advent of World War II.[105]

Indeed, the time of war and its aftermath became a period when traditional roles of wife and mother were dramatically altered by unprecedented labor needs. The defense industries' slogan, "For the Duration," took on new and ironic meaning for working women as thousands of "Rosie the Riveters" were arbitrarily fired after the war to make openings for returning male veterans and recent male high school graduates. The fact that many women wished to remain in the workplace did not deter Madison Avenue from glorifying housework and once again depicting women's only proper place as in the home. Postwar America witnessed a return to traditional sex conventions and consumerism rose to a quasi-religious fervor. The model of the middle-class homemaker—what Betty Friedan would later call the "feminine mystique"— swept public life, while active feminism and nontraditional pursuits for women ebbed in what one chronicler has aptly labeled feminism's "bleak and lonely years."[106]

The problems of women pursuing alternatives to the traditional middle-class model of homebound wife and consumer have contributed greatly in this century to keeping females within conventional protest spheres. As Blanche Wiesen Cook has concluded, historically American women committed to alternative lifestyles have hesitated to manifest their beliefs or actions in public for fear of incurring social scorn.[107] She uses the example of lesbianism—a term she defines as "women who love women, who choose women to nurture and support and to create a living environment in which to work creatively and independently"—to illustrate how vulnerable counterculture women have been to attacks by a disapproving society. Both legal and extralegal manifestations of repression, Cook suggested, have been prevalent throughout American history; they have helped provide for a general rejection of diversity and a long-standing repression of alternative lifestyles. This phenomenon has perhaps had a more profound effect on women and minorities than on any other group in America, a fact that has quite likely led black people and women to seek intragroup strength and solidarity in necessary "support networks."[108] Later in this study we will point out that female-oriented support networks have become the lynchpin of the modern feminist crusade.

The fact yet remains that after a generation of legal-oriented protest, which culminated in 1920 in the ratification of the Nineteenth Amendment, the visible forms of an extant feminist network, with the exception of the NWP, largely dissipated, or at least changed fundamentally in character from activist models to consensus-club and social-organization ones in the interwar years. Certainly there were other important social and economic reasons for the decline of feminism during this period. Still, most persons sympathetic to women's causes chose to manifest their interest primarily through reform and legal-oriented professional membership groups until the advent of a new generation of feminist activists in the 1960s.

SUMMARY

In the late 1960s the civil rights movement reached its peak of energy and effectiveness as blacks sought to achieve their goals through such ideologically disparate organizations as the NAACP, NUL, CORE, SCLC and SNCC—all of which pursued at some point in their evolution a commitment to legal and integrationist strategies. Among the legal-oriented groups, the NAACP grew to be the most visible because of its diligence in working for desegregation and its dramatic success in 1954 when the Supreme Court handed down a decision banning segregation in public schools. The backgrounds of SNCC and CORE, on the other hand, demonstrate how rapidly and fundamentally the intensity and approach of black protest changed in the 1960s from traditional consensus models to new or restated conflict ones. These changes can be summarized by comparing the judicial thrust of the NAACP with the more militant direct-action tactics of the younger black protest organizations of the early 1960s.

The very same decade witnessed a resurgence of historical black nationalism, which in large part can be traced back to Marcus Garvey's cultural awareness themes of black pride, power and Pan-Africanism. The cultural-oriented protest currents in the 1960s were generally led by young, angry activists who repudiated the ideological goals and tactics of the older, more firmly entrenched legal wing of the movement. During the late 1960s an increasing number of black Americans gravitated toward an ideology that recognized the hypocrisy of white America's "melting pot" myth. Almost simultaneously a new economic orientation resulted in blacks embracing their own dialectical strain of scientific socialism based upon Kwame Nkrumah's African-nationalist synthesis of race and class doctrines. Leaders like Black Power advocate Stokely Carmichael began to turn black protest into an altered ideological direction by arguing that blacks—indeed, all of the world's dispossessed—could achieve true equality only after the "total destruction of the racist capitalist system."[109] As we have seen, American communists had courted blacks for decades before black scientific socialism appeared but their ideology, as exemplified by the CP-USA, had frequently proved to be at odds with black priorities.

At this point it seems that the growing impact of black protest through the 1960s would have helped in many essential ways to generate and coordinate energies setting the stage for the emergence of the other social protests of the era, both by providing models for political activity and legal goals and by mobilizing a new consciousness against restraining concepts of proper place and role. Particularly representative of new social commitments in the 1960s was the reinvigorated women's movement, which attacked the notion that women's resources, desires and achievements should be limited to motherhood and corollary pursuits. However, to assume perfunctorily that the women's rights movement derived directly or coincidentally from the black civil rights movement would be to totally neglect women's own rich protest history, three important ideologies of which we have reviewed in this chapter.

We have seen, then, how the historical black civil rights and women's movements have both been shaped by three distinct strategical and tactical currents: the legal, the cultural and the economic. The following pages shall focus closely upon the orientations of feminism in the 1960s and the 1970s with the intent of examining more carefully the historical and contemporary ideological relationship and behavior between black civil rights and feminism. We shall continue to compare and contrast the 1960s' and early 1970s' ideological thrust of the two movements along legal, cultural and economic lines.

NOTES

1. Cited in Charles E. Silberman, *Crisis in Black and White* (New York: Vintage, 1964), 108.

2. Mary W. Ovington, *How the NAACP Began* (NAACP pamphlet, n.d.), NAACP Papers, Library of Congress, Washington, DC, and Ovington, *The Walls Came Tumbling Down* (New York: Harcourt, Brace, 1947), 100–146; Charles Flint Kellogg, *NAACP: A History of the National Association for the Advancement of Colored People*, Vol. 1: *1909–1920* (Baltimore: Johns Hopkins Press, 1967), 9–45; "National Association for the Advancement of Colored People, First Annual Report, January 1, 1911"; "National Association for the Advancement of Colored People, Second Annual Report, January 1, 1912," both in NAACP Papers.

3. John Morsell (former assistant executive director of the NAACP), taped interview, 1967, Ralph Johnson Bunche Oral History Collection, Moorland-Spingarn Research Center, Howard University, Washington, DC. See Robert L. Zangrando, "The NAACP and a Federal Antilynching Bill, 1934–1940," *The Journal of Negro History*, Vol. 50, No. 2 (1965), 116–17. For the NAACP's priorities through World War II, see the narrative of Langston Hughes, *Fight for Freedom: The Story of the NAACP* (New York: W.W. Norton, 1962), 25–89, and Minnie Finch, *The NAACP: Its Fight for Justice* (Metuchen, NJ: Scarecrow, 1981), 3–114.

4. Nancy J. Weiss, *The National Urban League, 1910–1940* (New York: Oxford University Press, 1974), 47–70.

5. "A Brief Statement Concerning the Activities of the NUL During 1935"(annual report), National Urban League Papers, Library of Congress, Washington, DC; Guichard Parris and Lester Brooks, *Blacks in the City: A History of the National Urban League* (Boston: Little, Brown, 1971), 56–293. A survey of the league's papers reveals that it often was eager to lend moral support to the NAACP, particularly in matters of adjudication, but it seldom undertook bold, independent initiatives on its own.

6. Lester B. Granger (former executive director of the NUL), taped interview, 1968, Bunche Oral History Collection.

7. E. David Cronon, *Black Moses: The Story of Marcus Garvey and the Universal Negro Improvement Association* (Madison: University of Wisconsin Press, 1969), 202–24. Cronon discounts Garvey's effectiveness in serving blacks' long-term needs. For a different perspective, consult Tony Martin, *Race First: The Ideological and Organizational Struggles of Marcus Garvey and the Universal Negro Improvement Association* (Westport, CT: Greenwood, 1976), 3–40.

8. Amy Jacques-Garvey, ed., *Philosophy and Opinions of Marcus Garvey*, Vol. 2 (New York: Universal, 1925), 12. See Laurence W. Levine, "Marcus Garvey and the Politics of Revitalization," in John Hope Franklin and August Meier, eds., *Black Leaders of the Twentieth Century* (Urbana: University of Illinois Press, 1982), 105–38.

9. Daniel Walden and Kenneth Wylie, "W.E.B. DuBois: Pan-Africanism's Intellectual Father," *Journal of Human Relations*, Vol. 14, No. 1 (1966), 28–41; George Shepperson, "Notes on Negro American Influences on the Emergence of African Nationalism," *Journal of African History*, Vol. 1, No. 2 (1960), 299–312; Ben F. Rogers, "William E. B. DuBois, Marcus Garvey, and Pan-Africa," *Journal of Negro History*, Vol. 40, No. 2 (1955), 154–65.

10. See Raymond L. Hall, *Black Separatism in the United States* (Hanover, NJ: University Press of New England, 1978), 1–3, 33–37.

11. Robert L. Zangrando, "From Civil Rights to Black Liberation: The Unsettled 1960's," *Current History*, Vol. 57, No. 339 (1969), 281–86, 299.

12. Lathan Starling, Sr., and Donald Franklin, "The Life and Works of Marcus Garvey," *Negro History Bulletin*, Vol. 26, No. 1 (1962–63), 36–38; C. Eric Lincoln, *The*

Black Muslims in America (Boston: Beacon, 1961), 66–67; Malcolm X with Alex Haley, *The Autobiography of Malcolm X* (New York: Grove, 1966), 6–7; Martin Luther King, Jr., *Where Do We Go from Here: Chaos or Community?* (New York: Bantam, 1968), 55; Theodore G. Vincent, *Black Power and the Garvey Movement* (Berkeley, CA: Ramparts, 1971), 217–48; Stokely Carmichael, interview with author, Akron, Ohio, November 10, 1977.

13. Raymond Wolters, *Negroes and the Great Depression: The Problem of Economic Recovery* (Westport, CT: Greenwood, 1970), ix; William Henry Chafe, *The American Woman: Her Changing Social, Economic, and Political Roles, 1920–1970* (New York: Oxford University Press, 1972), 107–11; Winifred D. Wandersee Bolin, "The Economics of Middle-Income Family Life: Working Women During the Great Depression," *Journal of American History*, Vol. 65, No. 1 (1978), 60–74.

14. "The Woman Wage Earner: Her Situation Today," *Women's Bureau Bulletin*, No. 172 (1939), 48.

15. Interestingly, the percentage of blacks supporting FDR continued to grow through the 1940s. See Leslie H. Fishel, Jr., "The Negro in the New Deal Era," in Bernard Sternsher, ed., *The Negro in Depression and War: Prelude to Revolution, 1930–1945* (Chicago: Quadrangle, 1969), 7–28; Allen Kifer, "The Negro Under the New Deal, 1933–1941" (Ph.D. dissertation, University of Wisconsin, 1961); Ralph J. Bunche, "Negro Political Activity in the North," in Dewey W. Grantham, ed., *The Political Status of the Negro in the Age of FDR* (Chicago: University of Chicago Press, 1973), 572–606, esp. 608–31.

16. Quote, "The Roosevelt Record" (editorial), *The Crisis*, Vol. 47 (November 1940), 343. See Zangrando, "Antilynching Bill," 106–17. The NAACP successfully lobbied two bills through the House (1937 and 1940), only to see them killed in the Senate. Nevertheless, Zangrando argues, the NAACP's relentless campaign acted as a deterrent to lynching and helped prepare the way for greater public acceptance of civil rights. See also, Zangrando's *The NAACP Crusade Against Lynching, 1909–1950* (Philadelphia: Temple University Press, 1980), 98–165.

17. See Wilson Record, *The Negro and the Communist Party* (Chapel Hill: University of North Carolina Press, 1951), 54–183, for events of the 1930s. For the post–World War II years, see Joseph C. Mouledous, "From Browderism to Peaceful Co-Existence: An Analysis of Developments in the Communist Position on the American Negro," *Phylon*, Vol. 25, No. 1 (1964), 79–90; Robert L. Allen, *Black Awakening in Capitalist America: An Analytic History* (Garden City, NY: Doubleday, 1969), 86–87; James S. Allen, *The Negro Question in the United States* (New York: International, 1936), 13–203; George Padmore, *Pan-Africanism or Communism* (Garden City, NY: Doubleday, 1971), 284–86; Hall, *Black Separatism*, 75; Brunetta R. Wolfman, "The Communist Party, Always Out of Step," in Raymond L. Hall, ed., *Black Separatism and Social Reality: Rhetoric and Reason* (New York: Pergamon, 1977), 109–14; T. H. Kennedy and T. F. Leary, "Communist Thought on the Negro," *Phylon*, Vol. 8, No. 2 (1947), 116–23; Wilson Record, *Race and Radicalism: The NAACP and the Communist Party in Conflict* (Ithaca, NY: Cornell University Press, 1964), 85–95. John Kosa and Clyde Z. Nunn, in "Race, Deprivation and Attitude Toward Communism," *Phylon*, Vol. 25, No. 4 (1964), 337–46, offer a plausible explanation of why communism never attracted mass support from the black community. Their contention is that communist ideology was too sophisticated for oppressed and poorly educated blacks. Although black

Americans were suffering from "classical deprivation," few could understand their plight, or have hope through Marxist solutions.

18. "The Opportunity Presidential Poll," *Opportunity*, Vol. 10 (May 1932), 141.

19. Padmore, *Pan-Africanism or Communism*, 440, 287; Allen, *Black Awakening in Capitalist America*, 87; Claude M. Lightfoot, *Racism and Human Survival: Lessons of Nazi Germany for Today's World* (New York: International, 1972), 288; Charles H. Martin, *The Angelo Herndon Case and Southern Justice* (Baton Rouge: Louisiana State University Press, 1976), xi–xiii.

20. Wilson C. Record, "The Development of the Communist Position on the Negro Question in the United States," *Phylon*, Vol. 19, No. 3 (1958), 306–26; David H. Bennett, "The Enigma of American Extremism," *Centennial Review*, Vol. 11, No. 2 (1967), 198–219. Milton Cantor found that blacks never accounted for more than 8 percent of the CP-USA's rank and file. See Cantor's *The Divided Left: American Radicalism, 1900–1975* (New York: Hill and Wang, 1978), 15.

21. Richard M. Dalfiume, "The 'Forgotten Years' of the Negro Revolution," *Journal of American History*, Vol. 55, No. 1 (1968), 90–106, and Dalfiume, *Desegregation of the U.S. Armed Forces: Fighting on Two Fronts, 1939–1953* (Columbia: University of Missouri Press, 1969), 25–43. See A. Russell Buchanan, *Black Americans in World War II* (Santa Barbara, CA: Clio, 1977), 59–101.

22. See Charles H. Thompson, "The American Negro and the National Defense" (Editorial Comment), *Journal of Negro Education*, Vol. 19, No. 4 (1940), 547–52; Robert C. Weaver, "Racial Employment Trends in National Defense," *Phylon*, Vol. 2, No. 4 (1941), 357–58; Louis Coleridge Kesselman, *The Social Politics of FEPC: A Study in Reform Pressure Movements* (Chapel Hill: University of North Carolina Press, 1948), 3–13; E. Franklin Frazier, "Ethnic and Minority Groups in Wartime: With Special Reference to the Negro," *American Journal of Sociology*, Vol. 48, No. 3 (1942), 373–77.

23. Frazier, "Ethnic and Minority Groups in Wartime," 375.

24. "For Manhood in National Defense" (Editorial), *The Crisis*, Vol. 47 (December 1940), 375. See Lee Finkle, "The Conservative Aims of Militant Rhetoric: Black Protest During World War II Years," *Journal of American History*, Vol. 60, No. 3 (1973), 692–713.

25. William H. Harris, *Keeping the Faith: A. Philip Randolph, Milton P. Webster, and the Brotherhood of Sleeping Car Porters, 1925–37* (Urbana : University of Illinois Press, 1977), 26–65, 136–38, 217–25; Jervis Anderson, *A. Philip Randolph: A Biographical Portrait* (New York: Harcourt Brace Jovanovich, 1973), 187–225, 241–64, 343. Randolph first became a socialist in 1916. See Philip S. Foner, *American Socialism and Black Americans: From the Age of Jackson to World War II* (Westport, CT: Greenwood, 1977), 268; Herbert Garfinkel, *When Negroes March: The March on Washington Movement in the Organizational Politics for FEPC* (New York: Atheneum, 1969), 8, 38–96.

26. Quote, A. Philip Randolph, "Call to Negro America 'To March on Washington for Jobs and Equal Participation in National Defense,' July 1, 1941," *The Black Worker*, May 1941.

27. A. Philip Randolph, "The Negro March on Washington," *The Black Worker*, July 1941; "Executive Order 8802," *Code of Federal Regulations* (1968), 957.

28. See Garfinkel, *When Negroes March*, 71–77; L.B. Granger, "The President, the

Negro and Defense," *Opportunity*, Vol. 19, No. 7 (1941), 204–7; "FEP Committee," *The Crisis*, Vol. 48 (September 1951), 291.

29. August Meier and Elliott Rudwick, *CORE: A Study in the Civil Rights Movement, 1942–1968* (New York: Oxford University Press, 1973), 409–31.

30. George M. Houser, "CORE: A Brief History" and "CORE Interview Sheet, November 17, 1942," CORE Papers, Social Action Collection, The State Historical Society of Wisconsin, Madison, WI (hereafter cited as SAC, SHSW). Meier and Rudwick, *CORE*, 7–8.

31. Originally a syndicalist term, "direct-action" was first used in the United States by the Industrial Workers of the World (IWW). However, CORE was the first protest group to adopt the term wholesale, and then only as an adjunct to "nonviolence," or nonviolent "resistance."

32. "James Russell Robinson to Night Manager of Jack Spratt Coffee House," Letter, May 14, 1942, James Farmer, "Report Sheet," November 11, 1942, George Houser, "Erasing the Color Line," 1945, "History of Stoner's Case," n.d., all in CORE Papers; "Sit-Down Strike Breaks South Side Jim Crow," *Chicago Bee*, May 16, 1943; August Meier and Elliott Rudwick, "How CORE Began," *Social Science Quarterly*, Vol. 49, No. 4 (1969), 789–99.

33. *Mitchell* v. *United States*, 313 U.S. 577 (1941); *Smith* v. *Allwright, Election Judge*, 321 U.S. 649 (1944). See Loren Miller, *The Petitioners: The Story of the Supreme Court of the United States and the Negro* (New York: Pantheon, 1966), 294–95, 365–66.

34. "N.A.A.C.P. 27th Annual Report for 1936," "N.A.A.C.P. 29th Annual Report for 1938" and "N.A.A.C.P. 30th Annual Report for 1940," all in NAACP Papers. Jack Greenberg, *Race Relations and American Law* (New York: Columbia University Press, 1959), 37–38; Randall W. Bland, *Private Pressure on Public Law: The Legal Career of Justice Thurgood Marshall* (Port Washington, NY: Kennikat, 1973), 13–98.

35. Alfred H. Kelly, "The Coming of *Brown* v. *Board of Education*," in Arnold M. Paul, ed., *Black Americans and the Supreme Court Since Emancipation: Betrayal or Protection?* (New York: Holt, Rinehart and Winston, 1972), 36–44.

36. *Brown* v. *Board of Education of Topeka, Shawnee County, Kan.*, 347 U.S. 483 (1954). On the evolutionary nature of the decision and Thurgood Marshall's pivotal role in the process, see Daniel M. Berman, *It Is So Ordered: The Supreme Court Rules on School Segregation* (New York: W. W. Norton, 1966), 1–51; Richard Kluger, *Simple Justice: The History of Brown v. Board of Education and Black America's Struggle for Equality* (New York: Alfred A. Knopf, 1976), 184–99, 214–17.

37. See Kluger, *Simple Justice*, 748–78. Although a complete discussion of the legal measures affecting the contemporary civil rights movement would be too massive to include in a study of this nature, it is helpful to note that Albert P. Blaustein and Robert L. Zangrando's *Civil Rights and the American Negro: A Documentary History* (New York: Washington Square, 1968), in addition to works already cited, is a useful source on the civil rights court cases. For additional information on the question of civil rights enforcement itself, see the annual issues, U.S. Commission on Civil Rights, *Federal Civil Rights Enforcement Effort* (Washington, DC: Government Printing Office, 1971–1975).

38. Gunnar Myrdal, *An American Dilemma: The Negro Problem and Modern Democracy* (New York: Harper and Brothers, 1944), 1014.

39. Rosa Parks, taped interview, 1967, Bunche Oral History Collection.

40. Martin Luther King, Jr., *Stride Toward Freedom: The Montgomery Story* (New

York: Harper and Row, 1958), 51, 53. See David L. Lewis, *King: A Critical Biography* (Baltimore: Penguin, 1970), 46–84; Lerone Bennett, Jr., "When the Man and the Hour Are Met," in C. Eric Lincoln, ed., *Martin Luther King, Jr.: A Profile* (New York: Hill and Wang, 1984), 40–71.

41. Ella J. Baker, "Memorandum to Committee on Administration (SCLC), October 23, 1959" (mimeographed), Ella Baker Papers, SAC, SHSW; Lewis, *King*, 88–89, 108–111.

42. "Negroes in South in Store Sitdown," *New York Times*, February 3, 1960; Tilman C. Cothran, "The Negro Protest Against Segregation in the South," *Annals of the American Academy*, Vol. 357 (January 1965), 68. The decision by Southern students to take an active part in social protest was due in large part to their perception of the sit-in tactic as being singularly successful, especially moreso than older forms of legislation and litigation. See Fredric Solomon and Jacob R. Fishman, "The Psycho-social Meaning of Nonviolence in Student Civil Rights Activities," *Psychiatry*, Vol. 27, No. 2 (1964), 91–99, and their "Youth and Social Action: II. Action and Identity Formation in the First Student Sit-in Demonstrations," *Journal of Social Issues*, Vol. 20, No. 2 (1964), 39–41; Helen Fuller, "Southern Students Take Over: 'The Creation of the Beloved Community,'" *New Republic*, Vol. 142 (May 2, 1961), 14–16.

43. "Student Nonviolent Coordinating Committee Constitution," and "Recommendations Passed By the Student Nonviolent Coordinating Committee Conference: Atlanta, Georgia, October 14–16, 1960," in Ann and Carl Braden Papers, SAC, SHSW; "Statement Submitted by the Student Nonviolent Coordinating Committee to the Platform Committee of the National Democratic Convention, Thursday Morning, July 7, 1960, Los Angeles, California," Ella Baker Papers. Howard Zinn, *SNCC: The New Abolitionists* (Boston: Beacon, 1965), 32–34; Marion Barry, Charles F. McDew and Julian Bond, taped interviews, 1967, 1967 and 1968, Bunche Oral History Collection. For an analysis of why SNCC became an independent organization, see Clayborne Carson, Jr., "Toward Freedom and Community: The Evolution of Ideas in the Student Nonviolent Coordinating Committee, 1960–1966" (Ph.D. dissertation, University of California, Los Angeles, 1975), 59–60, 76, 79.

44. "Riders Map Big Push," *Richmond Afro–American*, June 10, 1961; Meier and Rudwick, *CORE*, 135.

45. Anthony Lewis and the *New York Times, Portrait of a Decade: The Second American Revolution* (New York: Random House, 1964), 179–89; Lewis, *King*, 171–209. For the black view of Birmingham's notorious racism, see Fred L. Shuttlesworth, "Birmingham Shall be Free Some Day," *Freedomways*, Vol. 4, No. 1 (1964), 16–19.

46. "Dr. Martin Luther King, Jr., Southern Christian Leadership Conference," *New York Times*, August 29, 1963. See Robert L. Zangrando, "The Direction of the March," *Negro History Bulletin*, Vol. 27, No. 3 (1963), 60–64.

47. James Baldwin, *The Fire Next Time* (New York: Dial, 1963), 99.

48. "The Civil Rights Act of 1964," *U.S. Statutes At Large, 1964* (1965), 241–68; Clifford M. Lytle, "The History of the Civil Rights Bill of 1964," *Journal of Negro History*, Vol. 51, No. 4 (1966), 275–96. See Floyd M. Riddick and Murray Zweben, "The Eighty-eighth Congress: Second Session," *Western Political Quarterly*, Vol. 18, No. 2 (1965), 334–49.

49. "Mississippi: Structure of the Movement, Present Operations, and Prospectus for this Summer" and "Council of Federated Organizations: Mississippi Freedom Summer" (mimeographed), in CORE Papers. Pat Watters and Reese Cleghorn, *Climb-*

ing Jacob's Ladder: The Arrival of Negroes in Southern Politics (New York: Harcourt, Brace and World, 1967), 63–112; Neil R. McMillen, "Black Enfranchisement in Mississippi: Federal Enforcement and Black Protest in the 1960's," *Journal of Southern History*, Vol. 43, No. 3 (1977), 360–61; Lawrence Guyot and Mike Thelwell, "The Politics of Necessity and Survival in Mississippi," *Freedomways*, Vol. 6, No. 2 (1966), 120–32; James W. Silver, *Mississippi: The Closed Society* (New York: Harcourt, Brace and World, 1964), esp., vii–xxii, 83–104.

50. Sara Evans, "Women's Consciousness and the Southern Black Movement," *Southern Exposure*, Vol. 4, No. 4 (1977), 10–18; Mary Aickin Rothschild, "Northern Volunteers and the Southern 'Freedom Summers,' 1964–1965: A Social History" (Ph.D. dissertation, University of Washington, 1974), 177–84.

51. Bell Hooks, *Ain't I A Woman? Black Women and Feminism* (Boston: South End Press, 1982), Paula Gidding, *When and Where I Enter: The Impact of Black Women on Race and Sex in America* (New York: William Morrow, 1984), and Angela Y. Davis, *Women, Race and Class* (New York: Vintage, 1983) are three especially useful works regarding black women's perception of their influence on and role in the historical black struggle for equality.

52. Editorial, *New York Times*, August 16, 1964; "Negro Party Set to Push Its Drive," *New York Times*, October 11, 1964; "Mississippi and the NAACP," *The Crisis*, Vol. 73 (June–July 1966), 315–18; Jack Minnis, "The Mississippi Freedom Democratic Party: A New Declaration of Independence," *Freedomways*, Vol. 5, No. 2 (1965), 264–78; "The Mississippi Freedom Democratic Party" (mimeographed), Aviva Futorian Papers, SAC, SHSW; "Mississippi Freedom Democratic Party" (mimeographed), CORE Papers; Letter, "Fannie Lou Hamer to Friends, October 23, 1964" and "National Committee for Free Elections in Sunflower" (handbill), Fannie Lou Hamer Papers, SAC, SHSW.

53. Minnis, "Mississippi Freedom Democratic Party," 276.

54. Ibid., 277.

55. Stokely Carmichael, interview with author, Akron, OH, October 8, 1976. See Carmichael, "What We Want," *New York Review of Books*, September 22, 1966, "Stokely Carmichael Explains Black Power to a Black Audience in Detroit," and "Stokely Carmichael Explains Black Power to a White Audience in Whitewater, Wisconsin," in Robert L. Scott and Wayne Brockreide, *The Rhetoric of Black Power* (Westport, CT: Greenwood, 1969), 84–111, which gives a militant's nationalistic viewpoint respecting the growing restlessness and militancy of young blacks.

56. See "Talking About It . . . Black Power: The Widening Dialogue," *New South*, Vol. 21, No. 3 (1966), 65–80; Solomon P. Gethers, "Black Power: Three Years Later," *Negro Digest*, Vol. 19, No. 2 (1969), 4–10; Jack L. Walker and Joel D. Aberbach, "The Meanings of Black Power: A Comparison of White and Black Interpretations of a Political Slogan," *American Political Science Review*, Vol. 64, No. 2 (1970), 367–88. Carmichael admittedly borrowed the concept of self-defense from the black revolutionary president of the Monroe, North Carolina, NAACP chapter, Robert F. Williams, who was expelled from that position in 1959 after endorsing "self-defense" and meeting "violence with violence . . . lynching with lynching." By the mid–1960s Williams had become a cause célèbre for militant blacks; his *Negroes with Guns* served as a primer for black paramilitary and self-defense groups. Stokely Carmichael, interview with author, Akron, OH, November 10, 1977; Clinton P. Jones, "Black Power: An Analysis of Select Strategies for the Implementation of Concept" (Ph.D. dissertation,

Claremont Graduate School, 1971), 58–64; Robert F. Williams, *Negroes with Guns* (New York: Marzani and Musell, 1964), esp., 39–41, 120–24.

57. See J. Herman Blake, "Black Nationalism," *Annals of the American Academy*, Vol. 382 (1969), 15–25; James H. Laue, "A Contemporary Revitalization Movement in American Race Relations: The Black Muslims," *Social Forces*, Vol. 42, No. 3 (1964), 315–23; *Autobiography of Malcolm X*, esp. Haley's "Epilogue," 383–456; Samuel A. Weiss, "The Ordeal of Malcolm X," *South Atlantic Quarterly*, Vol. 67, No. 1 (1968), 53–63.

58. Carmichael, interview with author, November 10, 1977; Stokely Carmichael and Charles V. Hamilton, *Black Power: The Politics of Liberation in America* (New York: Vintage, 1967), xi–xii; Frantz Fanon, *The Wretched of the Earth* (New York: Grove, 1968 [1963]).

59. Carmichael and Hamilton, *Black Power*, 37, 39.

60. Huey P. Newton, *Revolutionary Suicide* (New York: Harcourt Brace Jovanovich, 1973), 113; Bobby Seale, taped interview, 1968, Bunche Oral History Collection.

61. Newton, *Revolutionary Suicide*, 111–12.

62. Locksley Edmondson, "The Internationalization of Black Power: Historical and Contemporary Perspectives," in Hall, *Black Separatism*, 183–94, quote, 186; Harold C. Relyea, "Black Power and Parallel Institutions: Ideological and Theoretical Considerations," *Journal of Human Relations*, Vol. 17, No. 2 (1969), 208–23, and Relyea, " 'Black Power': The Genesis and Future of Revolution," *Journal of Human Relations*, Vol. 16, No. 4 (1968), 502–13; Robert Blauner, *Racial Oppression in America* (New York: Harper and Row, 1972), 51–110. Quote, Gethers, "Black Power," 8.

63. See John H. Bracey, Jr., August Meier, and Elliott Rudwick eds., *Black Nationalism in America* (Indianapolis: Bobbs-Merrill, 1970), xlvii–lx; August Meier, "The Emergence of Negro Nationalism: A Study in Ideologies," in August Meier and Elliott Rudwick, eds., *Along the Color Line: Explorations in the Black Experience* (Urbana: University of Illinois Press, 1976), 198–91; Carmichael and Hamilton, *Black Power*, 41; Robert S. Brown, "A Case for Separatism," in Hall, *Black Separatism*, 24–28.

64. "The Founding Convention" (Republic of New Africa, Detroit, March 31, 1968) and "Position Paper of the Democratic Liberation Party of Politics, Third National Conference on Black Power," in Black Power Conference Papers, SAC, SHSW. See Robert S. Browne, "The Case for Black Separatism," *Ramparts*, Vol. 6 (December 1967), 46–51, for the conference resolutions. For a profile of the RNA, see Lionel Lokos, *The New Racism: Reverse Discrimination in America* (New Rochelle, NY: Arlington, 1971), 73–97.

65. See Alex Poinsett, "Roy Innis: Nation-Builder," *Ebony*, October 1969, 171–76; Ed Brown, "CORE and Garveyism," *CORE*, Vol. 3, No. 3 (1973), 41.

66. Stuart C. Gilman, "An Analysis of American Black Political Thought in the 1960s from a Marxist Perspective: The Phenomenological Approach" (Ph.D. dissertation, Miami University, Oxford, Ohio, 1974), 254–99; David Hillard (Panther Chief of Staff) on "Face the Nation," CBS, December 28, 1968, Bunche Oral History Collection; Lokos, *The New Racism*, iii; Bracey, Meier, and Rudwick, *Black Nationalism*, xlviii–lx; Newton, *Revolutionary Suicide*, 111–12; Hall, *Black Separatism*, 151–65.

67. James Forman, "The Black Manifesto," in Floyd B. Barbour, ed., *The Black Seventies* (Boston: Porter Sargent, 1970), 299, and Forman, "Control, Conflict and Change: The Underlying Concepts of the Black Manifesto," in Robert S. Lecky and H.

Eliott Wright, eds., *Black Manifesto: Religion, Racism, and Reparations* (New York: Sheed and Ward, 1969), 34–51.

68. Cited in Charlayne Hunter, "Black Intellectuals and Activists Split on Ideological Direction," *New York Times*, April 28, 1975.

69. Stokely Carmichael, "Marxism-Leninism and Nkrumahism," *The Black Scholar*, Vol. 4, No. 5 (1973), 42. For Nkrumah's position, see his *Neo-Colonialism: The Last Stage of Imperialism* (New York: International, 1965), esp., ix–xx; Carmichael, interview with author, November 10, 1977; "Carmichael: Blacks Must Make Move to Socialism," *Pittsburgh Courier*, November 12, 1977. Carmichael also had become known as Kwame Ture by the mid–1970s.

70. "Introducing the All-Afrikan People's Revolutionary Party" (pamphlet, n.d.), in Lodovic B. Kimble (founding member of A-APRP and active organizer of the Tennessee State University branch), personal papers, Nashville, TN; Stokely Carmichael, speech, Kent State University, Kent, OH, May 4, 1977; "Nkrumaism [*sic*]: The Ideology of the All-Afrikan People's Revolutionary Party" and "Pan-Afrikanism: Why Afrikans World-Wide Must Support It!" (mimeographed and mass distributed) author's personal papers; "The Political Education Program of the All-Afrikan People's Revolutionary Party," "All-Afrikan People's Revolutionary Party" and "Orientation Agenda" (pamphlets, n.d.), A-APRP "Memoranda and Press Releases," June 14, 1979, October 4, 1979, and November 15, 1979, all in Kimble personal papers.

71. The Douglass quote, to which italics have been added, is in Philip S. Foner, ed., *Frederick Douglass on Women's Rights* (Westport, CT: Greenwood, 1976), 105.

72. See Ellen Carol DuBois, *Feminism and Suffrage: The Emergence of an Independent Women's Movement in America, 1848–1869* (Ithaca, NY: Cornell University Press, 1978), 21–52; Keith E. Melder, *Beginnings of Sisterhood: The American Woman's Rights Movement, 1800–1850* (New York: Schocken, 1977), 1–11; Kathryn Kish Sklar, *Catharine Beecher: A Study in American Domesticity* (New Haven: Yale University Press, 1973), esp. 15–27; Carroll Smith-Rosenberg, "Beauty, the Beast and the Militant Woman: A Case Study in Sex Roles and Social Stress in Jacksonian America," *American Quarterly*, Vol. 23, No. 4 (1971), 562–84; Nancy F. Cott, *The Bonds of Womanhood: "Woman's Sphere" in New England, 1780–1835* (New Haven: Yale University Press, 1977), 197–206; Anne Firor Scott, *The Southern Lady: From Pedestal to Politics, 1830–1930* (Chicago: University of Chicago Press, 1970), 46–79, 135–84; Eleanor Flexner, *Century of Struggle: The Woman's Rights Movement in the United States* (New York: Atheneum, 1974), 62–101; Sheila M. Rothman, *Woman's Proper Place: A History of Changing Ideals and Practices, 1870 to the Present* (New York: Basic, 1978), 1–9; Linda K. Kerber, "Separate Spheres, Female Worlds, Woman's Place: The Rhetoric of Women's History," *Journal of American History*, Vol. 75, No. 1 (June 1988), 9–39.

73. Elizabeth Cady Stanton, Susan B. Anthony, and Matilda Joslyn Gage, eds., *History of Woman Suffrage*, Vol. 1 (New York: Arno and the New York Times, 1969 [1881]), 61–62.

74. Ibid., 69; Louis W. Banner, *Elizabeth Cady Stanton: A Radical for Women's Rights* (Boston: Little, Brown, 1980), 42; Mary Ann B. Oakley, *Elizabeth Cady Stanton* (Old Westbury, NY: The Feminist Press, 1972), 45–49.

75. See Flexner, *Century of Struggle*, xii, 74–75. "The Declaration of Sentiments and Resolutions" is sometimes referred to as the "Declaration of Sentiments," or, in Flexner's case, the "Declaration of Principles."

76. Flexner, *Century of Struggle*, 105–12; Oakley, *Stanton*, 69–79; Ida Husted Harper, *The Life and Work of Susan B. Anthony, Including Public Addresses, Her Own Letters and Many from Her Contemporaries During Fifty Years*, Vol. I (Indianapolis: Bowen-Merrill, 1888), 225–40.

77. The Fourteenth Amendment for the first time incorporated the word "male" into the United States Constitution. See Emily Hahn, *Once Upon a Pedestal* (New York: Thomas Y. Crowell, 1974), 180–85, for its effect on feminism.

78. Flexner, *Century of Struggle*, 145–46. For women's rejection of the "Negro's Hour" thesis, see Stanton, Anthony, and Gage, *History of Woman Suffrage*, Vol. II, 90–97, 256–58; Harper, *Life and Work of Susan B. Anthony*, Vol. I, 255–70.

79. Foner, *Frederick Douglass on Women's Rights*, esp. 25–43, quote, 32–33.

80. Stanton, Anthony, and Gage, *History of Woman Suffrage*, Vol. II, 267–68.

81. Information on the conservative and conventional trend in the movement is found in William L. O'Neill, *Everyone Was Brave: A History of Feminism in America* (Chicago: Quadrangle, 1971), 3–224.

82. Victoria Woodhull, "Editorial," *Woodhull and Claflin's Weekly*, January 14, 1871; Victoria Woodhull, "To Horace Greely," *Woodhull and Claflin's Weekly*, August 26, 1871.

83. Carol Hymowitz and Michaele Weissman, *A History of Women in America* (New York: Bantam, 1978), 222.

84. Charlotte Perkins Gilman, *The Living of Charlotte Perkins Gilman: An Autobiography* (New York: D. Appleton-Century, 1935), 3, 131, 187, 198–214, 247, 320, and Gilman, *The Home: Its Work and Influence* (New York: McClure, Phillips, 1903), esp. 3–13, 82–83.

85. Charlotte Perkins Stetson Gilman, *Women and Economics: A Study of the Economic Relation Between Men and Women as a Factor in Social Evolution* (Boston: Small, Maynard, 1899), 242–46, quote 225. See Carl N. Degler, "Charlotte Perkins Gilman on the Theory and Practice of Feminism," *American Quarterly*, Vol. 8, No. 1 (1956), 21–39.

86. See "Introduction," Alix Kates Shulman, ed., *Red Emma Speaks: Selected Writings and Speeches by Emma Goldman* (New York: Random House, 1972), 3–25; Richard Drinnon, *Rebel in Paradise: A Biography of Emma Goldman* (Chicago: The University of Chicago Press, 1961), 166–71.

87. Shulman, *Red Emma Speaks*, 142 and 43.

88. Ibid., 391.

89. Cited in Margaret S. Marsh, "The Anarchist-Feminist Response to the 'Woman Question' in Late Nineteenth-Century America," *American Quarterly*, Vol. 30, No. 4 (1978), 541.

90. August Bebel, *Woman Under Socialism*, trans. Daniel De Leon (New York: Labor News, 1904 [1883]); Frederick Engels, *The Origin of the Family, Private Property and the State* (New York: International, 1942 [1884]).

91. Olive M. Johnson, *Woman and the Socialist Movement* (New York: Socialist Labor Party, 1919), 18.

92. Kate Richards O'Hare, "Shall Women Vote?" *Social Revolution*, August 1914.

93. Elizabeth Gurley Flynn, *The Rebel Girl: An Autobiography, My First Life, 1906–1926* (New York: International, 1955), 57–58. See Alice Kessler-Harris, *Out to Work: A History of Wage-Earning Women in the United States* (New York: Oxford University Press, 1982), 225.

94. Cited in Harbor Allen, "The Flynn," *American Mercury*, Vol. 9 (December 1926), 426.

95. Elizabeth Gurley Flynn, *I Speak My Own Piece: Autobiography of "The Rebel Girl"* (New York: Masses and Mainstream, 1955), 103.

96. Quote, Freda Kirchwey, "The Pan-American Conference of Women," *The Nation*, May 10, 1922, 565; "Freda Kirchwey, 82, Dies; Long Editor of the Nation," *New York Times*, January 4, 1976.

97. "Rose Stokes Dies After Operation," *New York Times*, June 21, 1933; "Reds Honor Dead Leaders," *New York Times*, July 25, 1933; David A. Shannon, *The Socialist Party of America: A History* (Chicago: Quadrangle, 1955), 146–47; Edward T. James, et al., eds., *Notable American Women, 1607–1950: A Biographical Dictionary* (Cambridge, MA: Belknap, 1971), 384–86.

98. Quote, Flynn, *The Rebel Girl*, 280, see "Editor's Note," 9–11; "Red Leader Testifies," *New York Times*, October 4, 1952.

99. "U.S. Communists Assail 'Cold War,'" *New York Times*, August 5, 1955; "Elizabeth Flynn Freed," *New York Times*, May 26, 1957. "Elizabeth Gurley Flynn is Dead: Head of U.S. Communist Party," *New York Times*, September 6, 1964; "Miss Flynn is Cremated: Tribute in Moscow Today," *New York Times*, September 8, 1964; "Miss Flynn Given Moscow Tribute," *New York Times*, September 9, 1964.

100. The argument that suffrage became a moral reform crusade rather than a movement seeking a radical restructuring of society is discussed thoroughly in Aileen S. Kraditor, *The Ideas of the Woman Suffrage Movement, 1890–1920* (New York: Columbia University Press, 1965), esp., 249–64. See also, Glenda Gates Riley, "The Subtle Subversion: Changes in the Traditional Image of the American Woman," *The Historian*, Vol. 32, No. 2 (1970), 210–27; O'Neill, *Everyone Was Brave*, 146–68.

101. Jane Addams, "Why Women Should Vote," *Ladies' Home Journal*, January 1910, 21–22, quote, 22.

102. See Chafe, *The American Woman*, 112–32; J. Stanley Lemons, *The Woman Citizen: Social Feminism in the 1920s* (Urbana: University of Illinois Press, 1973), 49, 144, 181–208.

103. June Sochen, *Movers and Shakers: American Women Thinkers and Activists, 1900–1970* (New York: Quadrangle, 1973), 97–170.

104. O'Neill, *Everyone Was Brave*, 126–27; "Miss Alice Paul Retires," *New York Times*, February 20, 1921; Loretta Ellen Zimmerman, "Alice Paul and the National Woman's Party, 1912–1920" (Ph.D. dissertation, Tulane University, 1964), 162–322; Inez Haynes Irwin, *The Story of the Woman's Party* (New York: Harcourt, Brace, 1921), 193–476; Freda Kirchwey, "Alice Paul Pulls the Strings," *The Nation*, March 2, 1921, 332–33; "Declaration of Principles," *Equal Rights* (NWP Journal), Vol. 1 (February 17, 1923), 5; "Why the Argument?" *Equal Rights*, Vol. 1 (October 6, 1923), 268; "Drive for Equal Rights," *New York Times*, July 21, 1923. On the issue of protective legislation, also known as social welfare legislation, see Chafe, *The American Woman*, 79–83, 124–32, and the broader historical study of Judith A. Baer, *The Chains of Protection: The Judicial Response to Women's Labor Legislation* (Westport, CT: Greenwood, 1978).

105. Dorothy Elizabeth Johnson, "Organized Women and National Legislation, 1920–1941" (Ph.D. dissertation, Western Reserve University, 1960), esp. 504–28. Some researchers, for example Jo Freeman, have found that feminism died in the 1920s, not to be resurrected until the 1960s. However, a number of researchers, for example Leila J. Rupp and Verta Taylor, have shown that the feminist spirit clearly lived on in

this period, if not in dramatically altered form. Jo Freeman, "The Women's Liberation Movement: Its Origins, Organizations, Activities, and Ideas," in Jo Freeman, ed., *Women: A Feminist Perspective* (Palo Alto, CA: Mayfield, 1979), 557–74; Leila J. Rupp and Verta Taylor, *Survival in the Doldrums: The American Women's Rights Movement, 1945 to the 1960s* (New York: Oxford University Press, 1987), 187–206.

106. Sochen, *Movers and Shakers*, 171–228. On the issue of consumerism and domesticity being defined a woman's sphere after the war, see Chafe, *The American Woman*, 199–225.

107. Blanche Wiesen Cook, "Female Support Networks and Political Activism: Lillian Wald, Crystal Eastman, Emma Goldman," *Chrysalis*, No. 3 (Fall 1977), 43–61.

108. Ibid., 45–54; quote, 48.

109. Carmichael, interview with author, November 10, 1977.

Legal-Oriented Feminism

THE LEGAL APPROACH: INTRODUCTION

The most recent surge of American feminism, called "the rebirth of feminism," "the new feminism," "the resurgence of feminism," "the revival of feminism," and perhaps most commonly "the women's liberation movement," has reflected a particularly diverse and decentralized protest base.[1] It is comprised of a broad spectrum of organizations and individuals dedicated to a variety of ideological goals, tactics and strategies. In short, the new feminist drive can be described in many terms, but never as monolithic. As we have determined earlier in this study, contemporary feminist orientations have manifested themselves in three discernible wings based upon legal, cultural and economic orientations.

The three branches of the movement have gone about reaching their goals in different ways, yet there has been a certain unity of purpose and cross-pollination, as will be noted later. Since the legal model seemed to attract the largest number of members and reflected most closely the historical lessons of organized feminism, this chapter will address the ideological origins and development of the mass-membership phase of the contemporary movement. Nonetheless, it will be demonstrated in later chapters that even though the cultural and economic phases might have attracted fewer adherents relative to the legal model, certainly their members exhibited as much longevity and intensity as did the women active in the legal phase.

The legal-oriented aspects of contemporary feminism grew from a number of protest events and reformist actions of the early 1960s. During this time two public incidents in particular helped focus mass and private attention on the role of women in society. In 1961 President Kennedy established a Commission on the Status of Women—the first national commission of its kind, and arguably the most important national action with respect to women since the creation of the federal Women's Bureau in the Department of Labor in 1920.[2] Equally significant, however, was the impact of Betty Friedan's *The Feminine Mystique*, a 1963 best-seller which convinced many women that male America had perpetrated a hoax that convinced women that their greatest reward lay in being a "happy housewife,"[3] what others have subsequently labeled the modern "cult of domesticity." Though many of Friedan's basic arguments had been voiced previously, her articulate, blunt attack on the institution of "housewifery" stimulated many women to a new awareness of their inferior positions, as did the Kennedy commission's report of the same year.

The Kennedy Commission and Other Federal Actions

In his first year President Kennedy established a Commission on the Status of Women by signing Executive Order 10980, charged with "developing recommendations for overcoming discriminations in government and private employment on the basis of sex and for developing recommendations for services which will enable women to continue their role as wives and mothers while making a maximum contribution to the world around them."[4] Eleanor Roosevelt served as chairperson of the commission until her illness and death in 1962, at which time Esther Peterson, head of the Women's Bureau, assumed the reins of leadership. While Kennedy's exact personal or political reasons for creating such a commission remain a matter of scholarly conjecture, he possibly appointed it at the urging of Roosevelt and Peterson, both of whom argued that the president must act more than symbolically to repay women campaign workers and loyalists. Others have maintained that Kennedy acted to defuse the politically volatile and recently resurrected issue of an Equal Rights Amendment for women. Regardless of the reason, as Cynthia E. Harrison has indicated, the idea of a commission demonstrated the Kennedy administration's willingness to act explicitly on behalf of women and in this sense helped immeasurably to return women's issues squarely into the public policy arena.[5]

Even though the commission's report itself was mild in tone (e.g., it emphasized women's "role as wives and mothers"), it had a telling impact on female consciousness and commitment to feminist issues. With publication of the commission's final report, *American Women*, in October 1963, the widespread inequities of sex discrimination were brought clearly to the attention of a national audience. The report called for a "widely varied initiative, both private and public, in all parts of the country" to be undertaken to reverse common patterns of sex discrimination.[6] In many ways the well-documented findings served to underscore the deeply rooted discrimination that existed in the areas of employment and education, something the Women's Bureau had been documenting on a less grand scale for the previous four decades. At the behest of member Marguerite Rawalt, the commission left the question of a federal Equal Rights Amendment open for future consideration.[7] With the *Report* as a backdrop, capable spokespersons on women's issues became increasingly visible and vocal.[8]

Two of its recommendations were quickly implemented with the establishment of an Interdepartmental Committee on the Status of Women (IDCSW) and a Citizens' Advisory Council on the Status of Women (CACSW). The CACSW's Family Law and Policy Task Force, under the direction of feminist Marguerite Rawalt, soon gained the reputation of being "militant" in nature because of its nontraditional demands and its aggressive approach toward achieving those demands.[9] The IDCSW and the CACSW sponsored several national conferences of state commissions on the status of women. Consequently, the president's commission, the IDCSW, the CACSW and the various state commissions that emerged all made legislative proposals addressing the unequal treatment of American women in education and employment. Some of the recommendations were later enacted into law, but more important was the fact that the bodies themselves generated a new national climate conducive to women's own concerns and determinations. As the noted anthropologist and author Margaret Mead commented in the introduction to the 1965 commercial edition of *American Women*: "As in earlier years, when the movement for woman suffrage was linked with other reforms—in race relations . . . and so on—national needs in the 1960's have refocused attention on women." She continued: "The time was ripe for a new stocktaking."[10]

The "national needs" of which Mead spoke arose in large part not only from women's concerns, but also from an awareness of a reassertion by black Americans to gain their full rights as citizens. This awareness clearly stemmed from the increased protests and demands generated by the black community itself, which gave birth to an unprecedented legal and nonlegal "immediatism" that had never before characterized such a broad spectrum of black protest. This social phenomenon would soon apply similarly to women. An important distinction must be made here between the historical insight of Mead and the reality of contemporary social protest in America. Feminism frequently seemed to develop concurrently, but along separate organizational lines from the black movement. That is to say, although black civil rights historically might have lent inspiration to women by encouraging a new public awareness and setting a strong tone for social struggle, women themselves have customarily fashioned their own female-directed movements. We established the ideological parameters of this phenomenon along three protest lines as discussed earlier. We will now turn our focus toward the resurgence of feminism in the 1960s and 1970s to determine whether or not—and if so, to what extent—the civil rights movement cross-pollinated the women's movement, especially with respect to a legal-oriented ideology.

New Legislative Initiatives: State Commissions, The Equal Pay Act of 1963 and Title VII

Interest in the findings of the president's commission on women and the federal government's subsequent creation of the IDCSW and the CACSW created momentum that led to parallel actions at the state level. By 1964 forty-four governors had established state commissions. Within another three years all of the states as well as Puerto Rico, the Virgin Islands and the District of Columbia created similar agencies.[11] Women in all walks of life became increasingly aware of sex inequalities as identified in the reports issued by the various commissions. But more important for the developing movement, the commissions met in national conferences which brought together potential feminist organizers, theorists and spokespersons who otherwise might never have met. Kathryn Clarenbach, head of the Wisconsin State Commission on the Status of Women and later executive director of the National Commission on the Observance of International Women's Year, spoke to this: "Most of these state commissions included female leadership and staff, thus offering an unprecedented situation for articulate women's rights advocates to meet and exchange ideas."[12]

Later in 1963 Congress demonstrated a new public commitment to women's issues by augmenting executive actions with an unprecedented anti-sex-discrimination law, the Equal Pay Act of 1963.[13] This landmark measure required employers to pay equal wages to men and women for demonstrably equal work, efforts and responsibilities. Standard interpretation held that the act passed because of a favorable recommendation by the president's commission and the renewed vigorous support of organized labor.[14] However, Catherine East, executive secretary of the CACSW and aide to the Kennedy Commission and to Esther Peterson at the Women's Bureau, recalled that it was the dynamic Peterson who personally shepherded the legislation through Congress, an interpretation Peterson has not rejected.[15] Peterson acted, in East's words, "as an indomitable advocate for the bill; she used all her power and the power of the Kennedy Administration to focus both legislative and national support for the bill."[16]

Regardless of the legislative history of the act, its contemporary importance can hardly be overstated. For example, congressional testimony by women's rights advocates and organizational spokespersons further solidified the already growing women's communication network. Perhaps more important was the fact that nationally prominent women pushed for a law that would not have to compete for enforcement attention with the standard "race, religion, or national origin" clauses of past civil rights measures. The Equal Pay Act, then, set a legal precedent by addressing sex inequity specifically, and in this respect it became a working model for subsequent legal/reform actions at both the federal and state levels.

Within a year of these actions, women's rights partisans would applaud

President Johnson's active support of feminist causes. In fact, Johnson took meaningful executive action, promoting more women to high governmental positions than any previous president. Reflecting past civil rights assertions and his own administration's growing recognition that women were victims of a "special kind" of discrimination, Johnson stated in 1964, "My whole aim in promoting women ... in this Administration is to underline our profound belief that we can waste no talent, we can frustrate no creative power, we can neglect no skill in our search for an open and just and challenging society."[17] In 1965 Mary Keyserling, director of the federal Women's Bureau, noted that "all working women benefit from this showcase example of the Federal service."[18] Johnson further fueled the new feminist fires in 1968 by issuing an executive order forbidding federal contractors from discriminating against women and requiring business to create new programs aimed to increase their employment of women and minorities. These have subsequently become known as "affirmative action" programs. Certainly such actions provided inspiration for those who wished government and society to give females greater encouragement in their personal and collective aspirations. In this respect the actions taken by the federal government in establishing the president's commission, the Equal Pay Act of 1963 and Johnson's women's rights posture directly reflected a point of evolutionary divergence between civil rights and contemporary feminism: the latter grew largely from women's and their supporters' own energies. Furthermore, these actions demonstrated a new federal commitment to view sex discrimination as a bona fide policy-making arena in a pattern similar to, but contextually different from, the way in which government had been approaching the issue of race discrimination.

One of the most important legacies of this phenomenon grew from the addition of the word "sex" to the categories of race, religion and national origin in Title VII of the landmark 1964 Civil Rights Act.[19] Surely Title VII represented one direct and dramatic intersection between civil rights and feminism. Not only was the Act designed to eliminate a broad range of race discrimination, but it also included provisions to eliminate sex discrimination in employment. It was directly linked to the federal government's approach to bias based on racial and gender identity. As blacks' complaints appeared before the enforcement agency of Title VII, so did women's, which had the effect of leading the federal government to group the two concerns in the same policy-making arena based upon perceptions of similarly focused problems.

Congresswoman Martha Griffiths (D-MI) had originally sponsored the provision on sex in the Civil Rights Act in spite of the opposition of civil rights supporters, who felt that the "sex issue" might work to undercut support for the "more important race issue."[20] We can only speculate that Griffiths saw the parallel between this claim and those against such women's leaders as Susan B. Anthony and Elizabeth Cady Stanton for wanting to "selfishly" detract from the "Negro's Hour" during Reconstruction. In any event, Griffiths did defer action to conservative Howard Smith (D-VA), who, it has been claimed, intended to add "sex" as a "little joke" to ensure the bill's defeat. Obviously, Griffiths hoped the joke would backfire, as indeed it did. Title VII passed intact with the Civil Rights Act of 1964 and subsequently emerged as one of the most sweeping federal measures of contemporary times.[21]

Title VII gave the federal bureaucracy a mandate to guarantee women's equality in all aspects of employment. Further provisions created the Equal Employment Opportunity Commission (EEOC) to oversee implementation of and compliance with the act. Directed by five bipartisan presidential appointees, the EEOC held unprecedented authority to investigate written complaints of unjust employment practices and to issue employment guidelines. However, prior to 1972 the commission could only refer actions to the attorney general's office and advise on matters of sex discrimination. Alluding to the commission's initial impotence, Commissioner Aileen Hernandez mirrored the attitudes of many women's rights advocates when she stated, "It's the kind of law that raises the hopes of a lot of people, but doesn't provide any means of realizing those hopes."[22]

The EEOC further alienated many feminists by relegating sex charges to lowest priority. In instances where it did take action, the commission often exercised the "Bona Fide Occupational Qualification" guideline, which permitted unequal sex treatment if unavoidable, if the employer acted in good faith, or if relevant state laws claimed to "protect" rather than to discriminate against women. There were 551 such state laws in 1965.[23] As late as 1967 the commission in its *Annual Report* offended women by sidestepping the sex provision. In its own words, "the chief thrust of the statute was, of course, aimed at discrimination against the Negro."[24] In effect, the EEOC's apparent insensitivity to gender problems convinced many that government still lacked serious commitment to change. As will be seen, the EEOC was quickly forced into a new posture on the sex issue not by the actions of the federal government or by other protest phenomena, but rather by the direct actions and policies of feminists themselves.

A Renewed Feminist Articulation: *The Feminine Mystique* and Its Implications

In the fall of 1962 *Harper's* ran an editorial commenting on the phenomenon of female subservience to male promulgated standards of proper place and role. The magazine noted that an "extraordinary number" of women sought relief from such male-defined roles, yet most curiously exhibited little interest in organized feminism, choosing instead to identify with the male-defined goals of their husbands and, in some cases, sons.[25] Of course, to the extent that women lived in close proximity with men of the same family, ethnic and social class, there were few evident distinctions between them and the males in their lives in contrast to the visible differences between blacks and whites at all social levels. In the civil rights movement, as noted earlier, caste distinction often led to shared feelings of injustice. Women, by illustration, sometimes did not come to this "bonding by oppression," because many identified more with the status of their husbands, fathers, brothers and sons that with other women.

In 1963 Betty Friedan's best-seller *The Feminine Mystique* dramatically articulated many of the shared frustrations to which *Harper's* had alluded and from which the average woman of the day had shrunk. Friedan documented a post-World War II female image in the United States equated largely with motherhood and domestic creativity. She postulated that this image operated much along the lines of a social control system, the functional aspects of which manifested themselves in a blizzard of media stimuli designed to: (1) idealize marriage and motherhood, (2) always promote the husband's and son's careers over the ambitions of mother and daughter, (3) glorify housework, and (4) prepare a girl to emulate with joy her mother's own stultified life. Friedan concluded that this blind dedication to the husband, kitchen and child became a self-fulfilling prophecy—a "feminine mystique." In Friedan's words: "the core of the problem for women today is ... identity— a stunting or evasion of growth that is perpetuated by the feminine mystique. ...[O]ur culture does not permit women to accept or gratify their basic need to grow and fulfill their potentialities as human beings, a need which is not solely defined by their sexual role"[26] Friedan's book had a profound consciousness-raising effect on many women by inducing them to formulate new awarenesses of shared problems and feelings and by aiding in many respects to break down their own sense of frustration and personal isolation. By questioning the very gender norms of contemporary culture, *The Feminine Mystique* bluntly focused women's attention on feminist issues which, as *Harper's* had also pointed out, had received little attention for decades. The work quickly became central to a female-centered analysis and criticism of the reality that women's primary roles revolved around possibly invalid and alien assumptions.

By the mid–1960s the *feminine* mystique had metamorphosed somewhat into a *feminist* mystique. As a result of Friedan's book and the increasing federal and state actions, many women, like the noted civil rights attorney Pauli Murray, began to liken their protests to those of blacks, especially in the areas of economics and education.[27] Thus, developing from a relatively modest set of circumstances in the early 1960s, contemporary feminism rapidly expanded into advanced areas of awareness, theory and practice.

Relevant Social Indicators

The restrictions on women in education and employment in the early 1960s indeed mirrored their growing recognition of minority status throughout

American society. As studies have demonstrated, women, like blacks, had often been segregated in occupations thought "fitting" or "appropriate" for them based on social perception rather than on performance or reality. Also, like blacks, few women held positions of power or decision making. For example, there had never been a woman president, vice-president, or Supreme Court justice; only two women had held cabinet appointments. Throughout the 1960s women held fewer than 1 percent of federal circuit court and district court judgeships. Among foreign service officers, women constituted less than one-tenth of presidential appointees and only 1.4 percent of highest grade foreign service officers.[28]

A comparable situation existed at the state level. Prior to 1970 only three women had managed to win elections for governor and none had won election solely on her own credentials. Nellie Tayloe Ross of Wyoming, Miriam A. "Ma" Ferguson of Texas and Lurleen Wallace of Alabama each succeeded husbands vacating the gubernatorial office. In the early 1960s not a single woman mayor governed a major American city, although there were women piloting a number of smaller cities. Through the middle of that decade women held only 4 percent of 7,700 state legislative seats; of those 308 women, merely 45 served in the upper houses.[29]

The role of women in organized labor fared little better. In 1965 no woman sat on the executive council of the American Federation of Labor and Congress of Industrial Organizations (AFL-CIO), whose membership was 15.1 million. Similarly, only men chaired the council's sixteen standing committees. In fact, only one woman served on the staff of the standing committees. Even in the Amalgamated Clothing Workers of America (membership 377,000) and the International Ladies Garment Workers Union (membership 442,318), with over 80 percent female membership, no women held leadership positions.[30] As patterns of this type became more evident, new feminist visions of social and economic parity began to take hold. Moreover, researchers Karen S. Koziara and David A. Pierson have found that a dual labor commitment by women—one paid, the other in the home—coupled with childbearing often led to a general perception that women viewed unions only as an expediency that ranked behind family needs, which, of course, was a total misperception, as labor historian Alice Kessler-Harris has so aptly pointed out.[31] Indeed, legal feminist goals such as those of the National Organization for Women and similar new feminist groups in the 1960s flourished in large part because of the perceived need to eradicate such inequalities.

A New Organizational Thrust: The Creation of NOW

At this point we can conclude that during the early years of the 1960s the climate of expectations among women rose dramatically, partially as a result of their own new awakening to unequal status and actions and partially as a result of the government's restated general commitment to civil rights. Certainly it would be fair to say that women perceived that changing patterns in race relations and notions of proper social realms during the 1960s resulted primarily from the activities of protesters. Accordingly, concerned women exhibited new confidence that sex egalitarianism could be realized through similar collective protest actions.[32] In this sense the new feminists were not entirely ideologically divorced from both civil rights and other historical protest visionaries. Their characteristic approach was to extend the past questions of inequality toward new insights derived from the contemporary protest milieu.

When this milieu began to alter female consciousness, the efforts collectively sowed the seeds for a new action group dedicated to investigating and eradicating the ideology and practice of gender inequality. The movement for such an organization began in June 1966, when over two-hundred women from forty-four states met in Washington, D.C., for the Third National Conference of Commissions on the Status of Women, which provided an important forum for open discussion of feminist issues. During the conference twenty-six participants joined with Betty Friedan, an official observer from New York, to form the nucleus of what would become the first national feminist-action organization since the advent of the National Woman's Party. At the final luncheon Friedan and others formed the National Organization for Women (NOW), a legal-oriented group which grew to become the nation's largest and most active feminist-membership organization in the 1960s and 1970s.[33]

The new action group sprang from a rather haphazard set of circumstances. During the conference Friedan and a few friends discussed their mutual suspicions that the EEOC was not energetically enforcing Title VII in sex discrimination cases, a point Pauli Murray had carefully outlined in an earlier floor speech. On the second night of the conference Friedan invited Kathryn Clarenbach (head of the Wisconsin delegation), Inka O'Hanrahan of California, Catherine Conroy of Illinois and a few other interested persons to her hotel suite to "explore the need for a new action organization" for women, perhaps a "kind of NAACP" for them.[34] Yet many of those present agreed with Clarenbach, who had insisted all along it would be more efficacious for women's rights advocates to work for their goals through the existing state commissions.[35] Although those present tended to polarize behind either Friedan or Clarenbach, all did agree "that something immediate and urgent had to be done about the enforcement of Title VII in respect to sex discrimination."[36]

At a following session Clarenbach sought to address the Title VII question more directly by introducing a resolution attacking the EEOC's weak efforts to enforce sex discrimination laws. She also moved to commend EEOC commissioners Richard Graham and Aileen Hernandez for speaking out publicly against the commission's lack of a substantive policy concerning gender ex-plicit want-ads listings. In her closing statements, Clarenbach challenged the president to reappoint Graham, whose term was to expire shortly.[37]

Mary Keyserling, head of the federal Women's Bureau, which had spon-sored the conference, summarily dismissed Clarenbach's proposals (probably to prevent any antiadministration statements).[38] This "slap in the face," as Clarenbach recalled, convinced her that the type of civil rights organization proposed by Friedan the night before "indeed, did need creating after all."[39] Thereafter Friedan and Clarenbach began actively to recruit potential mem-bers for such an organization. At Friedan's somewhat offhand suggestion, the embryonic group took the name National Organization for Women (NOW: note the group's intent by adopting *for* women and not *of* women).[40] Clar-enbach accepted the position of temporary chair until an organizing confer-ence might be called. NOW's subsequent statement of purpose read: "To take action to bring women into full participation in the mainstream of American Society *now*, assuming all the privileges and responsibilities thereof in full equal partnership with men."[41] The statement meant to sound a note of urgency, and in this respect created a signpost for new legal-feminist com-mitments much as the creation of the Montgomery Improvement Association (1955) and the Southern Christian Leadership Conference (1957) had done earlier in civil rights. One need only to substitute "blacks" for "women" and "whites" for "men" in the statement of purpose to reach such a conclusion.

NOW held its first national organizing conference in Washington, D.C., October 29 and 30, 1966, where three hundred charter members adopted a constitution declaring:

We, men and women who hereby constitute ourselves as the National Organization for Women, believe that the time has come for a new movement toward true equality for all women in America, and toward a fully equal partnership of the sexes, as part of the worldwide revolution of human rights now taking place within and beyond our national borders.[42]

Delegates from twelve states and the District of Columbia endorsed Frie-dan's original theme of "NOW representing an NAACP for women." They agreed further to take "immediate action" against all forms of sex discrimi-nation in education and employment by using tactics that had proved effective in the civil rights movement—including sit-ins, marches and boycotts.[43] Clar-enbach, a die-hard proponent of legal measures only, chaired the board; Friedan, a similar die-hard proponent of legalism, assumed the presidency. Co-founder Pauli Murray closed the conference with a powerful address stressing the historical significance of the meeting within a black civil rights framework. Friedan later recalled that at that time "we shared a moving moment of realization that we had now indeed entered history."[44] Thus was reborn a new women's legal-oriented protest movement that centered its own drive and energy around a broad range of women's establishment causes largely apart from the civil rights and other policy-issue movements that comprised the sweeping protest milieu of the 1960s and 1970s.

Almost predictably NOW directed its first actions at forcing the government to comply with the sex provisions of Title VII of the 1964 Civil Rights Act. Indeed, many women activists of all commitments focused on Title VII as a target of opprobrium, and thus the measure grew to become one of the most important legal bridges between modern civil rights and feminism. Before the close of its first year, NOW pursued several sex discrimination cases under the dual sex and race mandate of Title VII. The organization immediately set up task forces to study and confront sex biases in employment, education, religion, poverty, law, politics and the media; special committees handled public relations, finance, legislation and legal activities.[45] In short, the approach demonstrated a typical legal-oriented pattern of protest for both blacks and women, i.e., the dual approach of pressing the government for meaningful commitment and then reviewing closely the government's actions to ensure strict compliance with stated policies.

Not only did NOW capitalize on the legal precedents established by civil rights, but it similarly focused its energies on the time-honored black tactic of lobbying and litigation. Friedan acknowledged another linkage with contemporary civil rights when she stated, "We don't even exclude the possibility of a mass march on Washington."[46]

Another point of contact with the older civil rights crusades occurred in NOW's second year when it created a tax-exempt legal arm patterned after the NAACP's "Inc. Fund," which had been founded on the eve of World War II. In this endeavor NOW's first general counsel, Marguerite Rawalt, communicated with Jack Greenberg of the Inc. Fund concerning organizational and logistical questions.[47] One of the legal section's first proposals involved the overturning of women's protective work laws, which, in the words of NOW's counsel, "could well result in a landmark decision in civil rights for women comparable to...*Brown* v. *Board of Education*."[48]

The committee controlling the arm undertook a number of key legal precedents. The conclusions and suggestions of its first annual report in November 1967 influenced and in large part set the tone for the movement's legal tactics over the years. It stated that

there has not been a single court decision which has enforced the sex-discrimination provisions of Title VII. Nor, to our knowledge, has there been a single instance in which the Attorney General of the United States has intervened, as he may do under Title VII, on grounds of sex discrimination. Nor, has there come...any instance of the Equal Employment Opportunity Commission entering or assisting in litigation where sex discrimination was at issue.

On the other hand, there have been adverse court decisions under Title VII.[49]

The report then outlined pending legal actions and recommended judicial redress in the following ways: assisting plaintiffs on appeal, having discriminatory state laws declared unconstitutional under the Fourteenth Amendment, pressuring the EEOC to issue definitive guidelines on classified advertising in newspapers, advertising state labor laws and pension and retirement plans and pursuing "face-to-face" interviews with all persons or directors of agencies or bureaus empowered to act on sex discrimination cases.[50] Concurrently, NOW proceeded to provide a national forum for such serious feminist reforms as legal abortion, equal employment opportunity, child care facilities, maternity leave, job training for displaced women and the right to equal educational opportunities.

As a result, the early experience of NOW demonstrated in a fundamental sense that feminists perceived a pressing need to resurrect their own indigenous legal-oriented civil rights movement. Not content simply to remain on the sidelines, women stepped forward and took the lead in creating such a force, and that organization not only formed along the lines of older groups like the NAACP and NAWSA, but it pursued a pressure and litigation approach that clearly reflected their experiences. Perhaps the most glaring similarity between NOW and the NAACP was this very preference for legal-oriented goals rather than for cultural and radical solutions. Moreover, NOW pursued a number of important legal "firsts" for women much as the NAACP had done for blacks. Before the close of the 1960s the new feminists had become actively involved in more than ten major court cases, most of which volunteer attorneys handled.[51]

We must conclude, then, that the real mission for NOW and other legal-oriented women was to organize a viable power base from which to pursue national legislation and court decisions strikingly similar in nature and intent to those historically demanded by black protesters. This legal model quickly grew to encompass other sectors of the movement. Let us now turn our attention to the new legal agenda, its collateral organizational growth and its impact on the feminist movement.

Legalism: Growth and Response

NOW's bold feminist critique had a significant impact on women as evidenced by its dramatic membership increases. The organization estimated that its membership had grown from 1,200 in 1967 to 15,000 in 1971. Actually these figures might have been on the conservative side. For instance, a 1972 special issue of *Time* placed NOW's membership at 18,000, distributed in some 255 chapters in forty-eight states.[52] By any standard, NOW had grown significantly during its first six years and certainly had become a beacon to many women denying the feminine mystique.

Partly in response to the resurrected feminism, President Lyndon Johnson in 1967 attacked the problem of sex discrimination by issuing Executive Order

11375, which prohibited gender bias by all employers holding federal contracts.[53] In addition, the order strengthened the enforcement powers of the Office of Federal Contract Compliance (OFCC) as delineated under Executive Order 11246. The "sex" provision assumed special importance since it assured female inclusion in Executive Order 11246, mandating that all employers holding federal contracts involving at least one-third of their personnel had to agree to OFCC nondiscrimination guidelines. In 1971 the OFCC issued Revised Order No. 4 (later amended in 1974), setting forth significant new policies on sex discrimination.[54] NOW widely publicized the OFCC's action as an affirmation of its success in pressuring the federal government to expand policies of fair employment for women and other minorities.[55] In fact, by 1978 the federal government adopted new guidelines delineating women as a "minority group" for statistical and demographic purposes even though their raw numbers had surpassed the male population in 1950.[56]

Revised Order No. 4 and its modifications carried new affirmative action enforcement provisions that were to revolutionize social crusades in America.[57] Almost immediately both blacks and women sensed the profound potential that the OFCC's action held as they sought to make the ruling on affirmative action programs for private employees a double-edged weapon against race and sex discrimination in a broad range of educational and employment areas. Here indeed was an important intersection between civil rights and feminism as both grasped almost simultaneously the federal government's new commitment to open previously closed doors for blacks and women. However, federal affirmative action policies, especially respecting the thorny issue of suggested hiring formulas, were often criticized by opponents as conferring hiring and promotion "quotas" on special groups, that is, blacks and women. Even as this study is being concluded the issue of affirmative action continues to evoke opposition, especially from those who see it as "reverse discrimination." They charge, as researcher Barry R. Gross has noted, that government and business are "giving special or preferred treatment to persons who are members of racial or religious and ethnic groups or a sex."[58]

NOW quickly undertook measures to force full public and private compliance with Order No. 4. In the months following the order's promulgation, NOW and other legal-oriented women filed blanket complaints of sex discrimination against some 1,300 corporations and institutions of higher learning holding federal contracts.[59] Charges of college and university discrimination sparked new government investigations and resulted in orders for educational institutions to provide affirmative action plans for hiring and promoting both blacks and women. A legal emphasis clearly permeated the reborn feminist movement from national to local levels by the late 1960s. One of the clearest examples of local legal initiative in the feminist tradition occurred in Pittsburgh, Pennsylvania.

In 1969 a local Pittsburgh chapter filed a class action suit against the *Pittsburgh Press* for alleged want-ads discrimination.[60] This initiative differed from NOW's national legal tactics in that it based its judicial brief on a recent Pennsylvania state human relations regulation and a similar municipal ordinance prohibiting sex discrimination.[61] One NOW officer recalled: "We in Pittsburgh were determined to take the bull by the horns, we felt we had the resources, know-how, and most important, the will. We drew sustenance for the action from within our own community and subsequently we made fighters and leaders out of previously mildly committed women."[62]

By drawing a black/woman analogy in its want-ads protest, the Pittsburgh chapter significantly broadened its appeal for support from a range of activists. To illustrate its point, the organization requested that offending newspapers

Take your "Notice to Job Seekers" and
　Substitute the word white for the word male
　Substitute the work [*sic*] black for the word female
　Substitute the word color for the word sex.
Your notice will now read
　Jobs are arranged under white and black classifications for the
　convenience of our readers. This is done because most jobs
　generally appeal more to persons of one *color* than the other.[63]

On July 24, 1970, the Pittsburgh Human Relations Commission ordered the *Pittsburgh Press* to cease its separate want-ads columns.[64] Through the 1970s NOW and other women's rights reform groups continued to press the EEOC to take a hard line against sex-segregated want ads as the Pittsburgh local had done, although most major newspapers by the late 1970s had voluntarily adopted nongender ads.[65]

The Pittsburgh NOW's local initiative demonstrated that the legal approach sought to use the power of government for the benefit of women at all levels. Here was a case where legal-oriented feminists of a branch organization influenced policy at both local and national levels. NOW itself had been conceived as a national action organization, but within a few years many of the women and men who belonged to NOW began to work for images of a new women's order by attacking both the national and local roots of discrimination. This strategy gave feminists at all levels a solid sense of purpose. But as in most social movements, conflict over style and thrust was destined to grow from within the ranks.

Conflicting Ideologies and Reproduction

The National Organization for Women had achieved a number of important legal and political successes by the early 1970s, yet the costs in terms of organizational unity were high. Signs of divisiveness among its pluralistic membership appeared as early as NOW's second annual conference once a final draft of "A Bill of Rights for Women in 1968" reached the floor.[66] The bill, proposed in large part by Betty Friedan, called for

I. An Equal Rights Amendment to the Constitution

II. Guarantees of equal employment opportunity

III. Guarantees of maternity leave rights including seniority, social security, and/or employee benefits

IV. Immediate revision of tax laws to permit the deduction of home and child care expenses for working parents

V. Guarantee of child care facilities

VI. The right of women to be educated to their full potential equally with men

VII. Rights of women in poverty to secure job training and other government provisions equal with men . . . and to dignity, privacy, and self-respect

VIII. The right of women to control their own reproductive lives.[67]

Plank eight of the bill predictably offended NOW's conservative wing, which had insisted that the organization restrict itself only to economic and legal issues. The entirely new social question posed by reproductive rights convinced many influential members that media interest on the controversial subject would totally destroy the political effectiveness of the organization. In the fall of 1968 this fear led the conservative faction under Cleveland attorney Elizabeth Boyer to break away from NOW. Here lay a certain parallel with the 1848 Seneca Falls Convention, when a minority of cautious delegates opposed Elizabeth Cady Stanton's insistence on the inclusion of suffrage rights for women in its "Declaration of Principles." In 1967 the reproductive rights controversy prompted some to withdraw from NOW rather than to defend an organizational stance in favor of safe and legal abortion; the suffrage proposal of 1848 had led to a similar splintering of personalities and forces.

As Lucinda Cisler, Wendy Brown and others have pointed out, the debate centered on changing feminist demands as first espoused by Emma Goldman and Margaret Sanger.[68] As a result of changing attitudes and pressures from a wide range of proponents, New York became the first state to liberalize its abortion laws in 1969. Despite such encouraging signs at the state level, feminist organizations like NOW continued to press for or divide over the goal of a definitive Supreme Court ruling on the issue of abortion as a choice to which all women were entitled regardless of residence or class.[69] By showing its awareness of the need to deal with such an important yet controversial issue, NOW adopted a position on reproduction that would bridge an ideological gap between the legal-oriented and radical wings of the movement. But while the issue continued to carry legal/radical overtones, the measure of true characterization came in the tactics the respective wings adopted in pursuit of their goals. NOW pressed for change through traditional legal and lobbying tactics; radicals opted for more nontraditional tactics.

The New York representation, always the most radical element of NOW, withdrew from the organization in 1968. Led by its outspoken president, Ti-Grace Atkinson, this faction stalked out of the convention after losing a sustained bid to "democratize" NOW's hierarchy by rotating routinely all decision-making positions in the organization. Their stinging defeat and their subsequent walkout nearly dealt a fatal blow to NOW, since the New York City chapter accounted for more than one-half its membership. NOW sought to woo back the dissidents, who decided to form an independent "radical" group, the October 17 Movement, later known as The Feminists.[70]

While the Atkinson faction moved quickly into radical-oriented politics, the Boyer group announced the formation of the Women's Equity Action League (WEAL), a women's rights organization with a more conservative posture than NOW that stressed solely "non-controversial legal issues, like employment and education equality."[71] In this sense the growing feminist movement began to exhibit the polarization and splintering that often typify maturing social movements, as Mayer N. Zeld and Roberta Ash have demonstrated, especially resurging social movements with deep roots and cyclic histories.[72]

WEAL incorporated under the laws of Ohio in late 1968. Its bylaws identified WEAL's purpose

to promote greater economic progress...to press for full enforcement of existing antidiscriminatory laws...to seek correction of de facto discrimination...and disseminate information and educational materials, to investigate instances of, and seek solutions to, economic, educational, tax, and employment problems affecting women, to urge that girls be prepared to enter more advanced career fields, to seek reappraisal of federal, state and local laws and practices limiting women's employment opportunities, to combat by all lawful means, job discriminations...in the pay, promotional or advancement policies of governmental or private employers...to attain these objectives, whether through legislation, litigation or other means.[73]

Elizabeth Boyer won election as first president, after which she quickly focused the organization's attention on systematic, legal battles against sex discrimination primarily in the areas of taxes, employment and education.[74]

Boyer, a former Ohio NOW official and activist in the national organization, had resolved to organize a conservative feminist wing in 1968 "because ordinary women . . . could not understand speakers from NOW or the radicals, and legislators were seeing them all as extremists and destructive forces, not as responsible people." WEAL's founder also recalled that "I, too, felt that many professional women did not want to get involved in issues that could smear them in the future—I could see this as a negative outcome of the black movement."[75] WEAL's second president, Nancy Dowding, stated more bluntly, "We don't take positions on issues that polarize people—like the Pill or abortion."[76]

In the spring of 1969 academic Bernice Sandler convinced WEAL to un-
dertake a significant legal action in the area of education.[77] In a letter to
Secretary of Labor George Schultz on January 31, 1970, WEAL began what
would become a significant and sustained campaign against sex discrimination
in academia. WEAL pointed out that statistics illustrated a continuing pattern
of sex discrimination against women at all levels of the campus community
and that over 90 percent of institutions of higher education held at least one
federal contract. With this real or perceived threat of federal leverage, the
league proposed specifically that the following areas be examined: (1) admission quotas to undergraduate and graduate school, (2) discrimination in
financial help for graduate study, (3) hiring practices, (4) promotions, and
(5) salary differentials.[78]

WEAL quickly filed class-action suits against more than sixty colleges and
universities, including Harvard, Radcliffe and the entire state university systems of California and Florida. In October 1970 WEAL filed class-action suits
challenging the admissions policies of all medical schools covered by federal
contracts. NOW later joined WEAL in these actions, but the more radical
feminist groups declined to endorse the tactic.[79] During the height of its
college challenges, WEAL, as NOW had done earlier, reflected a certain awareness of organizational black civil rights by creating a tax-exempt Legal Defense
Fund (LDF) patterned directly after the NAACP's Inc. Fund.[80]

By 1972 the federal Department of Health, Education and Welfare, which
had jurisdiction over the OFCC appellate process, had received over 350
complaints of sex discrimination, most of which involved class-action suits
patterned after WEAL's vanguard challenges. As a result of the appeals, the
department found it necessary to expand the OFCC's staff from approximately
twenty to sixty persons and to create a specific Higher Education Division.[81]
In a parallel action many women's rights advocates moved to force the OFCC
to enforce more stringently the sex provisions of affirmative action guidelines
on their respective campuses.

The feminist message carried by WEAL showed its awareness of the possible
divisiveness of certain sensitive feminist issues and in this respect offered
special attraction to professional women who had perhaps both the most to
gain from a successful feminist legal agenda and the most to lose from a
societal backlash to perceived radical feminist goals. WEAL's membership
grew to include many prominent national figures, including Congresswomen
Martha W. Griffiths (D-MI) and Shirley Chisholm (D-NY) and noted lawyers
Marguerite Rawalt and Pauli Murray.[82] The organization gained wide respect
on Capitol Hill for its "responsible" approach in contrast to the more dis-
ruptive antiwar and student protests of the era, and often was called on by
name to testify before legislative committees on women's rights. Because it
rejected confrontation politics in favor of working within and through the
system, some radicals denounced WEAL as the Aunt Janes of the feminist
movement—an epithet derived from the term Uncle Tom, used by black

militants to describe blacks seeking gradual, legal reform as opposed to immediate, total upheaval.[83] Although still smaller than NOW's membership in the 1970s, WEAL grew to include active grass-roots chapters in all but a handful of states and to count many local youth divisions and campus or-ganizations as well. League policy continued to eschew "controversial issues [such] as family structure and abortion . . . demonstrations . . . [and] flamboyant publicity tactics."[84]

While WEAL and NOW differed in tactics on how to attack barriers to woman's full and equal participation in society, both did agree on the par-amount goal of achieving a sweeping constitutional mandate for a new vision of total legal rights, to wit, a federal Equal Rights Amendment. A half century in the making, the ERA remained the predominant issue that united almost all feminist constituencies, whether radical, moderate, or conservative, like WEAL.

The ERA and the New Feminist Consciousness

As demonstrated by the uneasy alliance of NOW and WEAL, the ERA arose as the one issue around which all legal-oriented women's rights supporters could rally.[85] The symbolic relationship the ERA had with the total women's movement was especially important since it created an awareness in Congress of constituents' interest in women's rights. Also, both the political acknowl-edgment of the ERA and the respectable organizational support for the cause helped to dispel many negative impressions of feminism. The ERA lobbying effort not only provided opportunities for women at all levels of involvement to create working relationships with the like-minded—many of whom for-merly had been "woodwork" feminists—but also helped foster incipient communications networks among feminists eager to address other women's rights aspects and to establish liaisons between feminists and political forces.

Feminists convinced many legislators (although the ERA eventually failed ratification) that the ERA was a "bread and butter" civil rights issue, a veritable Fourteenth Amendment for women.[86] The ERA had won a few committee approvals since its introduction in Congress in 1923, but it did not receive unamended endorsement from both houses until the 92nd Congress com-pleted action in March 1972. A combination of factors, not the least of which was the dynamic leadership of Congresswoman Griffiths, prodded Congress to approve the amendment. The ERA passed the House 354 to 24 on October 12, 1971, and the Senate by 84 to 8 on March 22, 1972.[87]

An important ramification appeared at the local level as increasing numbers of women demanded accountability from their elected officials regarding state ratification debates. Women began organizing into new voting blocs and demanding recognition and response from their politicians. Partly in re-sponse, both parties revitalized their platforms' prowomen's planks. As a result of this and other efforts to secure more equal representation (e.g., the

so-called McGovern guidelines in the Democratic party), the number of female delegates to the Democratic convention increased from 13 percent in
1968 to 40 percent in 1972, and to the Republican convention from 17 percent
in 1968 to 30 percent in 1972.[88]

Similarly, an unprecedented number of women began running for office,
winning elections and accepting high appointive positions. Figures released
by the National Women's Education Fund, a clearinghouse for information
on women in politics, identified not only the measurable advances of women,
but also the degree to which women previously had been excluded from
positions of political authority. Through 1976, as an illustration, only 11
women had served in the United States Senate compared to 1,715 men; 87
women had been members of the House as opposed to 9,591 men. No women
had sat on the United States Supreme Court, and only 3 women (Frances
Perkins, Oveta Culp Hobby and Carla A. Hills) had served in the Cabinet.[89]

Equally significant shifts occurred at the state level. Between 1969 and 1976
the number of female state legislators doubled. By 1976 there were 610
women legislators, a figure accounting for 8.1 percent of all members. The
percentage of women officials ranged from a high of 27.6 in New Hampshire
to 1.2 in Mississippi. Only eight state senates (Alabama, Arkansas, California,
Michigan, Mississippi, South Carolina, Utah and Virginia) had no women
members in 1976. The number of women in the United States Congress rose
from 12 in 1968 to 18 in 1975. Between 1970 and 1974 the number of female
nominees of the two major parties increased by nearly 50 percent. Increased
political participation bridged race as well as sex divisions. For example, from
1969 to 1973 the number of black women elected officials in the United States
rose dramatically from 131 to 337.[90] The increases suggested that the Democratic and Republican parties had altered their policies regarding women
in accord with their perception of new power blocs and shifting protest
climates, although a number of their rank and file refused to work actively
at the state level for ratification of the ERA.

Judicial Moves Toward Women's Rights

As the ERA battle raged on, it became clear to many feminists that the
Supreme Court might ultimately provide the most decisive engine of change.
From the perspective of female observers, more barriers were now falling
in the courts in the late 1960s and the 1970s than ever before. From their
observation of the black experience, some women's advocates quickly perceived that judicial victories could be one of the most important indices of
change. Just as the Court had embarked on a series of precedent-setting
decisions on civil rights in the late 1940s and 1950s, culminating in the
sweeping *Brown* decision, women's rights advocates pressed the High Court
to address the issue of sex discrimination a little over a decade later.

Indeed, by 1973 the Supreme Court began to hand down a number of significant decisions affecting women. Specifically, in *Frontiero* v. *Richardson* (1973), the Court ruled almost unanimously that military fringe-benefit payments must be uniform regardless of the sex of the military personnel providing support. Reflecting a newfound judicial dualism, the Court addressed the issue with much the same sociological approach that it had inherited from earlier civil rights cases; its decision read: "Classifications based on sex, like classifications based on race . . . are inherently suspect, and must therefore be subjected to strict judicial scrutiny."[91] For their part, women continued to press the courts in much the way blacks had done and won a number of landmark cases through the late 1970s.

In many respects the Supreme Court's most far-reaching and controversial decisions concerned reproduction. In June 1965 the Court handed down a key statement on the reproductive question in *Griswold* v. *Connecticut*, in which it found that state laws regulating the distribution and use of contraceptives violated the "right to privacy." On January 22, 1973, the High Court announced in a seven-to-two decision in *Roe* v. *Wade* (later sustained in *Doe* v. *Bolton*, 1973) that states did not have regulative power over abortions during the first trimester of pregnancy. Although the ruling was cheered as a watershed victory for women, it precipitated a number of crucial legal questions with respect to the particulars of the abortion issue. Feminists pressed the Court for further clarification, and in 1976, in *Missouri* v. *Danforth*, the Supreme Court prohibited state requirements that a husband must consent to a wife's abortion.[92]

In the 1979 *Belloti* v. *Baird* decision, the Supreme Court further clarified the consent issue by striking down a Massachusetts law requiring minors to have written parental consent before proceeding with an abortion. In the wake of *Danforth* and *Baird*, however, the Court dealt a major setback to poor women by upholding the constitutionality of the so-called Hyde Amendment, which allowed legislators to withhold Medicaid funds for abortions. Shortly thereafter the Supreme Court in a six-to-three decision handed down on June 15, 1983, reaffirmed the 1973 *Roe* and *Doe* decisions by overturning an Akron, Ohio, ordinance that had sought to place a variety of restrictions on physicians and women seeking abortions.[93] Even as this study is being completed, the Supreme Court is continuing to consider various challenges to the reproduction question.

To ensure that the courts and government keep responding to these and other women's issues, feminists renewed efforts through various action groups. For the legally oriented, the principal thrust involved pressure-group tactics on the courts and legislature, an approach, to re-emphasize a point, not altogether new to organized feminism. Although women might not have borrowed the concept directly from the civil rights movement, Eleanor Holmes Norton, civil rights activist, feminist, and Chair of the EEOC, for one, suggested there was an important cross-fertilization between the two movements. She held that "women did observe that [black] pressure groups were effective designs for overcoming discrimination."[94] Later, as a recognized leader among black feminists, Norton would demonstrate the unique perspective of historical and unfolding race and gender protest by characterizing Friedan's *The Feminine Mystique* as the "*Uncle Tom's Cabin* of modern feminism."[95]

At this crossroad in contemporary feminism it clearly is seen that women came to share the conviction of much of black civil rights that grievances could be addressed effectively through legislation and litigation. This represented a consensus among legal-oriented protesters, and there were historical precedents to sustain their view. The tireless protests of the NAACP, for example, come readily to mind; but equally notable examples in feminism are found in the record of past initiatives, especially in regard to suffrage protests led by such groups as the American Woman Suffrage Association, the National Woman Suffrage Association, and their linear descendant, the National American Woman Suffrage Association. In other words, we may hypothesize that the emotional tone and direction of contemporary legal-oriented feminism found direction primarily in its own past as well as in modern models as set forth by black civil rights. Let us now turn our attention toward an expanded analysis of the goals and thrusts of legal-oriented feminism.

Special Groups and Spin-Offs: Toward a Multicentered Feminist Ideology

As contemporary feminism became more issue-oriented, it fostered the growth of many different organizations at both the local and the national levels. The development in numbers and scope of these groups represented many interests and also reflected the intent of feminists to institutionalize fully their goals through collectivist actions. The Women's Action Alliance, a national center for information on women's issues and programs, listed over one hundred issues groups in its 1979 *Women's Action Almanac*.[96] The groups covered a range of efforts, from the Women's Caucus for Art to the broad-based National Women's Political Caucus (NWPC), whose loose-knit umbrella organization of local, state and national women's caucuses sought to make a political impact without engaging directly in electoral activities.[97] The dynamics of this organization reflected in large part the aspirations and strategies of a wide range of similarly proliferating legal-oriented groups.

In July 1971 the NWPC held its founding convention in Washington, D.C., where more than two hundred women participants with different cultural backgrounds and political convictions heard founders Betty Friedan, Shirley Chisholm, Fannie Lou Hamer, Gloria Steinem and Bella Abzug exhort women to work more aggressively for political power at all levels of government. To stress their historical awareness, the founders reminded women that "a scant five years ago, political women stuffed envelopes, licked stamps, 'manned'

telephones and made coffee—not policy."[98] The NWPC served as a fundamental step to institutionalize and politicize the nurturing women's movement. Friedan hinted at such a mission during its founding convention when
she stated that her "internal, historical alarm clock" indicated that "the wom-
en's movement has crested now and must become political if it is not to
decline."[99] By 1973 every state plus the District of Columbia and Puerto Rico
had active caucuses. The national office maintained a mailing list of 30,000
to 35,000 names and estimated that additional thousands of supporters were
active in local caucuses.[100]

Initially the Caucus worked strictly for the purpose of realizing political
objectives, such as helping women win elections to public office. But by the
mid–1970s it expanded its priorities to include broad social causes, including
special emphasis on women's health care. Its services included publication
of a newsletter and a quarterly, *Women's Political Times*, and the dissemi-
nation of voluminous amounts of educational material and data pertaining
to women's political interests to local affiliates and other interested parties.
Like NOW and WEAL, the Caucus often testified before Republican and Democratic committees and federal and state legislative bodies. It operated under
an expanded social project mandate to include positions on family planning
services and contraceptive research.[101]

Jo Freeman has concluded that modern legal-oriented groups have grown
to a greater or lesser extent from overlapping memberships and a perceived
need for woman's organizational and political strengths to form what we may
now call the "mainstream" of traditional, organizational feminism. In this
sense there certainly does rise an analogy (a mother/daughter metaphor?)
between the new action groups like NOW, WEAL and the NWPC and such
precursors as the AWSA, NWSA and NAWSA.[102] It was inevitable that the now
surging legal-oriented branch of feminism would grow to encompass women
of unique or different backgrounds, from the middle-class orientation of the
Betty Friedans and Elizabeth Boyers to those of women of color, on which
we shall now focus.

The complications of race and gender frequently led black women to view
the new feminism from a dual perspective as victims both of racism and of
sexism: a unique class/caste consciousness. But new awareness as represented
by black presidential candidate Shirley Chisholm's statement in 1972, "I have
pointed out time and time again that the harshest discrimination I have
encountered in the political arena is antifeminism,"[103] seemed to be swinging
black female consciousness in a bold new course as many black women
began to advocate adopting feminist stances for political empowerment. As
an illustration, in May 1973 many leading black women gathered in New York
to create just such a new feminist group, the National Black Feminist Organization (NBFO). Former New York Human Rights Commissioner and then
Chair of the EEOC Eleanor Holmes Norton was especially instrumental in
creating the NBFO. In recalling the inception of that organization, Norton

said that she and other black women became convinced that they needed an organization independent of the existing civil rights and feminist structures of the day. They predicated their conclusion on the thesis that black women had a unique need for self-expression and self-determination apart from white middle-class orientations and structures.[104] NBFO President Margaret Sloan stated that the organization would serve to "remind the black-liberation move-ment that there can't be liberation for half a race."[105] Later Sloan noted another important principle behind the NBFO strategy: "This group can't be dismissed by black men as a play toy of white women"; another member added: "White women are white first and they have gained benefits—social, economic and psychological—from a racist society."[106] It was this belief, then, which led the NBFO to exclude white women as a matter of course. Its "Statement of Purpose" addressed these and other issues.

The Movement has been characterized as the exclusive property of so-called white middle-class women and any Black women seen involved in this Movement have been seen as "selling-out," "dividing the race," and an assortment of nonsensical epithets. Black feminists resent these charges. . . . Black women have suffered cruelly in this society from living the phenomenon of being Black and female, in a country that is *both* racist and sexist. . . . *We* . . . must define our own self-image as black women and not fall into the mistake of being placed upon the pedestal which is even being rejected by white women. . . . We must together, as a people, work to eliminate racism from without the black community, which is trying to destroy us as an entire people; but we must remember that sexism is destroying and crippling us from within.[107]

The declaration clearly delineated the major concern of self-definition and the development of positive self-images for black women. The organization grew in large part because black women, in the words of Eleanor Holmes Norton, "realized that racism and sexual exploitation [were] intricately inter-twined."[108] The NBFO remained a forum for black feminists until its frag-mentation in the latter 1970s, at which time its leadership, as Norton recalled, became increasingly involved in other valuable causes which drained their energies away from the NBFO's organizational and structural necessities.[109] Even so the NBFO experience demonstrated in a fundamental sense that black women were seeking to address their particular concerns through organizational means, albeit means apart from both civil rights and feminist pathfinders.

When labor women banded together into the Coalition of Labor Union Women (CLUW) to address their unique problems, the experience was not demonstrably unlike that of other special groups like the NBFO. Over three thousand female unionists participated in its creation in Chicago in 1974.[110] In some respects CLUW resembled the earlier Women's Trade Union League, with the exception that the new unionists would not accept nonwage earners into its membership. The latter occurred, as labor historian Alice Kessler-Harris surmised, because wage-earning women largely saw themselves as a

class apart from women who did not command a paycheck. Most women in
the paid labor force perceived their needs as financial in nature and thus
wanted the pay and other rewards—and protections—that were commonplace for men in the paid-labor sector. Women had only to look back into
their own history for models of forceful union activists and organizers, Rose
Schneiderman, Rose Pesotta, Fannia Cohn, Pauline Newman and Mary Harris
"Mother" Jones, to name but a few. Researcher Barbara Wertheimer and
others have demonstrated that labor women perceived a real need for class
solidarity and a desire to fight collectively for special women's interests within
a trade-union-only movement. Wertheimer found that they registered one
such policy victory in convincing the AFL-CIO to reverse its anti-ERA position.[111]

In this respect the new union voice of women continued legal-oriented
feminism's tradition of organizational tactics while adopting reformist positions and strategies (e.g., pressure-group approaches). Thus at the same time
that women—women of all socioeconomic groups and color—were entering
the paid labor force in unprecedented numbers (e.g., between 1960 and 1980
the female paid labor force almost doubled), a great many of them adopted
CLUW as one realistic manifestation of both historical and extant feminist
protest vehicles. Although CLUW would wither under various pressures over
the years, its life and history did demonstrate the new visibility and place of
legal-oriented women in the modern labor movement.

The trend toward legal-oriented organizational activity, then, obviously has
become a major perceived and tactical approach of contemporary feminism.
Of course feminists came to realize, just as civil rights groups like the NAACP
had, that court decisions, legislative actions and other governmental actions
could eliminate only those discriminatory practices falling directly under the
auspices of the legal system. In order to eradicate more pervasive discrimination, many women's organizations launched massive educational campaigns to win grass-roots support. The two approaches—legal and
educational—are mutually reinforcing, as civil rights partisans had successfully demonstrated by the mid–1960s. The importance of these and similar
events to the emerging feminist movement was to reveal a crucial attempt
by women to find their place in the mainstream of those institutions that
bequeathed not only fundamental but lasting change to society. Although the
range of such educational measures adopted by feminists is too great to
analyze in a study of this scope, a brief review of some ground-breaking
actions in this area will prove helpful.[112]

In 1969 a group of Pittsburgh area NOW members formed a dynamic work
collective, KNOW, Inc. (pronounced K-N-O-W), a reprint house for feminist
literature. The purpose of KNOW was to make available at low prices relevant
literature on the women's movement. KNOW specialized in collecting and
reprinting articles and other feminist materials at cost. From its meager beginnings in a member's basement, KNOW grew into a nationally recognized

and utilized clearinghouse for feminist literature. By 1975 KNOW numbered only one of twenty-six major women's presses across the United States and Canada. In addition to the outpouring of feminist presses, over one hundred women's periodicals appeared, including the mass-market *Ms.* magazine edited by Gloria Steinem and others. By 1980 the number of feminist-oriented national periodicals mushroomed to thirteen. These periodicals covered a wide range of female orientations, including culture, legislation and scholarship, and by so doing they and such publications as the *National NOW Times* served educational and functional purposes somewhat similar to NAACP's *The Crisis* and NUL's *Opportunity*. The increased supply of women's literature soon led to the opening of over thirty-eight women-oriented bookstores across the nation, all of which exemplified attempts by the women's movement to document its currents and offer continuing forums for feminist issues. Much like their Afro-American–oriented counterparts, feminist bookstores became powerful outlets for traditionally neglected history, cultural expression and other focused services. By 1979 women's bookstores numbered more than seventy in thirty-two states, almost double the number reported in a 1975 study.[113]

The Women's History Research Library, in its pioneering effort to collect, catalog and make available to women on request information, literature, documents and other data concerning their heritage and protest efforts, reflected one aspect of this phenomenon. Begun by activist Laura X, the Library opened in Berkeley, California, in 1969. It served as a vital repository for early movement literature until in 1974, when facing bankruptcy, its holdings were divided between Northwestern University and the University of Wyoming.[114]

In 1977 the National Women's Studies Association (NWSA) emerged as a further effort by women both to ensure the institutionalization and spread of feminist ideas and to offer common ground for those women and men interested in the teaching and scholarship of feminist praxis. Its stated goals were "to further the social, political, and professional development of women's studies throughout the country, at every educational level." Its sense of history was that "women's studies owes its existence to the movement for the liberation of women; the women's liberation movement exists because women are oppressed."[115]

Although few elementary and secondary schools offered women's courses per se, women's studies courses and programs proliferated in higher education. Following the original women's studies program at San Diego State in 1970, almost three hundred programs appeared in college and university curricula across the country. These programs soon consisted of some 4,658 catalogued courses.[116] Predictably, the new interest in women's studies resulted in an explosion of female-oriented scholarship. For example, in 1960 there were thirteen books dealing exclusively with American women's history; between 1960 and 1970, eleven more appeared; between 1970 and 1975, ten new studies surfaced; between 1975 and 1980, thirty-six new titles on women's history appeared, and the list mushroomed dramatically between 1981 and 1987.[117] Such new journals as *Women's Studies, Feminist Studies* and *Signs: A Journal of Women in Culture and Society* offered a further barometer of the growing acceptance and maturing dimensions of the organizational women's movement. The NWSA, new journals and other localized efforts such as new studies programs and campus women's centers notably represented attempts by feminists to ensure the institutionalization of feminism and to raise society's consciousness regarding social issues in America in a fashion strikingly similar to earlier and concurrent black studies and academic cultural thrusts on campuses throughout America.

The emphasis on scholarship and the creation of black studies and similar women's studies programs have been efforts by two groups to recover a heritage and significance independent of that of the white male. Since the traditional culture often taught blacks and women to defer to the achievements of white males and thereby to devalue themselves as human beings, new studies and publishing programs provided a forum whereby blacks and women could develop a positive self-image and a means to challenge the historical rationalization of the dominant cultural system. These programs were logical progressions of two movements that historically have sought to modify cultural norms used to justify a restricted, minority status for some. In many respects, women's actions of the 1960s and 1970s could be characterized as a new "women's spirit," much like an earlier "race spirit," which sought to increase the awareness of the black role in America through such vehicles as the Association for the Study of Negro Life and History, begun by Carter G. Woodson in 1915, and *The Journal of Negro History*, launched the following year.[118] The numerous studies on black life and culture that have been published since that time and the spate of women-centered works that have been appearing since the 1960s have been invaluable sources of information for scholars and for all students or would-be students of traditionally neglected black and women's history.

SUMMARY

In contemporary America blacks and women learned early in the evolution of their respective movements that organization and other collective behaviors were essential for achieving their goals. Lobbying and litigation often proved the best tactics for organizations committed to working within the system. As we have seen, the NAACP has been in the forefront of such black legal actions; NOW, WEAL and NWPC have represented feminist efforts to achieve meaningful change through the judicial, political and legislative processes. Indeed, in July 1978 feminists demonstrated their deep ideological commitment to pressure politics as they marched 100,000 strong on Capitol Hill to encourage the extension of the ERA, in a protest strikingly similar to

Randolph's threatened MOWM in the early 1940s and King's massive 1963 rally. The federal government also expanded its definition of *minority* to include women in 1978.[119] Later that fall Congress responded by extending the period for ratification of the ERA from March 1979 to June 30, 1982, so that proponents might gain the required votes in state legislatures in three more states. Despite this reprieve, the allotted time for ratification expired before the ERA was ratified by the states. Even so, the women's movement and its allies in Congress vowed to continue the fight. On January 3, 1983, Speaker of the House Thomas P. "Tip" O'Neil (D-MA) reintroduced the ERA into the new Congress as House Joint Resolution One. Reflecting this restated political commitment, the outgoing president of NOW, Eleanor Smeal, stated: "We are [in] this campaign stronger than we began. We are a majority. We are determined to play majority politics. . . . We are not going to be reduced again to the ladies' auxiliary."[120]

The determination to apply pressure through the courts, legislatures, political systems and academia is one, but not the only, similarity between modern black activism and contemporary feminism. Neither does the predilection of the two protest movements to develop and maintain institutionalized structures nor the determination to march in force on Washington exhaust the similarities. As these movements broadened their goals and stressed further activism as an operational tactic, both became subject to internal dissension. In the 1960s intense factional disputes erupted over goals and methods within the civil rights movements; similar divisions developed over the style and priorities of civil rights issues. CORE and SNCC especially modified their strategies to take on a more militant profile; Stokely Carmichael, for instance, moved from student activism to nationalism and then to Nkrumah-based socialism. For their part, women's rights advocates also witnessed both radical and conservative factionalism, as exemplified by the division at the 1968 National Organization for Women conference. Moreover, by the early 1970s NOW had been joined in the organizational wing by other rivals for constituent support, such as the National Women's Political Caucus and the race-, sex- and class-oriented National Black Feminist Organization.

As historian William Chafe suggested in one study, both the black and women's movements pursued substantive organizational models in an effort to combat prevailing systems of social control that worked to deprive the groups of similar rights, most fundamentally the right to strike down pernicious notions of proper spheres and the right to define their own existence, as blacks, as women, as human beings.[121] Underlying the legislative successes realized by the two social movements was the belief that judicial decisions and legislation in themselves could eliminate only legal discrimination. In order to eradicate the deeply entrenched de facto practices, many rights advocates launched massive new political and educational campaigns in hopes of further entrenching and institutionalizing the growing structures of the new social order.

At the same time there existed within these movements factions and individuals who shifted from conventional legal protest to unconventional radical approaches. Often these women joined with others who had adopted radical analyses to women's position and problems. Such groups will be considered within the context of contemporary feminism in the following chapter.

NOTES

1. Judith Hole and Ellen Levine, *Rebirth of Feminism* (New York: Quadrangle, 1971), 1–166; Carol Hymowitz and Michaele Weissman, *A History of Women in America* (New York: Bantam, 1978), 341–73; Lucy Komisar, *The New Feminism* (New York: Franklin Watts, 1971), 104–18; June Sochen, *Movers and Shakers: American Women Thinkers and Activists, 1900–1970* (New York: Quadrangle, 1973), 229–304; William Henry Chafe, *The American Woman: Her Changing Social, Economic, and Political Roles, 1920–1970* (New York: Oxford University Press, 1972), 226–44.

2. See Hole and Levine, *Rebirth of Feminism*, 19.

3. Betty Friedan, *The Feminine Mystique* (New York: Dell, 1963), esp. 28–61.

4. "Executive Order 10980, Establishing the President's Commission on the Status of Women," *Code of Federal Regulations, 1961* (1962), 138.

5. Esther Peterson, interview with author, Washington, DC, October 27, 1978; Hole and Levine, *Rebirth of Feminism*, 19; Catherine East, interview with author, Arlington, VA, October 1, 1978; Marguerite Rawalt, interview with author, Arlington, VA, October 6, 1978. Catherine East through 1978 had held key positions on all the presidentially appointed commissions on women beginning with the Kennedy Commission; attorney Marguerite Rawalt co-chaired the Kennedy Commission's Committee on Political and Civil Rights. See Cynthia E. Harrison, "A 'New Frontier' for Women: The Public Policy of the Kennedy Administration," *Journal of American History*, Vol. 67, No. 3 (1980), 634.

6. *American Women: Report of the President's Commission on the Status of Women* (Washington, DC: Government Printing Office, 1963), v.

7. Rawalt, interview with author; East, interview with author.

8. See Harrison, "A 'New Frontier' for Women," 630–46.

9. "Executive Order 11126: Establishing a Committee and a Council Relating to the Status of Women," *Code of Federal Regulations, 1963* (1964), 202–04. See *American Women, 1963–1968: Report of the Interdepartmental Committee on the Status of Women* (Washington, DC: Government Printing Office, 1968), vii–ix, 1–31, esp. 18–19. Rawalt, interview with author; East, interview with author.

10. Margaret Mead and Frances Balgley Kaplan, eds., *American Women: The Report of the President's Commission on the Status of Women and Other Publications of the Commission* (New York: Charles Scribner's Sons, 1965), 4.

11. Women's Bureau, *1975 Handbook on Women Workers*, Bulletin 297 (Washington, DC: U.S. Department of Labor, 1975), 402; Komisar, *New Feminism*, 112.

12. Kathryn Clarenbach, interview with author, Washington, DC, October 28, 1977.

13. "Equal Pay Act of 1963," *Statutes at Large, 1963* (1964), 56–57. See Morag MacLeod Simchak, "Equal Pay in the United States," *International Labor Review*, Vol. 103, No. 6 (1971), 541–57. This act did not lay to rest the issue of equal pay since it

left open a number of areas to reinterpretation. In the 1980s feminists attacked the inequities of persistent nonequal pay by broadening the concept to equal pay for work of comparable worth. See Helen Remick, ed., *Comparable Worth and Wage Discrimination* (Philadelphia: Temple University Press, 1984).

14. In essence, the male-dominated unions supported the bill, hoping that it would prevent women's wages from undercutting men's wages. See Elizabeth Faulkner Baker, *Technology and Woman's Work* (New York: Columbia University Press, 1964), 411–24; Simchak, "Equal Pay," 541–57.

15. East, interview with author. Peterson did not deny East's recollections. Peterson, interview with author.

16. East, interview with author.

17. Cited in Mary Dublin Keyserling, "Facing the Facts about Women's Lives Today," in Women's Bureau and Office of Education, *New Approaches to Counseling Girls in the 1960s* (Washington, DC: Government Printing Office, 1965), 9. See Alice Kessler-Harris, *Out to Work: A History of Wage-Earning Women in the United States* (New York: Oxford University Press, 1982), 315.

18. Keyserling, "Facing the Facts About Women's Lives Today," 9.

19. "Civil Rights Act of 1964," *Statutes at Large, 1964* (1965), 241–68.

20. Rawalt, interview with author. Attorney Rawalt served as an unpaid legal advisor to Griffiths during the 1964 debate over Title VII.

21. See Caroline Bird, *Born Female: The High Cost of Keeping Women Down* (New York: Pocket, 1971), 1–10. An example of the use of Title VII was the *Norris* case, in which the Supreme Court found that federal law requires that men and women be treated equally by pension plans. In stating the majority opinion, Justice Thurgood Marshall centered the argument almost solely around Title VII guarantees of equal protection for the sexes and a similar decision in the 1978 *Manhart* case. Feminist groups immediately hailed the decision as a victory for supporters of equal rights and vowed to use the Court's arguments in their own struggle to obtain federal guarantees of nondiscrimination in all areas of private and public insurance—the so-called unisex insurance plan. See "The Battle Over Unisex Insurance," *The Washington Post*, July 18, 1983; *Arizona Governing Committee for Tax Deferred Annuity and Deferred Compensation Plans, etc., et al., Petitioners* v. *Nathalie Norris etc., No. 82–52, The United States Law Week*, Vol. 52, No. 50, Extra Edition No. 6 (1983), 5243–53; *City of Los Angeles, Department of Water and Power* v. *Manhart*, 435 U.S. 702 (1978).

22. Cited in Hole and Levine, *Rebirth of Feminism*, 31.

23. *Report on Progress in 1965 on the Status of Women: Second Annual Report of Interdepartmental Committee and Citizens' Advisory Council on the Status of Women, December 31, 1965* (Washington, DC: Government Printing Office, 1965), 25–26.

24. Rawalt, interview with author. Quote, Equal Employment Opportunity Commission, *1st Annual Report* (Washington, DC: Government Printing Office, 1967), 5. A good source for policy and legal decisions affecting black and female Americans is the EEOC's year-end reports beginning with Equal Employment Opportunity Commission, *Equal Employment Opportunity, Report No. 1: Job Patterns for Minorities and Women in Private Industry, 1966* (Washington, DC: Government Printing Office, 1967).

25. Editorial, *Harper's*, Vol. 225 (October 1962), 117–19, see the special supplement, "The American Female," 120–80.

26. Friedan, *The Feminine Mystique*, 28–72, quote, 69.

27. Pauli Murray, interview with author, Alexandria, VA, October 30, 1977. Insight into this area is provided in Gayle Rubin, "Woman as Nigger," in Betty Roszak and Theodore Roszak, eds., *Masculine/Feminine: Readings in Sexual Mythology and the Liberation of Women* (New York: Harper and Row, 1969), 230–40; Catharine Stimpson, " 'Thy Neighbor's Wife, Thy Neighbor's Servants': Women's Liberation and Black Civil Rights," in Vivian Gornick and Barbara K. Moran, eds., *Woman in Sexist Society: Studies in Power and Powerlessness* (New York: Mentor, 1972), 622–57; and William H. Chafe's section "Sex and Race: The Analogy of Social Control," in his *Women and Equality: Changing Patterns in American Culture* (New York: Oxford University Press, 1977), 45–78.

28. New York Commission on Human Rights, *Women's Role in Contemporary Society* (New York: Avon, 1971), 354; U.S. Civil Service Commission, *Federal Employment of Women* (Washington, DC: Government Printing Office 1966), 7. Useful compendiums of the stark disparity in education and employment of women are U.S. Commission on Civil Rights, *Social Indicators of Equality for Minorities and Women* (Washington, DC: Government Printing Office, 1978), especially, 5–33; U.S. Department of Labor, Women's Bureau, *Time of Change: 1983 Handbook on Women Workers*, Bulletin 298 (Washington, DC: Government Printing Office, n.d.), 5–135.

29. Martin Gruberg, *Women in American Politics: An Assessment and Sourcebook* (Oshkosh, WI: Academia, 1968), 189–90, 169–70, 206–10; *American Women*, 51, which reported the number of women in state legislatures at 234 in 1962.

30. Alice Kessler-Harris, *Women Have Always Worked: A Historical Overview* (Old Westbury, NY: The Feminist Press, 1981), 62–70; U.S. Department of Labor, *Directory of National and International Labor Unions in the United States, 1965: Listing of National and International Unions, State Labor Organizations, Developments Since 1963, Structure and Membership* (Washington, DC: Government Printing Office, 1966), 1–2, 18, 20, 40. See Barbara M. Wertheimer, "Search for a Partnership Role: Women in Labor Unions Today," in Jane Roberts Chapman, ed., *Economic Independence for Women: The Foundation for Equal Rights* (Beverly Hills, CA: Sage, 1976), 191–209.

31. Karen S. Koziara and David A. Pierson, "The Lack of Female Union Leaders: A Look At Some Reasons," *Monthly Labor Review*, Vol. 104, No. 5 (1981), 30–32; Kessler-Harris, *Out to Work*, 300–319.

32. This suggestion emerged as a common denominator from interviews with 1960s women's rights activists. For example, Clarenbach, interview with author; Murray, interview with author, October 30, 1977.

33. Interdepartmental Committee on the Status of Women and the Citizens' Advisory Council on the Status of Women, *Targets for Action: The Report of the Third National Conference of Commissions on the Status of Women* (Washington, DC: Government Printing Office, 1966), 83–89; Hole and Levine, *Rebirth of Feminism*, 81–95.

34. Betty Friedan, "How NOW Began" (mimeographed, n.d.), Betty Friedan Papers (partly restricted), Schlesinger Library, Cambridge, MA; Betty Friedan, *It Changed My Life: Writings on the Women's Movement* (New York: Dell, 1977), 115, 119–23; Murray, interview with author, October 30, 1977; Rawalt, interview with author; Clarenbach, interview with author.

35. Clarenbach, interview with author; Friedan, "How NOW Began"; Friedan, *It Changed My Life*, 117–19.

36. Quote, Friedan, "How NOW Began," Friedan, *It Changed My Life*, 117–19; Murray, interview with author, October 30, 1977; Clarenbach, interview with author.

37. Clarenbach, interview with author.

38. Rawalt, interview with author.

39. Clarenbach, interview with author.

40. "NOW Origins: A Summary Description of How 28 Women Changed the World by Reviving a Revolution Everyone Thought was Dead!" (pamphlet), National Organization for Women Papers (partly restricted), Schlesinger Library, Cambridge, MA; Friedan, "How NOW Began"; Murray, interview with author, October 30, 1977; Clarenbach, interview with author; Friedan, *It Changed My Life*, 119–20. Admittedly, those women and men founding the organization were unaware that "NOW" was an unoriginal acronym. Six years earlier a little-known organization of women educators had chosen "NOW," which stood for "National Organizations of Women for Equality in Education" (pamphlet), Mimi Feingold Papers, Social Action Collection, State Historical Society of Wisconsin, Madison, WI (hereafter cited as SAC, SHSW); "17 Women's Groups Organize to Combat School Segregation," *New York Times*, January 19, 1960.

41. "NOW Origins: A Summary Description."

42. "The National Organization for Women (NOW) Statement of Purpose, (Adopted at the organizing conference in Washington, D.C., October 29, 1966)," Friedan Papers.

43. Rawalt, interview with author.

44. Quote, Friedan, "How NOW Began"; Clarenbach, interview with author; Murray, interview with author, October 30, 1977; Rawalt, interview with author; "National Organization for Women Formed to Press for 'True Equality,'" *New York Times*, November 22, 1966; "NOW May Use Sit-Ins, Pickets to Get Equality," *Newsday*, November 25, 1966. For further development of its leadership viewing NOW as an NAACP for women, see "They Meet in Victorian Parlor to Demand 'True Equality'—NOW," *New York Times*, November 22, 1966.

45. "An Invitation to Join N.O.W., National Organization for Women" (mimeographed), probably 1968, and "National Organization for Women, Inc. (NOW): By-Laws," February 23, 1967, Friedan Papers.

46. Cited in *National Observer*, December 26, 1966.

47. Rawalt, interview with author. It took the Fund four years to achieve tax-exempt status similar to the senior NAACP Inc. Fund.

48. "NOW Press Release," January 13, 1967, NOW Papers.

49. Marguerite Rawalt, "Report . . . of the Legal Committee, National Organization for Women," November 18–19, 1967. Friedan Papers.

50. *Ibid*.

51. In 1967 NOW operated on a $2,522.08 legal budget. *NOW Act* (newsletter), Fall 1968; "NOW Press Release" (no month), 1967; "Legal Committee Report," Second Annual Convention, December 6–7, 1968, both in NOW Papers.

52. "NOW Origins"; "Financial Statement of the National Organization for Women," December 31, 1972, NOW Papers; "Women's Liberation Revisited," *Time*, March 20, 1972, 29.

53. "Executive Order 11375 Amending Executive Order No. 11246, Relating to Equal Employment Opportunity," *Code of Federal Regulations, 1966–1970* (1971), 684–86.

54. Women's Bureau, *1975 Handbook on Women Workers*, 294–95.

55. National Organization for Women, "Background on Federal Action Toward Equal Opportunity for Women" (pamphlet), June 1971, NOW Papers.

56. The 1950 federal census for the first time confirmed that there were more female than male Americans. Its findings listed 75,864,122 women and 74,833,239 men. By 1960 the figure had risen to 90,599,726 women and 87,864,510 men. U.S. Bureau of the Census, *U.S. Census of Population: 1960, Subject Reports, Nativity and Parentage* (Washington, DC: Government Printing Office, 1965), 2. On the classical aspects of women's oppression as a minority, see Helen Mayer Hacker's "Women as a Minority Group," *Social Forces*, Vol. 30, No. 1 (1951), 60–69.

57. The OFCC amended Revised Order No. 4 on July 12, 1974, and established new standard compliance review procedures in Revised Order No. 14, May 15, 1974. Women's Bureau, *1975 Handbook on Women Workers*, 294–95.

58. Barry R. Gross discusses this issue in the general introduction to his edited work, *Reverse Discrimination* (Buffalo, NY: Prometheus, 1977), 3.

59. Jo Freeman, *The Politics of Women's Liberation: A Case Study of an Emerging Social Movement and Its Relation to the Policy Process* (New York: David McKay, 1975), 76.

60. For background on the want-ads issue, see Elizabeth Boyer, "Help-wanted Advertising—Every Woman's Barriers," *Hastings Law Journal*, Vol. 23, No. 5 (1971), 221–31.

61. *NOW Hear This* (Pittsburgh Area NOW monthly newsletter), June 1970, Women's Center, University of Pittsburgh.

62. Flo Scardenia (Pittsburgh Area NOW official at the time of the want-ads controversy), interview with author, Pittsburgh, PA, February 22, 1977.

63. *NOW Hear This*, October 1969.

64. "Classifying Ads 'By Sex' Ruled Out," *Pittsburgh Press*, July 24, 1970. The *Pittsburgh Press* subsequently appealed as far as the United States Supreme Court.

65. Eleanor Holmes Norton (Chair, Equal Employment Opportunity Commission), interview with author, Washington, DC, October 30, 1978.

66. Rawalt, interview with author.

67. Betty Friedan, "A Bill of Rights for Women in 1968" (mimeographed), Friedan Papers; Rawalt, interview with author.

68. Lucinda Cisler, "Unfinished Business: Birth Control and Women's Liberation," in Robin Morgan, ed., *Sisterhood Is Powerful: An Anthology of Writings from the Women's Liberation Movement* (New York: Vintage, 1970), 274–323; Wendy Brown, "Reproductive Freedom and the Right to Privacy: A Paradox for Feminists," in Irene Diamond, ed., *Families, Politics, and Public Policy: A Feminist Dialogue on Women and the State* (New York: Longman, 1983), 322–338.

69. See Barbara Hayler, "Abortion," *Signs*, Vol. 5, No. 2 (1979), 307–23, esp. 313–14.

70. Hole and Levine, *Rebirth of Feminism*, 89–90; Freeman, *The Politics of Women's Liberation*, 81–82; Cellestine Ware, *Woman Power: The Movement for Women's Liberation* (New York: Tower, 1970), 24–25; Ti-Grace Atkinson, *Amazon Odyssey* (New York: Links, 1974), 9–11. See Betty Friedan's interesting recollection of these events in *It Changed My Life*, 152–53.

71. Elizabeth Boyer (founder and first president of WEAL), interview with author, Cleveland, OH, August 11, 1977; Lizabeth Moody (founding member and early pres-

ident of WEAL), interview with author, Cleveland, OH, November 17, 1977; Rawalt, interview with author.

72. Mayer N. Zald and Roberta Ash, "Social Movement Organizations: Growth, Decay and Change," *Social Forces*, Vol. 44, No. 3 (1966), 327–41.

73. "By-Laws of the *Women's Equity Action League*" (1968), Women's Equity Action League Papers, Schlesinger Library, Cambridge, MA (hereafter cited as WEAL Papers).

74. Boyer, interview with author; Moody, interview with author; WEAL Position Papers and Press Releases, 1968–1969, WEAL Papers.

75. Boyer, interview with author.

76. Cited in "Another Lib Voice Heard From," *The Plain Dealer* (Cleveland), June 28, 1970.

77. Letter, Bernice Sandler to Elizabeth Boyer, May 19, 1969, Bernice Sandler Papers (partly restricted), Schlesinger Library, Cambridge, MA; Boyer, interview with author.

78. Letter, Nancy E. Dowding (President of WEAL) to George P. Schultz (Secretary of Labor), January 31, 1970, WEAL Papers.

79. Bernice Sandler, "Universities and Colleges Charged with Sex Discrimination under Executive Orders 11246 and 11375 (filed by WEAL unless otherwise indicated)," (mimeographed), probably 1970, WEAL Papers; Bernice Sandler, "A Little Help from Our Government: WEAL and Contract Compliance," in Alice S. Rossi and Ann Calderwood, eds., *Academic Women on the Move* (New York: Russell Sage Foundation, 1973), 439–55.

80. Boyer, interview with author; Moody, interview with author.

81. Freeman, *The Politics of Women's Liberation*, 199–200.

82. Boyer, interview with author; Moody, interview with author; Rawalt, interview with author; Pauli Murray, interview with author, Alexandria, VA, September 22, 1978; "Another Lib Voice Heard From."

83. Murray, interview with author, September 22, 1978.

84. "WEAL: Women's Equity Action League" (pamphlet), probably 1972, WEAL Papers.

85. See analysis of the ERA as a national issue in National Commission on the Observance of International Women's Year, *To Form a More Perfect Union: Justice for American Women* (Washington, DC: Government Printing Office, 1976), 218–20, 373–77; National Commission on the Observance of International Women's Year, *The Spirit of Houston: The First National Women's Conference* (Washington, DC: Government Printing Office, 1978), 49–52, 128–52.

86. Indeed, the forces of reaction, including the Ku Klux Klan, acted against the women's movement in much the same manner that they had acted against black civil rights. That is to say, reactionaries opposed feminism with vituperation, demagoguery, sabotage and frequent violence. The most glaring demonstration of this occurred in 1977 when reactionaries led by the Klan did everything in their power to intimidate International Women's Year state committees and provide a "war between women," thus creating divisiveness in the women's movement much as they had sought to cultivate factionalism in the black movement. See National Commission on the Observance of International Women's Year, *The Spirit of Houston*, 109–10; "ERA Opponents Rail Against Women's Meeting," *The Atlanta Journal and Constitution*, May 14, 1977; "Klan Cardholder Wanted to Help," *Today* (Brevard County, FL), July 7, 1977; "Militant Conservatives form New Coalitions," *Delta Democratic-Times* (Green-

ville, MS), July 14, 1977; "Women's Year: Peril on the Right," *Philadelphia Inquirer*, August 23, 1977; "Klan's 'Spies' Plan to Disrupt Feminist Parley," *Detroit News*, September 1, 1977; "KKK Infiltrates Women's Groups," *The Washington Star*, September 2, 1977. Also, East, interview with author; Rawalt, interview with author; Murray, interview with author, September 22, 1978.

87. U.S. Commission on Civil Rights, *Statement on the Equal Rights Amendment* (Washington, DC: Government Printing Office, 1978), 2; East, interview with author; Rawalt, interview with author.

88. Nancy Gager, ed., *Women's Rights Almanac* (New York: Harper and Row, 1974), 384–86; National Commission on the Observance of International Women's Year, *The Spirit of Houston*, 41.

89. Betsey Wright (Director, National Women's Education Fund), interview with author, Washington, DC, September 18, 1978. For background information on women's political objectives, see Jeane J. Kirkpatrick, *Political Woman* (New York: Basic, 1974), 217–53.

90. National Women's Education Fund, "Facts: Women and Public Life, 1978" (data sheet); National Women's Education Fund, "Women's Election Central" (press release), November 8, 1976; National Women's Education Fund, "Women's Election Central" (press release), October 1976. Data obtained from the national office of the National Women's Education Fund in Washington, DC. See Gager, *Women's Rights Almanac*, 383.

91. *Frontiero* v. *Richardson, Secretary of Defense*, 411 U.S. 677 (1973); U.S. Commission on Civil Rights, *Women's Rights in the United States of America* (Washington, DC: Government Printing Office, 1979), 1–15, provided important background information on women and the Supreme Court.

92. *Griswold* v. *Connecticut*, 381 U.S. 479 (1965); *Roe* v. *Wade, District Attorney of Dallas County*, 410 U.S. 113 (1973); *Doe* v. *Bolton, Attorney General of Georgia*, 410 U.S. 179 (1973); "States' Bans Ruled Out Until Last 10 Weeks," *New York Times*, January 23, 1973; Kirstin Booth Glen, "Abortion in the Courts: A Laywoman's Historical Guide to the New Disaster Area," *Feminist Studies*, Vol. 4, No. 1 (1978), 1–26; *Planned Parenthood of Central Missouri* v. *Danforth, Attorney General of Missouri*, 428 U.S. 52 (1976); "High Court Bars Giving a Husband Veto on Abortion," *New York Times*, July 2, 1976; Hayler, "Abortion," 308–9.

93. *Bellotti, Attorney General of Massachusetts* v. *Baird*, 428 U.S. 132 (1979); "Parental Consent Law on Abortion Is Struck Down," *New York Times*, July 3, 1979; Hayler, "Abortion," 309; and *Harris* v. *McRae*, 448 U.S. 297 (1980); see *Harris* v. *McRae, No. 79–1268. The United States Law Week*, Vol. 48, No. 50 (1980), 4941–60; "H.E.W. Funds Bill Stalled in House by Abortion Issue," *New York Times*, August 11, 1976; Hayler, "Abortion," 309–11; *City of Akron* v. *Akron Center for Reproductive Health, Inc., Nos. 81–746 and 81–1172, The United States Law Week*, Vol. 51, No. 48 (1983), 4762–83; "The Court Stands by Abortion," *Newsweek*, June 27, 1983, 62–63; "Supreme Court Reaffirms 1973 Abortion Decision," *The Washington Post*, June 16, 1983.

94. Norton, interview with author.

95. Eleanor Holmes Norton, interview, "The MacNeil/Lehrer News Hour," Corporation for Public Broadcasting (PBS), February 12, 1988.

96. Women's Action Alliance, *Women's Action Almanac: A Complete Resource Guide* (New York: William Morrow, 1979), 343–420.

97. See "Up from the Kitchen Floor," *New York Times Magazine* (March 4, 1973),

8–9, 28–37, and further data on women's election and appointment to positions of authority in National Commission on the Observance of International Women's Year, *To Form a More Perfect Union*, 341–48.

98. Quote, "The National Women's Political Caucus" (pamphlet), probably 1972. See "Articles of Incorporation of National Women's Political Caucus, Inc."; "Bylaws of the National Women's Political Caucus, Inc." (revised 1977). All obtained from the national office of the National Women's Political Caucus, Washington, DC. See also, "Women Organize for Political Power," *New York Times*, July 11, 1971.

99. Cited in "Women Organize for Political Power." See "The National Women's Political Caucus"; "Texan Will Head Women's Caucus," *New York Times*, February 12, 1973; "Now a Wide Spectrum of Groups," *New York Times*, February 25, 1973. For Betty Friedan's account of the creation of the NWPC, her role in it and her subsequent disinterest in it, see *It Changed My Life*, 218–40.

100. Maren Lockwood Carden, *The New Feminist Movement* (New York: Russell Sage Foundation, 1974), 139.

101. "The National Women's Political Caucus"; National Women's Political Caucus, "Health Care Services: A Position Paper," probably 1975; and National Women's Political Caucus, "Position Papers," probably 1975. All obtained from the national office of the National Women's Political Caucus, Washington, DC.

102. Freeman, *The Politics of Women's Liberation*, 162.

103. Shirley Chisholm speech to the Conference on Women's Employment, Hearings before the Special Subcommittee on Education of the Committee on Education and Labor, House, 91st., 2d sess. (Washington, DC: U.S. Government Printing Office, 1970), 909–15. See Pauline Terrelonge Stone, "Feminist Consciousness and Black Women," in Jo Freeman, *Women: A Feminist Perspective* (Palo Alto, CA: Mayfield, 1979), 575–88.

104. Norton, interview with author; "Feminism: 'The Black Nuance,' " *Newsweek*, December 17, 1973, 89–90; "Black Feminism: A New Mandate," *Ms.*, May 1974, 97–100; "Black Feminists Prepare Policies," *New York Times*, December 3, 1973; Michele Wallace, "On the National Black Feminist Organization," in Redstockings of the Women's Liberation Movement, ed., *Feminist Revolution* (New York: Random House, 1978), 174. See Pauli Murray, "The Liberation of Black Women," in Mary Lou Thompson, ed., *Voices of the New Feminism* (Boston: Beacon, 1970), 89–90, and the entire article for the black women issues discussed throughout this study; Dara Abubakari, Renee Ferguson, Pauli Murray, Patricia Robinson, Shirley Chisholm, Margaret Wright and Fannie Lou Hamer in Gerda Lerner, ed., *Black Women in White America: A Documentary History* (New York: Pantheon, 1972), 585–614.

105. Cited in "Black Feminists Form Group Here: National Body Hopes to End 'Myths' and Intimidation," *New York Times*, August 16, 1973.

106. Cited in "They're Black, So Feminism Has Even More Obstacles than Usual," *New York Times*, November 7, 1973.

107. National Black Feminist Organization, "Statement of Purpose," in Ella Lasky, ed., *Humanness: An Exploration into the Mythologies about Women and Men* (Borough of Manhattan: Community College of CUNY, 1975), 410. For a more detailed account of these and other such issues, see "Black Women's Plan of Action," in National Commission on the Observance of International Women's Year, *The Spirit of Houston*, 272–77; Diane K. Lewis, "A Response to Inequality: Black Women, Racism, and Sexism,"

Signs, Vol. 3, No. 2 (1977), 339–61; Bonnie Thornton Dill, "The Dialectics of Black Womanhood," *Signs*, Vol. 4, No. 3 (1979), 543–55.

108. Norton, interview with author.

109. Ibid.

110. "3,000 Delegates at Chicago Meeting Organize a National Coalition of Labor Union Women," *New York Times*, March 25, 1974; Patricia Cayo Sexton, "Workers (Female) Arise!: On Founding the Coalition of Labor Union Women," *Dissent*, Vol. 21, No. 3 (1974), 381–82.

111. Kessler-Harris, *Women Have Always Worked*, 147–48. Alice Kessler-Harris provides a useful analysis of the tensions between such activist women and the problems of union organizing in "Organizing the Unorganizable: Three Jewish Women and Their Union," *Labor History*, Vol. 17, No. 1 (1976), 5–23. See Barbara Mayer Wertheimer, *We Were There: The Story of Working Women in America* (New York: Pantheon, 1977), 372–76; Annemarie Troger, "Coalition of Labor Union Women: Strategic Hope, Tactical Despair," *Radical America*, Vol. 9, No. 6 (1975), 111–14; Barbara M. Wertheimer, "'Union Power': Sketches from Women's Labor History," in Jo Freeman, *Women: A Feminist Perspective*, 353–357.

112. For a breakdown of the movement's various educational and publicity programs, see Kirsten Grimstad and Susan Rennie, *The New Woman's Survival Catalog* (New York: Coward, McCann and Geoghegan, 1973), 9–45, 123–43, 183–201.

113. Information on KNOW, Inc. obtained from Flo Scardina (co-founder of KNOW, Inc.), interview with author, and *KNOW News* (September 1975), KNOW, Inc. Library (partly restricted), Pittsburgh. Grimstad and Rennie, *The New Woman's Survival Catalog*, 9–15; Susan Rennie and Kirsten Grimstad, eds., *The New Woman's Survival Sourcebook* (New York: Alfred A. Knopf, 1975), 10, 144–50; Gager, *Women's Rights Almanac*, 588–90; Women's Action Alliance, *Women's Action Almanac*, 316–19.

114. Freeman, *The Politics of Women's Liberation*, 157; Carden, *The New Feminist Movement*, 194, n.18.

115. "Constitution of the NWSA," *Women's Studies Newsletter*, Vol. 5, Nos. 1 and 2 (1977), 6.

116. "Programs," *Women's Studies Newsletter*, Vol. 5, No. 3 (1977), 23–28; "Fact Sheet on Women's Studies Programs in 1977," *Women's Studies Newsletter*, Vol. 5, No. 4 (1977), 17; Tammar Berkovitz, Jean Mangi, and Jane Williamson, eds., *Who's Who and Where in Women's Studies* (Old Westbury, NY: The Feminist Press, 1974), vii; Hole and Levine, *Rebirth of Feminism*, 327.

117. Gerda Lerner, "Priorities and Challenges in Women's History Research," *Perspectives*, Vol. 26, No. 4 (April 1988), 17–18.

118. See C. G. Woodson, "An Accounting for Twenty-Five Years," *The Journal of Negro History*, Vol. 25, No. 4 (1940), 422–31; Barton J. Bernstein, "Fiftieth Anniversary of *The Journal of Negro History*," *The Journal of Negro History*, Vol. 51, No. 2 (1966), 75–97.

119. "100,000 Join March for Extension of Rights Amendment Deadline," *New York Times*, July 10, 1978; "Government Expands 'Minority' Definition; Some Groups Protest," *New York Times*, July 30, 1978.

120. "E.R.A. Needs Extra Innings," *New York Times*, November 6, 1978. If the ratification period had not been extended, the amendment would have died three states short of the thirty-eight required for ratification on March 22, 1979. U.S. Congress, House, "House Joint Resolution Proposing an Amendment to the Constitution of the United States Relative to Equal Rights for Men and Women, to the Committee of the

Judiciary," H. J. Res. 1, 98th Cong., 1st sess., January 3, 1983; *Congressional Record*, Vol. 129, No. 1 (1983), 46; "Congress Back, So Is ERA," *USA Today*, January 4, 1983; "House Applause for ERA Stops in Middle of the Aisle," *The Washington Post*, January 4, 1983; quotes, "ERA Senate Battle Brews," *USA Today*, January 5, 1983; "What Killed Equal Rights: A Ten-Year Struggle Teaches American Women the Art of Politics," *Time*, July 14, 1982, 32. On the failure of the ERA to win ratification, see Jane J. Mansbridge, *Why We Lost the ERA* (Chicago: University of Chicago Press, 1986); Mary Francis Berry, *Why ERA Failed: Politics, Women's Rights and the Amending Process of the Constitution* (Bloomington: Indiana University Press, 1986).

121. Chafe, *Women and Equality*, 45–78, esp. 77–78.

Cultural-Oriented Feminism

THE CULTURAL APPROACH: INTRODUCTION

The new feminism included a classic radical side that rejected many organizational reform goals in favor of a theoretical analysis of gender based on intragroup strength and solidarity and attacks on normative cultural values, most notably those that sustained the notions of women's proper sphere as one solely of reproduction, domesticity and family.[1] This radical ideology, militantly class and caste conscious, revolved in particular around a critical framework of an identifiable women's culture and a militant view of male domination as the source of women's oppression. The radicals' strategy often rejected the legal-oriented consensus models of protest in favor of conflict models, many of which came to be characterized as "zap actions." Cultural norms based upon class and caste analysis, group identity, intragroup strength and a theory that men subordinate women through myriad cultural controls gave this segment of modern feminism an ideologically eclectic and often dramatic public quality. In essence, the radicals created a huge protest umbrella for a wide cultural-oriented thrust ranging from small consciousness-raising "rap groups" to outright separatist ventures. In the introduction to *Sisterhood Is Powerful*, an anthology of the best-known early essays on contemporary feminism, Robin Morgan suggested that radical feminism was as much an act of female self-assertion as an anticonsensus movement:

This is not a movement one "joins." There are no rigid structures or membership cards. The Women's Liberation Movement exists where three or four friends or neighbors decide to meet regularly over coffee and talk about their personal lives. It also exists in the cells of women's jails, on the welfare lines, in the supermarket, the factory, the convent, the farm, the maternity ward, the streetcorner, the old ladies' home, the kitchen, the steno pool, the bed. It exists in your mind, and in the political and personal insights that you can contribute to change and shape and help its growth. It is frightening. It is very exhilarating. It is creating history, or rather, *herstory*.[2]

In retrospect, the cutting edge of both black militancy and radical feminism has been autonomous cultural movements rather than consensus legal-oriented ones. Both blacks and women persisted in efforts to testify to their separate social and political worlds quite apart from the protest spheres of other 1960s activists. It is impossible to establish the numbers of radical women, since many of them operated at different levels of feminism and not infrequently varied the degree of their involvement and their group affiliations over time. Judging from the tremendous outpouring of radical-based literature, the number of radical women and those with radical leanings must have been extensive. Researcher Maren Lockwood Carden concluded that the total participants in the legal phase and the cultural phase of the movement (what she called Women's Rights and Women's Liberation groups) in 1973 was between 80,000 and 100,000, with radical-oriented groups accounting for as many as 20,000 of that figure.[3] There is, however, no way of establishing actual numbers of participants in the radical phases of the movement, particularly radical organizations, since they were so decentralized as compared to NOW, WEAL, the NWPC and other membership organizations of the legal-oriented camp.

The term *radical* is used here in its traditional sense to connote "a disturber of the peace."[4] *Peace* itself must be considered a cultural-laden term in that it includes a society's prevailing, normative standards of "correct behavior." As a result, any behavior that upsets recognized norms may be considered radical. Richard Greaves and Robert Zaller speak directly to this: "In the proper etymological sense of the term, we may define radicals as those [seeking] fundamental change by striking at the very root of contemporary assumptions and institutions, often in order to revert to what they judged to be the proper historic roots."[5] One must be careful not to fall into the semantic trap of excluding completely reform-minded legalists from the radical category. Certainly, legal-oriented reformists' goals at various junctures of American history must be considered radical. For example, the Republican reforms following the Civil War, certain Progressive ideas, and most organized-labor actions prior to the New Deal were seen as radical.

The true measure of radical action in contemporary feminism lies in the degree of militancy and other behavior meant not solely to reform but to "disturb" society into new modes of self-definition and self-expression. For the purposes of this study, accordingly, radical feminism describes a generally nonconventional, women-centered method of protest, an effort to change fundamentally the framework and prevailing values of society. Consequently, radicalism for women, much as it has been for blacks, arose as a matter of style as much as of ideology. This "going to the roots" thesis of black and female radicals gave rise to a commitment that focused on long-standing external realities different from those concerning other historical protest movements challenging the American consensus.

THE ROOTS OF CULTURAL/RADICAL FEMINISM

As Sara Evans and others have demonstrated, it was primarily women in civil rights and the New Left whose perception of unequal protest spheres laid the basis for a new radical feminist constituency.[6] Women active in these movements derived important political lessons from male leaders practicing overt sexism. Indeed, most of the protest movements of the early 1960s were controlled and defined by male leaders, many of whom exhibited a penchant for dominance over women. The reaction of female activists to the idea that they should be subservient to men served as one of the most important catalysts for modern radical feminism. It led to the sense of women as a caste, linked inextricably by their sex and shared injustices. Their involvement in civil rights and the New Left taught women the meaning of psychological oppression and served as a prelude to their seeking out and challenging the perceived sources of that oppression. Moreover, women's involvement in civil rights and the Left not only brought them to new levels of awareness about the restrictions of sex, but also served as a training ground for many future radical feminists.

In many ways women's renewed awareness of the legalists' circumscribed visions paralleled the development of feminism in the years prior to and directly following the Civil War. As we have already seen, the first wave of American feminism grew in large part from male abolitionists' ambivalence toward women's interests. In 1840 most American male delegates to the World Anti-Slavery Convention in London refused to challenge the convention's majority decision not to seat women representatives. After the Civil War many male leaders declined to support women's causes for fear of jeopardizing support for the Negro's Hour. Consequently, women were sensitive to such issues; in this respect, the 1960s simply wrote another chapter in women's own protest odyssey.

Early signs of a radical consciousness appeared during the early 1960s civil rights summer projects, many of which were led or influenced by groups like the Student Nonviolent Coordinating Committee and the Council of Federated Organizations (COFO). Women involved in the southern phase of the broad movement found themselves treated as second-class citizens and consigned to inferior roles. The male leadership almost invariably directed women's energies into the most menial, domestic-oriented chores (what many women termed "shitwork"), including typing and duplicating, making and serving coffee and cooking and cleaning. Women resented the domestic chores which had the overall effect of casting them as movement "house-keepers."[7] In a letter home, one female COFO worker summed up this disenchantment as follows: "We didn't come down here to work as a maid this summer, we came down to work in the field of civil rights."[8] In addition to stereotyping based upon an earlier era's notion of proper spheres, white women often faced a nettlesome problem: the "sexual test," or their ability to handle diplomatically unwelcomed sexual advances from black males.[9]

Women in the civil rights movement found themselves systematically excluded from policy-making positions, an especially intolerable practice for a professionally egalitarian movement. In 1964 Ruby Doris Smith Robinson, a founding member of SNCC, addressed this issue in a memorable female position paper titled, "The Position of Women in SNCC," which allegedly prodded Stokely Carmichael to respond that "the only position for women in SNCC is prone."[10] The "prone" story stimulated female unrest. Indeed, there was evidence indicating that the new phrase "women's liberation" was first coined as a reaction to Carmichael's purported statement.[11]

In 1965 two white female members of SNCC, Casey Hayden and Mary King, circulated a paper ingeniously comparing the inferior role of women in the civil rights movement to that of blacks in society at large.[12] In so doing, King and Hayden fashioned one of the first effective arguments against the pervasive gender/class/caste systems in the southern civil rights crusade. Like Smith Robinson's position paper on SNCC sexism, their protests met with male scorn and ridicule and served as further catalysts for the formation of new radical groups. Following this incident women's caucuses began appearing within the movement and female workers began drawing together for solace and fellowship, known later as "networking."

Women in the New Left experienced strikingly similar treatment to those in civil rights. They were seldom represented in the Left hierarchy and were routinely assigned clerical chores and other menial tasks.[13] When women sought to place a discussion of their subordinate status on the agenda of a Students for Democratic Society (SDS) conference in December 1965, men reacted derisively, retorting: "She just needs a good screw."[14] At a similar convention in 1966 female SDS supporters of a proposed "women's plank" again suffered verbal abuse; some were even pelted with tomatoes. Subsequent attempts by New Left women to gain stature and recognition within the movement met with similar male responses, which in turn led to their forming autonomous women's caucuses and awareness groups.[15] Author Robin Morgan, active in both civil rights and the Left, reflected the feelings of many such women as follows: "Thinking we were involved in the struggle to build a new society, it was a slowly dawning and depressing realization that we were doing the same work and playing the same roles *in* the Movement as out of it: typing the speeches that men delivered, making coffee but not policy, being accessories to the men whose politics would supposedly replace the Old Order. But whose New Order? Not ours, certainly."[16]

One of the most revealing incidents of women's political actions within the New Left occurred in late summer of 1967 at the National Conference for a New Politics (NCNP) in Chicago. Although it recognized over two hundred civil rights and peace groups, the new women's caucus achieved only informal status.[17] In direct reaction to this snub, a group of Chicago feminists formed one of women's liberation's first cells, which like a magnet, quickly attracted disenchanted radical women from throughout the country and set in motion a chain of events culminating in a dramatic schism between the New Left and the new feminists.[18] Such women concluded that working for their own freedom within existing male-dominated protest structures was impossible. If women wanted to achieve true liberation, they would have to go it alone. Accordingly, this core of politically active radicals, like their foremothers in the second half of the nineteenth century, grew to accept a strategy rejecting the extant protest framework. Looking back on the events, radical theorist Shulamith Firestone concluded, "The most analogous movement in America, [was] Black Power."[19] Firestone's analysis of the restatement of Black Power and radical feminism in the 1960s showed certain useful insights by illustrating that each action grew from an ideological cornerstone based on new group consciousness, new militant actions and new defiant rhetoric.

As a result modern radical women have confronted American cultural standards with substantially more sophisticated theories and broader programs than did their forebears. Central to their ideology has been a determination to repudiate coalitions with men in favor of an all-women's movement, a stance which in itself paralleled a concurrent series of events occurring in black civil rights. For example, by 1967 Black Power advocates such as Stokely Carmichael had also rejected the politics of coalition. SNCC even ejected long-active whites from the organization. This rejection of coalition politics represented an important watershed in militant black activism and feminism that was predicated on the belief that the goal of self-determination was indisputable and that the radical approach was the only viable means for success. To pursue this end, new styles of leadership arose in both movements, initiated by blacks like Stokely Carmichael, H. Rap Brown and Huey Newton, and by new feminists, to whom we shall now turn our discussion.

VWLM Signals a Beginning

Late in 1967 Jo Freeman, one of the women prevented from speaking at the NCNP, founded the first national radical newsletter, *Voice of the Women's Liberation Movement (VWLM)*. It quickly reached a circulation of two thousand, demonstrating that cultural-oriented women sought communication bridges in much the way that NOW, WEAL, and the NWPC had done in the legal phase.[20] In its sixteen months of existence, *VWLM* pioneered an important radical communications network that reached out to women of various localities and ideologies. One convert to feminism comments about her first encounter with *VWLM*: "I read it.... I said, 'My God, here are women who are not just sitting around.' " She continued: "I got the faith, like religion, with that first publication."[21]

VWLM further signaled a new women-centered movement by demanding that the phrase "women's liberation" be adapted to replace the more historical and conventional "women's rights" rhetoric of the legal-oriented camp. The term *women's liberation*, therefore, originated with the radical wing of the women's movement; but as time wore on others not associated with the radicals also adopted the term. Today the two concepts (i.e., women's rights and women's liberation) are somewhat synonymous, although militant feminists continue to define themselves almost exclusively in women's liberation terminology.

Shortly after the publication of *VWLM*, three other radical feminist journals appeared: *No More Fun and Games* (Boston); *Notes from the First Year* (New York); and *Lilith* (Seattle). These journals spoke to a new national audience. *Notes from the First Year* and its successor *Notes from the Second Year* became especially invaluable sources of well-articulated, militant feminist thought during the radicals' formative years. Over one hundred feminist publications appeared by 1973, many of which appealed primarily to the militant branch of the movement.[22] Such publications served a key function in creating a widespread awareness of a viable women's movement with radical overtones. In another sense the journals convinced an array of women that their oppression was political in nature and deserved as much attention as any of the other 1960s' reform causes.

The continuing proliferation of radical periodicals provided one measure of the radical wing's growth. Within two years of the first edition of *VWLM*, radical feminist groups were emerging at a startling rate. The most rapid increases came in cities with articulate radical publications, such as Chicago (thirty groups), Boston (twenty-five groups) and especially New York (fifty groups).[23] Shulamith Firestone, one of the incipient feminists at the National Conference for a New Politics, quickly arose as an important force among New York radicals. Like Freeman, Firestone left the conference convinced that women radicals must organize apart from the male-controlled Left. In late 1967 Firestone and Pamela Allen shaped an initial group of about twenty or thirty women into New York City's first radical feminist organization, New York Radical Women (NYRW). NYRW later evolved into Redstockings and New York Radical Feminists (not to be confused with The Feminists).[24]

The founders of NYRW chose their name to reflect a clear image of their purposes, three of which appeared in the group's "Principles": "We take as our source the hitherto unrecognized culture of women....We regard our feelings as our most important source of political understanding....We see the key to our liberation in our collective wisdom and our collective strength."[25] Most of NYRW's members were under twenty-five years of age and were veterans of civil rights and the Left. Years later a founder of NYRW recalled: "What brought them [NYRW] together to a women-only discussion and action group was a sense of abuse suffered at the hands of the very protest movements that had spawned them. As 'movement women' they were tired of doing the typing and fixing the food while 'movement men' did the writing and leading."[26]

The advent of NYRW, an extended group of some fifty or sixty women, of whom about twenty to thirty attended weekly meetings, marked a turning point in the radical movement.[27] It signaled the abandonment of women's caucus-type actions in favor of formal action-oriented liberation groups divorced completely from extant protest structures. NYRW quickly formed ties with a burgeoning nationwide network; but it was a network of loosely knit, usually fiercely independent groups, many of which were short-lived. Implicit in their ideology was the notion that women could operate independently of the larger society and should operate independently of nationwide reform groups like NOW and WEAL, as well.

The history of The Feminists, the group which parted with NOW in October 1968, in many ways illustrates the central issues and experiences of radical feminism. The Feminists' raison d'être covered a wide range of women-centered goals, most of which involved aggressive theoretical attacks on women's spheres and oppression—an approach we are calling cultural-oriented. In this sense The Feminists arose as one group particularly illustrative of how some women moved from one current of protest to another, to wit, from legal-oriented protest to cultural-oriented protest.

The Feminists and Other Early Radical Experiences

In Ti-Grace Atkinson's words, The Feminists left NOW after serious "deep-rooted value conflicts...between those who want women to have the opportunity to be oppressors...and those who want to destroy oppression itself."[28] Returning to New York City as the October 17th Movement, the group later changed its name to The Feminists, which evolved quickly into one of the nation's most militant women's organizations. One of The Feminists' early position papers stated that "what we [are] groping for [is] not the sum of current ideas on women, but an approach altogether new not only to feminism but to political theory as well."[29]

The Feminists' structure and rhetoric reflected its abhorrence of traditional hierarchical schemes. The chair and secretary changed with each meeting; the treasurer served for a month after being chosen by lot. Work tasks also changed on a monthly basis.[30] Each member would theoretically occupy every position through one cycle. Feminist Jessica Furie described the system as follows: "It says that some work is better than other work—but no person is better than any other.... It also says women—all women—are capable of power—of leadership—but that we no longer want the male values imposed on us—that of hierarchy."[31]

The Feminists' ethos ushered in what would become the widespread radical practices of promoting cooperation and discouraging competition among like-minded women. Its concepts of "leaderless" organization and autonomy of branches came to characterize a wide spectrum of the movement. The very diversity that The Feminists symbolized lent new strength to the radical movement. No one group became dependent upon individual "stars," nor did radical feminists themselves become dependent upon any single group. Radical women's liberation consisted primarily of small groups of women meeting informally to discuss a growing militant opposition to sexism. This faction of the movement had a tendency to reject cooperation between itself and legal-based groups like NOW and WEAL, which were seen as typifying all that had been ineffective and odious in the traditional reform structure.

At this point it is easy to draw comparisons between the new feminists and the ideology of young, militant blacks of the early 1960s who, like members of SNCC, for example, had manifested an antiorganizational strategy in favor of direct encounter.[32] This leaderless quality in both movements spawned an essentially broad-based allegiance and encouraged development of individual talents rather than dependence upon the type of hierarchical structure in which a few leaders would articulate and embody the ideas of many. Inherent in this approach was the principle that power should be shared in the battle against the larger oppressor, not monopolized by a few. In this sense the internal dynamics of protest came to reflect the character of its external demands against society at large.

As a result of their antiorganizational structure, women's groups like The Feminists found themselves squeezed between their adversaries and more moderate organizations. They frequently responded by turning inward for sustenance and strength. For its part the legal-oriented branch of the women's movement came to disapprove of the radicals' agenda and tactics as "self-defeating and extremist in nature."[33] Similarly, "to some it is abhorrent, to others dynamic; to some it is repugnant, to others exhilarating; to some it is destructive, to others it is useful," Dr. Martin Luther King, Jr., once wrote about militant Black Power demands.[34] His words described not only civil rights experiences, but a similar split in ideological directions between radical and reform feminism. The parallel may be developed further by noting that both black and women reformers sought to destroy the legal structure of racism and sexism, and both black and women radicals sought to go beyond this agenda by attacking the psychological assumption of inequality at its very cultural roots.

The 1968 Miss America Pageant in Atlantic City generated one of the earliest of such attacks. Radical women gathered there for perhaps their first mass militant demonstration against prevailing cultural assumptions of beauty. Led by sixty NYRW, approximately two hundred demonstrators from as far away as Florida and Iowa formed a loose coalition to picket what was termed the "Pageant's obscene exploitation of women."[35] One participant commented that the protests at Atlantic City were specifically planned to publicize that "we women are all *forced* to play the Miss America role—not by beautiful women but by men who we have to act that way for, and by a system that has so well institutionalized male supremacy for its own ends."[36]

Women protesters established a picket line directly in front of the pageant's headquarters, where they marched brandishing such signs as Miss America Sells It and Atlantic City Is a Town with Class—They Raise Your Morals While They Judge Your Ass. In one action designed to parody the pageant's closing ceremony, radicals crowned a sheep as Miss America. Other direct actions in the hall itself resulted in six arrests.[37] When the protesters dropped girdles, false eyelashes and other implements of fashion into a "freedom trashcan," the press so misrepresented the act that a persistent myth of feminists as "bra burners" resulted.[38] One participant recalled coming away from the protest with surging feelings that probably applied to many: "Thus I learned, with terrifying immediacy, the meaning of the new term 'sex object,' and how, henceforth, to regard both the physical flattery and the physical insults of men. From that moment, I have never smiled back at a flirting construction worker or truck driver, nor given a damn about the way I appear, physically, in the eyes of men."[39]

By squarely affronting a number of deep-seated gender notions, the Miss America demonstration made the hopes of both active and latent cultural-oriented feminists a feasible reality. Moreover, many women came to realize the paradoxes of a cultural system that rewarded extragroup notions of proper appearance and conduct in just the way blacks had come to view the paradigm. Blacks had long been faced with the Sambo myth of a happy, carefree, shuffling, irresponsible scamp. Whites and some blacks came to expect such behavior and for some it did, indeed, become a self-fulfilling prophecy. Likewise, the "cult of true womanhood" prescribed "proper" female behavior, emphasizing a devotion to piety, purity, domesticity and beauty (by the 1960s perhaps beauty above all else). Both myths imposed behavioral criteria on their subjects with the demands of submission, subservience and extragroup standards of beauty and docility in the presence of white males. Women had been so propagandized to accept this nineteenth-century notion that it, like the Sambo stereotype, took on aspects of a self-fulfilling prophecy.

The radicals' actions at Atlantic City took shape against a 1960s backdrop of sustained shifting social demands and actions against such myths. As the current of protest standards changed, the contours of personal commitment and group and individual challenges took on an increasingly militant nature. The tactics of protest that the radical women used were more reminiscent of the earlier street style of SNCC and other black militants, who emphasized a shift from negotiation to personal confrontation, than they were of the concurrent massive and sometimes fragmented antiwar and student protests. SNCC labeled this its "eyeball-to-eyeball" tactic; Huey Newton and the Black Panthers called it their "shock-a-buku" tactic.[40] Radical women used the term "zap action" to describe similar tactics. Thus the Miss America protest was in many ways the first radical "zap action" to focus the nation's attention on the growing militancy of 1960s women in attacking stereotypes and by so doing encouraged many women to join ranks both physically and spiritually with newly committed radicals.

GENERAL PROGRESSION OF SEMINAL RADICAL GROUPS

Civil Rights and the New Left

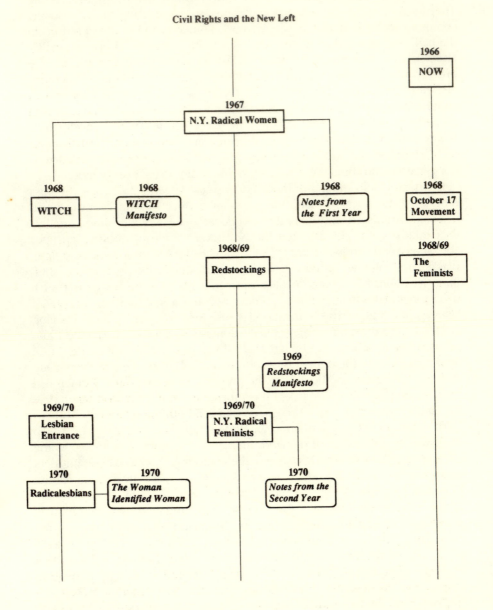

1966
NOW

1967
N.Y. Radical Women

1968
WITCH

1968
WITCH Manifesto

1968
Notes from the First Year

1968
October 17 Movement

1968/69
Redstockings

1968/69
The Feminists

1969
Redstockings Manifesto

1969/70
Lesbian Entrance

1969/70
N.Y. Radical Feminists

1970
Radicalesbians

1970
The Woman Identified Woman

1970
Notes from the Second Year

Source: Sarachild, "The Power of History," 43; Carden, **The New Feminist Movement**, 87; author's personal papers.

New Currents of Radical Feminism

After Atlantic City, radical actions were typified by encounter protest or zap actions against perceived cultural oppressions. In no small way the new campaigns reflected earlier feminist protest themes: group-centered actions, collective strength, self-defined goals and rejection of coalition politics.

Historically, Alice Paul and her followers best exemplified this type of protest. Paul led a small band of militant suffragists to dramatize the struggle for the vote by engaging in street demonstrations on the day of Woodrow Wilson's inauguration in 1913. The group, then known as the Congressional Union, and later as the National Woman's Party (NWP), flatly rejected the strategy of negotiation that characterized the organizationally inclined National American Woman Suffrage Association. The NWP organized high-visibility protests designed to force the vote to be granted rather than bargained for. After the American entry in the war in 1917, while the NAWSA combined the call to patriotic service with its own lobbying efforts for suffrage, Paul and others marched in front of the White House, were arrested for disturbing the peace, and were incarcerated and force-fed.[41] These women represented a dramatic example of contextual radicalism and militancy and a rejection of the more moderate legalist wing's tactics, a division that would characterize feminism through the appearance of its third wave in the 1960s.

In the fall of 1968 several founders of NYRW formed a new group on which the spirit and zeal of such earlier protests as Paul's lived. Reflecting the decentralized nature of radical feminism, WITCH (Women's International Terrorist Conspiracy from Hell) had neither an organizational hierarchy nor a true communication network among the dozens of local "covens" springing up in emulation of the parent group.[42] The unifying chain among the various WITCH covens seemed to be the universal commitment to aggressive public female behavior on behalf of radical causes. The direct WITCH tactics drew sustained media attention to the radical cause and served to announce a new phase of local and national initiatives. Robin Morgan noted, "WITCH would seem to be the striking arm of the Women's Liberation Movement, and as such is firing women's imagination in totally unrelated places where covens have sprung up and Witch guerrilla actions have occurred."[43]

The first WITCH zap action occurred, appropriately, on Halloween 1968. Women in witches' costumes circled the entrance to the stock exchange, where they "hexed and spooked" all who entered. WITCH had chosen Wall Street because it represented the most visible symbol of the male power structure. This and subsequent zap actions caught the imagination of women across the country, some of whom emulated these protests through local covens.[44] All were autonomous from the New York group, yet centered their ideology on "The WITCH Manifesto," a document that came to symbolize many of the central currents of radical feminism. This lengthy position paper stated that "WITCH is an all-women Everything." In a subsequent passage the "Manifesto" continued: "Your Power comes from your own self as a woman, and it is activated by working in concert with your sisters. The power of the Coven is more than the sum of its individual members, because it is *together*."[45] The last reported WITCH actions were simultaneous protests against the Valentine's Day bridal fairs in New York and San Francisco in 1969, by which time WITCH had become almost a byword for feminist cultural-oriented encounter tactics.[46]

The Rise of Consciousness Raising

About the time of the bridal fair incidents, Redstockings (a group of other women who had left NYRW), took a step that quickly would become the most lasting heritage and widely used activity of cultural-oriented women. Redstockings abandoned WITCH-type guerrilla tactics in favor of new intragroup consciousness-raising techniques (alternately known as CR). This ideal had taken similar form in the United States during the southern civil rights campaigns in the early 1960s. Carol Hanish and Kathie Amatniek (Kathie Sarachild), members of New York Radical Women, drew the parallel from their SNCC days in Mississippi when blacks used to "rap" about white injustice as symbolized by "the Man."[47] Thus consciousness raising for both blacks and women became a strategy whereby they discussed theory and sought unity.

Redstockings was also one of the first radical feminist groups to argue forcefully the culturally wrenching notion that not only were men at the root of the problem, but that they were the *enemy* of the movement as well. A classic document of women's liberation, the "Redstockings Manifesto," spoke for many radicals on this in excerpts from articles II, III and V:

II. Women are an oppressed class....We are exploited as sex objects, breeders, domestic servants, and cheap labor. We are considered inferior beings, whose only purpose is to enhance men's lives.

III. We identify the agents of our oppression as men. Male supremacy is the oldest, most basic form of domination. All other forms of exploitation and oppression (racism, capitalism, imperialism, etc.) are extensions of male supremacy: men dominate....*All men* receive economic, sexual, and psychological benefits from male supremacy. *All men* have oppressed women...

V.   We regard our personal experience, and our feelings about that experience, as the basis for an analysis of our common situation....Our chief task at present is to develop female class consciousness through sharing experience and publicly exposing the sexist foundation of all our institutions. Consciousness-raising is not "therapy," which implies the existence of individual solutions and falsely assumes that the male-female relationship is purely personal, but the only method by which we can ensure that our program for liberation is based on the concrete realities of our lives.[48]

Consciousness raising carried on in cells, affinity groups, rap groups, collectives, support groups, small groups, or simply women's liberation groups, emerged as an important engine of growth regarding feelings of a new cultural-feminist sisterhood. The very act of meeting away from men became a feminist act for some women. Often their sharing of experiences led them to understand that their grievances were derived from systemic and not merely personal shortcomings, a realization that induced them to work actively for the cause of liberation. Usually groups of five to twelve women comprised a consciousness-raising cell. Their purpose was to discuss intimately and openly any feelings of frustration and to speculate on the underlying causes for women's lack of fulfillment. Initially CR relied on spontaneity for catharsis, but by the early 1970s many groups centered their issues and discussions around burgeoning movement literature such as Redstockings's radical "Manifesto." Redstockings itself pursued a stridently prowoman line in its pronouncements, but this interpretation did not always surface as a legitimate issue in the full range and scope of CR practices.[49]

Consciousness raising provided energy for the entire radical movement much as it had done for Black Power advocates. As women shared their common experiences and expectations, many came to realize that only through self-initiated and collective actions could they redress their grievances. Some radical groups used CR techniques only for short periods before moving into more visible direct actions; others used the method for longer periods in a sustained effort to create new feminist praxis. In many ways the wide range of topics introduced in consciousness-raising groups led to a broadening and diversifying of the basic issues of radical/cultural feminism to include numerous fresh personal challenges to women's traditional spheres. Carol Hymowitz and Michaele Weissman estimated that upwards of 100,000 women had joined such groups; it would be impossible to estimate how many more thousands of women participated briefly in and were influenced by such groups.[50]

One of the more profound results of the radical/cultural consciousness-raising movement was that its ideas did become institutionalized through a corpus of "radical handbooks," including essays, books, position papers and other reference works whose range and appeal transcended the CR era itself. To illustrate this, we will examine briefly three landmark works.

Consciousness Raising and Social Analysis: De Beauvoir, Firestone and Millett as Inspiration

Within the ranks of contemporary feminism, Simone de Beauvoir's *The Second Sex* (1952) has provided the ideological wellspring for a cultural-oriented praxis, although de Beauvoir's work, like the other two under discussion, also attracted vast audiences in all feminist circles.[51] De Beauvoir's conclusions on female liberation and independence, in particular, have provided a discernible body of radical feminist analysis and have led many contemporary feminists to label her their "spiritual mother." The immensely popular *Second Sex*, which sold more than a million copies in America through 1980, supplied the biology-equates-to-class-oppression framework from which radical feminism eventually adopted its most basic tenets.[52]

De Beauvoir's work finds its centrifugal pull in an adoption of dialectical Marxism's class consciousness framework to a biological and historical analysis of gender based on existential categories of eminence and transcendence. Her section on "History" offers an especially felicitous example of this by tracing the rise of oppressive patriarchal and matriarchal theories from the ancient nomads to contemporary society. To keep women in their "place," de Beauvoir surmised, male-oriented theories of patriarchy were propounded on the assumption that the female sphere reflected nature's biological dictates. Therefore, in her theoretical framework the Marxian dialectic converted to a distinct biology-is-history paradigm: class and gender became synonymous; material motivations and patriarchal oppressions similarly assumed interchangeable qualities.

In retrospect, de Beauvoir's new critical analysis of gender oppression provided radical feminists with their most useful mode of analysis. It triggered not only new conceptual attacks on women's cultural-based oppressions, but simultaneously offered cross-currents of awareness to those women who had always suspected a stultifying, patriarchal hidden agenda as being the invisible controlling factor in their own lives. Clearly this new sense of conceptual and spiritual sisterhood provided the ideological underpinnings for a great mass of cultural-oriented feminism. Roxanne Dunbar, author of many widely circulated women's liberation works, wrote that "for many of us Simone de Beauvoir's *The Second Sex* changed our lives." Dunbar added, "*The Second Sex* is still the most intelligent, human, and thorough document written on Female oppression and masculine supremacy."[53] Kathie (Amatniek) Sarachild, a distinct force in the radical movement, stated: "Beauvoir's book was the best, most radical and comprehensive analysis up to its time and remains so. It was crucial to the development of the WLM." Sarachild continued, "But we took our more recent derivation for granted—Beauvoir and the black movement."[54]

In 1970 Redstockings cofounder Shulamith Firestone's *Dialectic of Sex* presented one of contemporary feminism's first and most masterful political analyses of the source of women's oppression, based in large part on this de Beauvoir model, which Firestone called "the most comprehensive and far-reaching" with respect to women's ideas on culture.[55] At first glance Firestone's "sex class" methodology seemed to mirror de Beauvoir's with regard to a materialistic view of history. In fact, Firestone felt that economic determinism was useful as a methodology only in that it supplied a theoretical structure for analysis—that in and of itself a materialist construct could not supply totally feminist solutions. In an introductory passage she commented that "an economic diagnosis traced to ownership of the means of production, even of the means of *re*production, does not explain everything. There is a level of reality that does not stem directly from economics."[56]

Firestone theorized, and almost all radicals came to argue, that all oppression, especially racism and sexism, sprang from sexual inequalities. She argued that biological differences led to male dominance, which in turn spawned an omnipotent patriarchy. In the beginning, according to the author, woman, because of her biological nature with its recurring cycles of menstruation and childbirth, was forced into a physical dependence on man analogous to a mother-child relationship. Men's dominance of women created a prototype of other power relationships, especially racism and sexism: "Thus, *racism is sexism extended*."[57]

Robin Morgan recalled Firestone's study as "a lucid political analysis... more revolutionary, in fact, than any theory I had yet encountered. Today, *Dialectic* seems almost axiomatic to current feminist thought; it is a basic building block."[58]

Firestone's ideas had an impact at another level by pointing out that the contemporary radical feminist position was a direct descendant of an earlier radical feminist line, notably that of Stanton and Anthony and of Alice Paul and the National Woman's Party. By so tracing their roots, Firestone provided radical feminists with an important sense of protest legacy. In talking of her feminist awareness prior to reading *Dialectic of Sex* and Simone de Beauvoir's *Second Sex*, radical Kathie Sarachild postulated that "too few of us had enough of a sense of history, particularly our own history, to see the political importance of making our tradition clear."[59]

Kate Millett's writings represented a further radical feminist progression to the historical basis of women's oppression. Millett gave added voice to radical thought by defining anew the theory of patriarchy and the need for feminist revolution to throw off the chains of what was becoming rapidly known by radicals as their "psychosexual" oppression. In *Sexual Politics* (1971) Millett effectively synthesized the heretofore atomized radical position on biological/patriarchal-based oppression, and gave to it, as well, a new gender-based revolutionary tone.[60] She cited social myths, women's radical protest past, anthropological writings, psychology and, finally, some selected literary giants to substantiate her theory that male domination was rooted in male-fomented roles and not in nature. "Conditioning runs in a circle of self-perpetuation and self-fulfilling prophecy," Millett noted of patriarchal domination.[61] "We are speaking, then," Millett further stated, "of a cultural revolution, which, while it must necessarily involve the political and economic reorganization traditionally implied by the term revolution, must go far beyond this as well."[62]

Millett's political theory on dominance and revolution, along with de Beauvoir's and Firestone's theories of the same, had a critical impact on the growing radical movement. As Sarachild noted about her CR group's early exposure to such writers: "Most of us had thought we were already radicals;

but we were discovering that we were only beginning to have a radical understanding of women—and of other issues of class, race and revolutionary change."[63]

De Beauvoir, Firestone and Millett were singularly influential feminists whose works helped convince radicals that females' inferior position in society was purely a result of male desire and design. The resultant radical paradigm held that women must unite solidly as an oppressed class in order to foment revolution against the oppressive patriarchy. This pervasive radical ideology became, as one student of the subject concluded, a paradigm of "women-over-against-men," or of "men as the enemy."[64] To this concept we shall add the category of women physically seeking to live apart from male society.

The Women-Over/Apart-from-Men Paradigm: Paternalism Attacked

A wide range of literature demonstrated some contemporary feminists' antipathy for men, yet it was the radical movement that seemed to fuse most solidly around this issue as a rallying cry and political postulate. The radicals held that, since men sought to dominate women and could relate only to traditional gender roles, women would find the most effective movement as one purged of such unnatural allies.[65] As SNCC and other Black Power groups had excluded whites, radical women concluded similarly that men would be antithetical to their cause. *Ms.* magazine commented on this point in 1972 as follows: "Even well-meaning men tend to adopt an attitude of helpful paternalism, and less enlightened ones take over the focus of a group by becoming adversaries—symbolic enemies to be defeated or convinced.... Men who really want to be helpful will care for houses and children so that women may be free to take part, or they will start rap groups of their own, to discuss the ways they are restricted by their 'masculine' role."[66] Black Power advocates like Stokely Carmichael had long stated flatly that a "white question" existed in the movement, and thus whites should return to their own communities and work for change, leaving blacks free to lead their own struggle. "We did not," Carmichael recalled, "want pampered white kids or condescending white liberals who knew nothing about black oppression trying to dominate our meetings."[67] A similar "man question"—the determination by radicals of what role(s) males would play in the movement—surfaced as early as the NOW organizing convention in 1966. With little dissension, NOW resolved the question in favor of full participation by men.[68] Its decision set the precedent for total participation by men on an equal basis, a position subsequently adopted almost perfunctorily by most legal-oriented feminist organizations. The man question, therefore, never proved divisive within the traditional wing of the movement.

Unlike members of the organizational branch, many of the radicals had especially bitter recollections of experiences with men, namely in regard to civil rights and the Left, and argued as an outgrowth of those experiences that full participation by men in their movement would only serve to co-opt women's self-defined prerogatives. The argument went that men could not really empathize with the unique problems of women, would try to secure the positions of leadership within the feminist movement for themselves as they had done in past movements, and would, in general, add an unnecessary psychological burden to movement women. Many radicals even declared outright ideological and cultural warfare against males. This attitude gave rise to a number of sharp epithets like "male chauvinist," "male chauvinist pig" (MCP) and "the oppressor." Often the terms were meant to reverse the traditional patterns of gender-based social insults, but the radicals' use of the term "oppressor" carried deeper political connotations. Oppression for them meant odious sex-based inequalities. To be sure, not all radicals were antimen. Many argued for the inclusion of men in the movement, but critics of the movement have often capitalized on the "man-hater" theme or myth as a means of derogating all radically inclined feminists.[69]

Ti-Grace Atkinson's The Feminists took one of the earliest collective hard-line postures against men. The Feminists stated flatly that men were oppressors of women and were, as such, the enemy. Theirs was an interpretation that reinforced the theory of women as victims of a historical male conspiracy. In many respects The Feminists' 1968 slogan Men Are the Enemy presaged radical feminism's most criticized ideological stance. Yet as one member concluded, "In order to have a revolution you must have a revolutionary theory."[70]

Unlike legalists and Marxist women, most radicals went to great lengths to underscore their antimen policies. Atkinson refused to appear in public with men unless the meeting encompassed a matter of "class confrontation." The Feminists' ideology itself focused on marriage as the institution most symbolic of male oppression. The organization enforced a one-third marriage rule, which stated that no more than one-third of its membership might be married or in cohabitation with males.[71] Shortly after its inception, The Feminists held a sit-in at the New York City Marriage Bureau and confronted Mayor John Lindsay with a list of charges purporting that "women [were] being illegally made sex slaves in the unholy state of matrimony."[72]

As a result of such protests, the antimen question provided a demarcation line along which feminists split over the very nature of institutionalized oppression. Those opposed to misandry (hatred of *man*kind) maintained that women could—and did—understand the nature of the institutional structure of inequality and that anger could be vented against that institutional structure without hating all members of the opposite sex. Even so, this question became so abhorrent to legalist women that it led Betty Friedan to conclude, "It was harder to fight than male oppression. The pathology caused by oppressive institutions was being mistaken for, and was in danger of perverting, the revolution women needed to change those institutions."[73] Conversely, the antimen argument led to the institutionalization of a discernible pro-women line resting on the cultural assumption of women's need for identity and autonomy from what was viewed as perhaps an irreversible historical oppression.

Some of the reactions to the "man issue" were quite notable. On this subject New York Radical Feminists stated openly what many movement women were discussing privately: "We recognize that we are engaged in a power struggle with men, and that the agent of our oppression is man insofar as he identifies with and carries out the supremacy privileges of the male role."[74] Accordingly, NYRF clearly predicated its politics on the theory that a historical male-female role-typing had led to women's oppression and that such power relationships must be destroyed through female revolutionary action.

Long-time activist Valerie Solanas best symbolized this prowomen/antimen line, carrying the antimen stance to its extreme in a widely circulated polemic titled the "SCUM Manifesto."[75] Solanas had previously gained notoriety for shooting pop artist Andy Warhol, for which she became a cause célèbre to many radicals who felt she had committed a political act. In the SCUM (Society for Cutting Up Men) polemic, Solanas exhorted women to "eliminate" men, because males were the very antithesis of women's liberation.[76] In one passage Solanas predicted that "the sick, irrational men, those who attempt to defend against their disgustingness, when they see SCUM barreling down on them, will cling in terror to Big Mama . . . [who'll] be clinging to Big Daddy, who'll be in the corner, shitting his forceful, dynamic pants. Men who are rational, however, won't kick or struggle or raise a distressing fuss, but will just sit back, relax, enjoy the show and ride the waves to their demise."[77] Author Joanna Russ summed up the general reaction to the SCUM statement as follows: "While every woman is not Valerie Solanas, Solanas is Everywoman— this means that nobody can escape the general situation."[78] But in that many of the radicals did adopt the antimen line for shock purposes, in reality their ideology embraced a greater cultural autonomy from males rather than a society based upon Solanas's female totalitarianism.

The idea of cultural autonomy was not novel to contemporary protest. As we have seen, Black Power advocates called for both psychological and phys-ical cultural autonomy, the latter perhaps best demonstrated by the black "nation within a nation" idea of the Republic of New Africa. While some Black Power advocates sought simply to adopt personal commitments to community and group separatism, the Republic of New Africa called for the separation of five southern states to create its black nation. Of course, just as cultural autonomy embraced a whole range of commitments and ideas throughout the black movement, the same general observation can be made about the women's movement. Even though radical feminists manifested the strongest and most thorough commitment to cultural autonomy, other women sought answers to their problems in similar terms.

Feminists and academics have argued this point for years. Historians Carroll Smith-Rosenberg, Gerda Lerner and Jessie Bernard have, among others, thoroughly explored the "separate cultures" and "female world" themes. Smith-Rosenberg found that middle-class, nineteenth-century women were often united by shared experiences and biological imperatives that led to the evolution of an identifiable, mutually supportive "women's culture." She acknowledged that women had learned to coexist functionally with the predominant male culture; yet over generations, the women in her study displayed a sustained camaraderie exclusive of men. Consequently, Smith-Rosenberg argued, women's culture was a refuge from thralldom, women's culture was a domestic world in which men merely played outside roles.[79]

In complementary studies, Gerda Lerner dwelled on the psychological dynamics of a separate women's culture in which she delineated a divergent male-female consciousness, and Jessie Bernard postulated in *The Female World* that the "female world is worthy of study in and of itself, quite apart from its impact on the male world."[80] In "Sexuality, Class and Role," Charles Rosenberg suggested that women's recognition of a separateness had caused them to shift concerns from behavior traditionally defined as deviant to configurations of approved female behavior.[81] Within this framework the concept of women's culture became for many radicals the true measure of group identity and resulted in both physical and psychological expressions of solidarity and awareness. The manifestations of cultural identity ran the gamut from new personal commitments to an insistence on redefining women as a cultural group to outright separatist ventures. It now becomes instructive to identify some examples of these approaches.

Women, History and Cultural Separatism

In the early 1970s radical women began to call for a significant revision of history that, in turn, would lead to new theories of women regarding their past, present and future roles. The movement reached an ideological watershed of sorts with radical women's attacks on traditional history and concurrent calls for a history of women based upon their unique personal, social and political lives. Conventional male-centered history, or what Robin Morgan castigated as "mytho-history," came under increasing attack by a wide segment of radicals who sought to show the origins of prevailing oppression and to use history as an important (mass) consciousness-raising tool.[82] Militant radicals such as Firestone and Millett saw history as an especially propitious means for "demythologizing" women's past. The attention given to women's history paralleled that of other protest groups' experiences, such as the developments in black history in the 1960s, which sought both to integrate black experiences into American history and to provide a conceptual framework for exploring in greater depth the special characteristics and themes of people of African ancestry. In this regard, blacks and women notably moved toward redefining past events with the purpose of presenting themselves as a cohesive group of active players in history. Cultural-oriented women, in particular, began to shift their emphasis from zap actions and protests to theories and practices designed to institutionalize a woman's own sense of history and self. Tracts like Sheila Rowbotham's *Hidden from History* and Linda Gordon's "Towards a Radical Feminist History" reflected this theme and became immensely popular reading. Gordon struck to the heart of this theme in her "Towards a Radical Feminist History": "I think we need a women's history, but I also think it will be impossible to create one without a radical transformation of the whole historical discipline and profession—a radical feminist perspective on all of history." She continued: "If this suggests similar conclusions about the history of black people, brown people, and working class people, please feel free to draw them."[83]

To combat what they considered a whitewashing of their history, radicals demanded that women's studies become an integral part of the college curricula just as black studies had in the 1960s. The demands of blacks, like those of women a decade later, were grounded on the assumption that history had been used by the powerful to perpetuate their control of those minority groups denied an equal access to power. In any consideration of the need for black studies or women's studies, two incontrovertible facts surfaced: blacks often knew more about white history than their own, and women often knew more about male history than their own.

Consequently, as the 1960s marked the coming of age for black studies, the first half of the 1970s witnessed the same for women's studies. The rapid growth of courses testified to the fact that cultural-conscious females were determined to expound and institutionalize new visions about women's past and future. Between the years 1971 and 1975 the number of gender-oriented courses increased dramatically. By mid-decade more than 5,000 new courses appeared. By 1978, 301 women's studies programs were available in forty-one states.[84] The new National Women's Studies Association (begun in 1977) disseminated important information about women's studies efforts, as did the *Women's Studies Abstract* and the *Women's Studies Newsletter*. Also, much as in the black movement, women's studies became the intellectual and research arm of the movement. Through the tools of research, teaching and writing, feminists have attempted to credit women with their rightful positions in all facets of history and scholarship. One radical spoke of the proliferation of women's studies as a mark that the movement was "growing up." She summed up the position on women's studies as follows: "Most of us were also seriously committed to a Feminist Movement which could transform our culture; and this meant study and respect for intelligence—as in the trends expressed... [in] women's studies."[85] Like black studies, women's curricula have grown to become an integral part of higher education and are now enjoyed and found useful by women and men of many personal and ideological commitments (as black studies is by both blacks and whites).

Sexism in language was another cultural area, like that of history, for which radical feminists in particular proposed alternative models. Radicals took the lead in arguing that nouns, pronouns and titles in the language often conveyed both overt and covert senses of male supremacy. Kate Millett observed that "in many patriarchies, language, as well as cultural tradition, reserve the human condition for the male."[86] Millett and others argued that gender identity in language had become a powerful aspect of culture and demonstrably influenced the way one talked, acted and felt about the opposite sex. Radicals especially argued that language tended to depreciate female dignity and self-concept and set women apart from the traditional power structure.

This belief led radical women to spearhead a drive to eliminate gender-oriented pronouns from the English language. Like some black militants before them, radical women argued that language too often transformed symbolism into convoluted reality. For example, in the early twentieth century black activists almost always considered the term "colored" as reflecting the white concepts of Afro-Americans. The nationalist Marcus Garvey rejected words like "colored" and adopted "Negro" with the upper case "N" much as the scholar W.E.B. DuBois had done. Later Garvey embraced "Black" solely to describe his race and adopted models for alternative institutions with names like the Black Cross Navigation and Trading Company, Black Cross Nurses and Black Star Line; Garvey's newspaper, *Negro World*, subsequently gave way to his *Black Man*.[87] By 1969 H. Rap Brown wrote anew about this phenomenon: "Negroes and whites have wished death to all Blacks, to all niggers. Their sentiment is 'Die Nigger Die!'—either by becoming a negro or by institutionalized or active genocide."[88] For Brown and other nationalists of the late 1960s, the words *Negro* and *nigger* had become unacceptable white images of and for blacks.

In some respects radical women's attempts to reform the language manifested the same nationalistic solidarity characterizing blacks like Garvey and Brown. This was further demonstrated in their determination to eliminate from common usage words, phrases and titles based solely on male-defined images of sex and marital status. Both blacks and women, then, paid unique homage to George Orwell's observation, "If thought corrupts language, language can also corrupt thought."[89]

In "Manglish," a column published in *Everywoman*, Varda One offered antidotes to traditional gender-oriented phraseology. In one typical article she wrote:

1. Use man specifically only, use a new word for woman, use person or human when referring to both sexes.
2. Use man generically only, specify when referring to one sex by using a modifier such as male man or female man.

3. Use man generically only, invent a new word for man in the specific sense and for "woman." While waiting for the solution, we can replace man used as a suffix with male or human depending on whether usage is specific or generic.

FROM	TO
Specific: man-child, man of means, man of the house, manhood	male child, male of means, male of the house, malehood
Generic: mankind, manhunt, man-made, man-eating, manhole	humankind, humanhunt, human-made, human-eating, humanhole[90]

In earlier columns Varda One had suggested similar changes for gender-oriented nouns like "statesman," "congressman," "policeman" and "chairman," changes that indeed reflected a long stream of feminist consciousness regarding gender-prone language (e.g., the "Womenfesto" drafted by the organizer of the 1848 Seneca Falls Conference) and changes that would become accepted standards in a later time (e.g., statesperson, member of Congress and police officer).

Radicals also questioned the validity of, or necessity for, marital distinctions in titles—the fact that no such delineation applied to males made the titles particularly objectionable. Varda One suggested using *Pn.* (Person) in place of Mrs. or Miss.[91] However, by 1970 *Ms.* came to be accepted much more readily than the more awkward *Pn.* Even so, the appropriate application of *Ms.* seemed to cause endless problems for both speakers and writers of the English language. The editors of *Ms.* magazine proposed to settle the issue in 1972:

In practice, *Ms.* is used with a woman's given name: *Ms. Jane Jones*, say, or *Ms. Jane Wilson Jones*. Obviously, it doesn't make sense to say *Ms. John Jones*: a woman identified only as her husband's wife must remain a Mrs.

The use of *Ms.* isn't meant to protect either the married or the unmarried woman from social pressure—only to signify a female human being. It's symbolic, and important. There's a lot in a name.[92]

Without doubt, many women from all branches of the movement found fault with the custom that a bride forfeit her family name in favor of the husband's surname. This was not a new issue to feminism. In 1855 women's rights activist Lucy Stone became one of the first women in the United States to retain her maiden name after marriage to abolitionist Henry Blackwell. Even after her death Lucy Stone continued to be known simply as Lucy Stone and not as Mrs. Blackwell and in this respect offered an important model for women who followed her practice, for example, the "Lucy Stoners." When contemporary feminists attempted to resurrect the Lucy Stoners' practice, however, many encountered widespread social pressure to accept quietly the traditional usage of Mrs. and the husband's surname. In addition, they initially met much legal resistance from government bodies, which, based on centuries of English common law, viewed married women as wards of their husbands. The women who persisted in retaining family names after matrimony, and even those who adopted hyphenated surnames (e.g., Mary Jones-Smith) at first encountered endless roadblocks. But the practice of name retention by cultural-oriented females had become fairly common practice for a wide range of women by the end of the 1970s.[93]

The subtle revolution in language grew into a second direction as radical women increasingly began to take "revolutionary" or "liberation" names. Some merely recast their surnames, like Betsy Warrior and Ann Fury; Kathie Amatniek merged the concept of mother and daughter into Sarachild; Laura X's choice represented the female chromosome; Sylvia Preston Cary Ostrovsky Hartman used all her maiden and married names to demonstrate the curious way in which some women, especially those in high society, heaped name upon name; Varda One (Varda Murrell) simply provided a "resting name until I could come up with something better."[94]

The use of such liberation names was not unique to the women's movement; black nationalists and members of the Nation of Islam often had followed the same practice. For instance, in the 1930s Elijah Poole became Elijah Muhammad, "Messenger of Allah" and Supreme Minister of the Nation of Islam. Malcolm Little, at one time perhaps the Nation of Islam's most effective speaker, adopted the initial X to replace "the white slavemaster name of 'Little' which some blue-eyed devil named Little had imposed upon my paternal forebears."[95] Young nationalists of the 1960s, like author and playwright Imamu Amiri Baraka (formerly LeRoi Jones), defiantly adopted Pan-African names to symbolize their ancestry and black pride.

By the late 1960s women were militantly challenging not only language distinctions and self-concepts but entire life-styles and value systems as well. By the early 1970s this momentum carried women toward openly addressing a new, heretofore taboo, feminist issue: lesbianism. Lesbianism soon became one of the most visible means by which women redefined their lives beyond the boundaries of traditional male-designated roles, and arose as one of the most controversial elements of the new radical feminism

Lesbianism, Separatism and Alternative Living Ventures

It is incorrect to assume that lesbianism was identified solely with radical feminism, since many contemporary feminists have endorsed it as an option even if they themselves choose to be heterosexual. For example, at its 1971 national conference the National Organization for Women formally acknowledged "the oppression of lesbians as a legitimate concern of feminism."[96] Still, by the mid–1970s radical feminists had come to view lesbianism as a political statement against the oppression by men of women in general, and of alternative–life-style women in particular. Charlotte Bunch commented on the political aspects of lesbianism/feminism in *The Furies*, a network paper started in 1972 by a lesbian collective, as follows: "The Lesbian has recognized that giving support and love to men over women perpetuates the system that oppresses her. . . . Women-identified Lesbianism is, then, more than a sexual preference, it is a political choice."[97]

Such broadsides caused lesbianism to surface as a contentious issue within the women's rights movement. In February 1970 lesbian Del Martin shocked many legal-oriented feminists with her election as secretary of the San Francisco chapter of NOW. Shortly thereafter lesbian author Rita Mae Brown, long active in the New York chapter of NOW, resigned from the organization amid a storm of reactionary protests linked to her public disclosure of homosexuality. Later the Women's Caucus of the Los Angeles Gay Liberation Front separated from that organization to form the Lesbian Feminists.[98] Not all feminists supported these attempts to politicize the personal priorities of certain women. Opposing feminists argued that lesbianism was not a bona fide movement issue, that it would encourage McCarthy-like attacks in the form of "lesbian baiting" and that ultimately the "lavender herring" of lesbianism would destroy the movement.[99]

The lesbianism tide surged, nonetheless. Following her renunciation of NOW, Rita Mae Brown called a meeting of lesbians from which Radicalesbians emerged.[100] The new group drew national attention by taking the position that lesbianism was the purest expression of feminism since heterosexual women were actually consorting with the enemy. The group articulated its ideology in "The Woman Identified Woman," now one of the definitive position papers on contemporary lesbianism/feminism. In it Radicalesbians stated: "As the source of self-hate and the lack of real self are rooted in our male-given identity, we must create a new sense of self. . . . It is the primacy of women relating to women, of women creating a new consciousness of and with each other, which is at the heart of women's liberation."[101]

Lesbians themselves spearheaded drives to create alternative living patterns to "help us learn about ourselves and about better ways of living."[102] As a result of this philosophy the radical movement in the 1970s became characterized by an increasing number of women's separatist living arrangements based on intragroup norms of role and place.

Radical separatists—and separatism was a uniquely radical phenomenon in the women's movement as it had been in the black movement—based their allegiance on an ethnocentric view of women's culture and heritage. Elements of separatism and communalism, including work collectives, seemed to coalesce around many of the characteristic features of radical feminism: female autonomy and self-sufficiency, freedom from patriarchal dominance, various antimale perspectives, lesbian unity, consciousness-raising tactics and the notion of women as an oppressed class. Inherent in these theories was the belief that association with men of any plane corrupts women; to wit, women must define their identity as human beings through contact with others of their sex only. Consequently, liberation could be achieved solely within unorthodox living and working arrangements. In many respects this position was reminiscent of the theories of the Republic of New Africa and the Nation of Islam, which had sought to achieve similar autonomy and independence through various forms of physical separation from white society. The right to exercise dominion over community and self coupled with the power to preserve that existence free from outside interference moved both blacks and women in identifiable ways toward restated visions of independent lives.

In a large sense lesbian priorities were chosen as political statements. One participant of the 1960s and 1970s movement recalled, "Many radical feminists seized onto lesbianism almost by instinct as the ultimate means of self-determination." Another feminist described the lesbian psychology in more detail: "A lesbian, I would suggest, is a woman who...cannot feel at ease with herself while worshipping The Male. At least at such close quarters. I do think that lesbians have been in a real sense a feminist avant garde, but our refusal to worship The Male has of course been far from complete."[103]

A variety of separatist experiments emerged. The new ventures ranged from houses with a few separatist women, to women-only retreats, to fully functioning separatist communities. Alternative lifestyle advocates held that pride, self-expression, sexual fulfillment and all the other ingredients of human dignity could be achieved best—perhaps only—through separation from the male patriarchal system.

Women's centers, which often served as temporary settlement houses for movement women, appeared as the first institutional separatist ventures. The centers offered a supportive atmosphere where women of all interests could associate with others who shared their basic ideas and feelings. Some of the houses began work collectives centered around key aspects of the movement, such as publishing ventures, women's health education and day care facilities. Women had long gathered into such self-interest groups—consider, as an illustration, Anne Hutchinson's religious gatherings in New England in 1636— but the new attempts of contemporary feminism were significant because they allowed women the option of fully integrating feminism into their lifestyles.

In July 1970 *Everywoman* ran a full-page feature describing one of the more comprehensive women's separatist ventures in the United States, the Women's Collective, located near the University of Iowa. Its philosophy, as outlined in *Everywoman*, conveyed an interesting sense of utopian hopefulness.

Living together makes us physically close, enabling us to study together, work together, share the shit work, and to share the exciting moments together. We formed the collective hoping that it would be a place where all our sisters and us could come together and eventually find alternative life styles and philosophies for the future.

Women, by forming their own collectives are saying two things at the same time: "Fuck men" and "Up with the new revolution."[104]

Located in California's San Bernadino Valley, Califia represented another important separatist venture. Women, most of whom were lesbians from the Los Angeles area, created Califia in the mid–1970s.[105] Here community members practiced the purest form of separatism by rejecting all voluntary contact with men. Lesbianism itself did not appear to be as important for entrance into the community as a strong commitment to feminist ideology. It operated on a nonprofit basis; and like Ti-Grace Atkinson's group The Feminists, duties rotated from member to member. Participants shared equally any profit from crafts and outside jobs.[106] The community held mandatory business and political discussions every Saturday, and in classic radical fashion it sponsored periodic "institutes" designed to raise the political consciousness of members and visitors. The institutes thus provided a setting for those wishing to pursue alternative lifestyles and/or escape from male dominance. One participant from the Midwest described her experience, based on her conversations with the other women, as typical:

Heaven on earth. It proved that women can do things without men. It proved independence to visiting women. *It was* the first time in my life I could feel totally free. I have never been the same since the experience. I can't walk in a public place now without consciously feeling the presence of men. If it were not for their economic dependence on men, I believe a majority of American women would choose to live apart from them—most of the political women I've spoken to would.[107]

The Lesbian Power Authority emerged as an East Coast counterpart to Califia. It closely paralleled the Califia West Coast experience except that it took an extreme stand on the lesbian question by excluding heterosexual women. Author and composer Alix Dobkin, founder and a spokesperson for the Authority, recorded the collective's ambitions in an album (for women only) distributed solely through women's outlets. This recording stated that for the lesbians in this community "separatism is a technique which offers a frame of reference . . . for developing a special consciousness."[108]

Daughters, Inc., of Plainfield, Vermont, represented a tactical departure from these kinds of ventures. The Daughters collective tacitly admitted that its goals at that stage of the revolution could not be achieved without some working contact with men. By the late 1970s the collective grew as an important feminist book publishing concern. A *New York Times Magazine* article explained Daughters's eclectic approach to separatism: "They believe they are building the working models for the critical next stage of feminism: full independence from the control and influence of 'male-dominated' institutions—the news media, the health, education and legal systems, the art, theater and literary worlds, the banks."[109]

The fact that the collective collaborated with men in the business world, albeit reluctantly, demonstrated flexibility in the separatist position. Some black militants had also learned the imperative of dealing with the dominant white culture even though they choose to withdraw from it. In the 1920s, by way of illustration, Marcus Garvey accepted white support for his UNIA and other separatist ventures, although white support itself was not always tendered for ethical reasons.[110] The Black Panthers, as discussed earlier, practiced a sort of psychological separatism and sought working coalitions with white radicals, whereas some black nationalist organizations like the Republic of New Africa and the Nation of Islam flatly rejected any collaboration with whites. Female separatism shows some examples of the Panthers's type of psychological separatism, as well.

A New Women's Focus: Multicentered Self-Sufficiency

During the 1970s feminists increasingly worked cooperatively to create and spread educational and cultural information by and for women only. Illustrative of the new emphasis were women's attempts to deal with female sexuality in forthright woman-centered ways. In publications like the Boston Women's Health Book Collective's *Our Bodies, Ourselves*, Susan Brownmiller's *Against Our Will*, Shere Hite's *The Hite Report*, Adrienne Rich's *Of Woman Born* and Anne Kent Rush's *Getting Clear*, special emphasis was placed on demystifying gynecological matters and other female concerns such as rape and spouse abuse. Concurrently, women's health centers rapidly became fixtures in most communities.[111] Although one feminist described the new thrust as "the insistence of radical feminists that we deal with our bodies—the sexual and reproductive systems—first,"[112] it was obvious from the wide commercial availability of these books that they were being digested by no single feminist audience in particular. Other women took alternative measures to manifest their sense of separatedness through a number of compendium-type publications for women. Representative of these attempts to disseminate useful bodies of information through mass-market techniques in the 1970s were the *Women's Rights Almanac, Woman's Almanac, Women's Action Almanac* and *New Woman's Survival Catalog*.[113]

As women increased their efforts to reach out psychologically and materially to each other, a number of feminist-oriented presses appeared, such as the Feminist Press in Old Westbury, New York, and the lesbian-oriented Diana Press in Baltimore. By the mid–1970s there were at least ten publishing concerns adding bound literature to the twenty-six major women's periodicals.[114] Many radicals chose to use female presses for their literary outlets; others—like Redstockings in its *Feminist Revolution* (published by Random House)—continued to disseminate ideas and information through the older commercial publishing houses. Regardless of whether these works were published by feminist or conventional houses, however, the 1970s can be seen as a period during which a wide range and scope of female-only literature appeared in unprecedented volume and commanded equally unprecedented audiences. Robin Morgan's *Monster*, a seminal collection of radical protest poems published in 1972, seemed to embody the new spirit in traditional verse. In Morgan's words:

> One thing I know:
> there is no atom that is not political,
> and poetry can be quite dangerous propaganda,
> especially since all worthwhile propaganda
> ought to move its readers like a poem.
> Graffiti do that; so do some songs,
> and rarely, poems on a page.[115]

SUMMARY

Both contemporary black and feminist radicalism have passed through similar stages as protesters disenchanted with traditional goals, values and strategies pursued alternative "radical" solutions. The analogy of race and sex appears particularly fitting in terms of a "new militancy"—an activist approach based on rejection, either in whole or in part, of the mass-membership, legal-oriented groups and of generally accepted traditional protest norms. Priorities in each movement turned to self-sufficiency and collective loyalties and personal commitments, usually by a handful of activists at first. This subsequently evolved into a rejection of coalition politics (e.g., antiwhites and antimen) and an embracing of black-centered and women-centered solutions by increasingly larger numbers of adherents. In the process black radicals and women radicals produced decentralized organizational structures.

As a result, the experience of radical women during the 1960s and 1970s can be seen as an extension of goals generated by the mass-membership phase of contemporary feminism. While the legal-oriented camp grew primarily from national reform efforts, the radical wing evolved from the dissatisfaction women felt with their roles in civil rights and the New Left and to a lesser extent from a disaffection with the pace and priorities of the legalists in their effort to graft feminism onto the stem of patriarchal society. The real cutting edge of feminist radicalism became its determination to attack the very roots of cultural-based sexism. Although some women came to that realization while participating (or attempting to participate) in different protest movements, there is little evidence to indicate that radical feminists sought to move back into those movements or to form working coalitions with them.

Moreover, as we have noted, women like Shulamith Firestone and Kate Millett offered a kind of synthesis of political theories of female autonomy akin to black nationalism. Other groups and individuals, such as Redstockings, NYRW, Robin Morgan, Ti-Grace Atkinson and Adrienne Rich, reflected a determination by women in the late 1960s and the 1970s to define for themselves a new sense of history and community and to gain control of certain cultural-defined imperatives. Some groups, like Califia and Lesbian Power Authority, rejected traditional gender arrangements in favor of alternative living patterns unfettered by intractable males.

In recent decades, then, both blacks and women have sought greater cultural or "community" control and self-identity and have looked inward for energy and direction more than had been the norm prior to the 1960s. All these attempts reflected the diversity of views encompassed by radicalism; all stemmed from protests and ideologies considered alien to the traditional American consensus. Within this context, the slogans Black Power and Sisterhood Is Powerful took on important politician and psychological overtones.

In the following chapter the focus will shift to an analysis of how other feminists attempted to assess and implement purely economic (i.e., Marxist) solutions to feminist concerns. Unlike the legalists and radicals, and generally smaller in numbers, these women spoke of socialist-revolutionary remedies that would finally and permanently end "male capitalist oppression."

NOTES

1. Jo Freeman, "The Origins of the Women's Liberation Movement," *American Journal of Sociology*, Vol. 78, No. 4 (1973), 795–97; Maren Lockwood Carden, *The New Feminist Movement* (New York: Russell Sage Foundation, 1974), 47–56. The preponderance of scholarship on contemporary feminism identifies the two wings of the movement as "reform" and "radical," "women's rights" and "women's liberation," and, as Freeman finds, simply the "older" and "younger" (p. 795). Since this study focuses primarily on the goals and tactics of the two wings relative to traditional social protest, the terms "legal/reform" and "cultural/radical" will be used to describe the two branches. Many of the lasting goals and tactics of radical feminism were first spelled out in Anne Koedt, "Women and the Radical Movement," *Notes from the First Year* (1968), and Jo Freeman, "The Women's Liberation Movement: Its Origins, Structure and Ideas," KNOW, Inc., reprint (n.d.). Robin Morgan, in the introduction to her compendium of personal experiences in the radical movement provides an overview of the contemporary radical feminism experience, *Going Too Far: The Personal Chronicle of a Feminist* (New York: Vintage, 1978), 3–17. See Bonnie Kreps, "Radical Feminism I," in Anne Koedt, Ellen Levine, and Anita Rapone, eds., *Radical Feminism* (New York: Quadrangle, 1973), 234–39; Alix Kates Shulman, "Sex and Power: Sexual Basis of Radical Feminism," *Signs*, Vol. 5, No. 4 (1980), 590–604.

2. Robin Morgan, ed., *Sisterhood Is Powerful: An Anthology of Writings from the Women's Liberation Movement* (New York: Vintage, 1970), xli. See "Defining Women's Culture: Interview with Robin Morgan," in Gayle Kimball, ed., *Women's Culture: The Women's Renaissance of the Seventies* (Metuchen, NJ: Scarecrow, 1981), 30–40, and the entire book for firsthand accounts of women's new culture themes.

3. Carden, *The New Feminist Movement*, 140.

4. Hans Sperber and Travis Trittschuh, *American Political Terms: An Historical Dictionary* (Detroit: Wayne State University Press, 1962), 349.

5. Richard L. Greaves and Robert Zaller, eds., *Biographical Dictionary of British Radicals in the Seventeenth Century*, Vol. 1 (Brighton, England: Harvester, 1982), viii.

6. Sara Margaret Evans, "Personal Politics: The Roots of Women's Liberation in the Civil Rights Movement and the New Left" (Ph.D. dissertation, University of North Carolina, 1976), 48–133; Evans's dissertation later appeared as *Personal Politics: The Roots of Women's Liberation in the Civil Rights Movement and the New Left* (New York: Vintage, 1979). See also, Anne Koedt, "Women and the Radical Movement."

7. Evans, *Personal Politics*, 24–82. The objection by women to male stereotyping and subordination to menial office and household chores is a common thread running through civil rights workers' papers found in the Social Action Collection of the State Historical Society of Wisconsin, Madison, WI (hereafter cited as SAC, SHSW). In particular, read the letters in the Mimi Feingold Papers, Aviva Futorian Papers, Lillian Hamwee Papers, Sandra Dugan Hard Papers, and Linda Seese Papers. See Mary Aickin Rothschild, "Northern Volunteers and the Southern 'Freedom Summers,' 1964–1965: A Social History" (Ph.D. dissertation, University of Washington, 1974), 177–99.

8. Cited in Rothschild, "Northern Volunteers," 185, see 177–84.

9. Eldridge Cleaver deals forthrightly with the phenomenon of the black male attraction for the white female in *Soul on Ice* (New York: Delta, 1968), 155–210. Michele Wallace provides a retort to Cleaver's views in *Black Macho and the Myth of the Superwoman* (New York: Warner, 1979), 13–126.

10. See Morgan, *Sisterhood Is Powerful*, xxiv; Carden, *The New Feminist Movement*, 60; Wallace, *Black Macho*, 18; Judith Hole and Ellen Levine, *Rebirth of Feminism* (New York: Quadrangle, 1971), 110. Carmichael later claimed that the story had been fabricated by the FBI to discredit him among women and create divisiveness in the movement. Carmichael interview with author, Akron, OH, November 10, 1977.

11. Kathie Sarachild, "The Power of History," in Redstockings of the Women's Liberation Movement, ed., *Feminist Revolution: An Abridged Edition with Additional Writings* (New York: Random House, 1978), 17; Barbara Leon, "Separate to Integrate," in Redstockings, *Feminist Revolution*, 152.

12. Subsequently printed as Casey Hayden and Mary King, "Sex and Caste: A Kind of Memo from Casey Hayden and Mary King to a Number of Other Women in the Peace and Freedom Movements," *Liberation* (April 1966), 35–36. See Evans, *Personal Politics*, 98–101.

13. Marge Piercy, "The Grand Coolie Dam," *Leviathan*, October–November, 1969.

14. Cited in Marlene Dixon, "On Women's Liberation: Where Are We Going?" *Radical America*, Vol. 4, No. 2 (1970), 27.

15. Hole and Levine, *Rebirth of Feminism*, 111–22; Evans, *Personal Politics*, 126–211, esp. 197–99.

16. Morgan, *Sisterhood Is Powerful*, xxiii.

17. "Third Party Convention," *The Seed* (Chicago), August 26 to September 21, 1967, for the NCNP's initial program, which emphasized the peace and civil rights struggles; "New Politics—Too Late?" *The Seed*, September 22–October 12, 1967; Hole and Levine, *Rebirth of Feminism*, 113. The NCNP Convention never did extend formal recognition to the women's caucus. See "Summary of NCNP Resolutions," *The Seed* (Chicago), September 22–October 12, 1967.

18. Hole and Levine, *Rebirth and Feminism*, 113.

19. Shulamith Firestone, "On American Feminism," in Vivian Gornick and Barbara K. Moran, eds., *Woman in Sexist Society: Studies in Power and Powerlessness* (New York: Mentor, 1971), 684.

20. Jo Freeman, *The Politics of Women's Liberation: A Case Study of an Emerging*

Social Movement and Its Relation to the Policy Process (New York: David McKay, 1975), xiii, 109–11; Freeman, "The Origins of the Women's Liberation Movement," 794, n.3; Cellestine Ware, *Woman Power: The Movement for Women's Liberation* (New York: Tower, 1970), 20; Hole and Levine, *Rebirth of Feminism*, 115.

21. Cited in Carden, *The New Feminist Movement*, 39.

22. Hole and Levine, *Rebirth of Feminism*, 271; Carden, *The New Feminist Movement*, 65.

23. "The New Feminists: Revolt Against 'Sexism,' " *Time*, November 21, 1969, 54.

24. Carol Hanish, "The Liberal Takeover of Women's Liberation," in Redstockings, *Feminist Revolution*, 164; Carden, *The New Feminist Movement*, 87; Leah Fritz, *Dreamers and Dealers: An Intimate Appraisal of the Women's Movement* (Boston: Beacon, 1979), 26–27; Sarachild, "The Power of History," 43; Ware, *Woman Power*, 24–32.

25. New York Radical Women, "Principles" (mimeographed), probably 1967, Vertical File, Schlesinger Library, Cambridge, MA.

26. Susan Brownmiller, " 'Sisterhood Is Powerful': A Member of the Women's Liberation Movement Explains What It's All About," *New York Times Magazine*, March 15, 1970, 27, 128.

27. Hanish, "The Liberal Takeover of Women's Liberation," 164.

28. Ti-Grace Atkinson, *Amazon Odyssey* (New York: Links, 1974), 9 and 10.

29. "The Feminists: A Political Organization to Annihilate Sex Roles," *Notes from the Second Year* (1970), 114; see Ware, *Woman Power*, 25.

30. "The Feminists," *Notes from the Second Year*, 115.

31. Cited in Ware, *Woman Power*, 27.

32. Carmichael, interview with author, November 10, 1977. See Cleveland Sellers, *The River of No Return: The Autobiography of a Black Militant and the Life and Death of SNCC* (New York: William Morrow, 1973), 183–219, 240–67.

33. Elizabeth Boyer (first president of WEAL), interview with author, Cleveland, OH, August 11, 1977.

34. Martin Luther King, Jr., *Where Do We Go from Here: Chaos or Community?* (New York: Bantam, 1968), 37–38.

35. "Who Will Miss America?" *Rat*, September 6–September 19, 1968; Robin Morgan, "Miss America Goes Down," *Rat*, September 20–October 3, 1968; Morgan, *Going Too Far*, 62–67.

36. Carol Hanish, "A Critique of the Miss America Protest," *Notes from the Second Year* (1970), 86–88, quote, 87.

37. Morgan, "Miss America Goes Down"; "WLM vs Miss America," *Voice of the Women's Liberation Movement* (October 1968).

38. See Hole and Levine, *Rebirth of Feminism*, 123–24; Morgan, *Going Too Far*, 62–67.

39. Fritz, *Dreamers and Dealers*, 24. For amplification of the "beauty role myth," see Nora Scott Kinzer, *Put Down and Ripped Off: The American Woman and the Beauty Cult* (New York: Thomas Y. Crowell, 1977), 1–24, 181–99.

40. Huey P. Newton, *Revolutionary Suicide* (New York: Harcourt Brace Jovanovich, 1973), 122.

41. Inez Haynes Irwin, *Up Hill with Banners Flying* (Penobscot, ME: Traversity, 1964), 270–99.

42. Morgan, *Going Too Far*, 71–81; Ware, *Woman Power*, 46–49; Carden, *The New Feminist Movement*, 87.

43. Morgan, *Going Too Far*, 69.

44. Ibid., 71–81; "WITCH Power," *Rat*, November 15–November 28, 1968; Ware, *Woman Power*, 46; "Witch," in Morgan, *Sisterhood Is Powerful*, 603–04.

45. Women's International Terrorist Conspiracy from Hell, "The WITCH Manifesto" (mimeographed), probably 1968, Vertical File, Schlesinger Library.

46. "National News," *Voice of the Women's Liberation Movement* (February 1969); "It Was A Special Show—and the Audience Was Special, Too," *New York Times*, February 17, 1969; Morgan, *Going Too Far*, 71–75, 80–81; Hole and Levine, *Rebirth of Feminism*, 126.

47. Brownmiller, " 'Sisterhood Is Powerful,' " 128.

48. "Redstockings Manifesto," (mimeographed), 1969, Vertical File, Schlesinger Library, and *Notes from the Second Year* (1970), 112–13. This document has been reproduced, sometimes with grammatical inconsistencies, in numerous secondary sources. Further insight into Redstockings's political program may be found in "Redstockings" (mimeographed), 1970, Vertical File, Schlesinger Library, and in the Joan Jordan Papers, SAC, SHSW.

49. Carden presented one of the better analyses of consciousness raising in *The New Feminist Movement*, 33–37. See Ware, *Woman Power*, 108–119.

50. Carol Hymowitz and Michaele Weissman, *A History of Women in America* (New York: Bantam, 1978), 368. Ware, *Woman Power*, 108–13. A typical consciousness-raising process is identified in "Consciousness-Raising," in Koedt, Levine, and Rapone, *Radical Feminism*, 280–81.

51. Simone de Beauvoir, *The Second Sex*, trans. and ed. by H. M. Parshley (New York: Vintage, 1974 [1952]).

52. See Caroline Moorehead, "A Talk with Simone de Beauvoir," *New York Times Magazine*, June 2, 1974, 16, 18, 22, 26–34; Mary Lowenthall Felstiner, "Seeing *The Second Sex* Through the Second Wave," *Feminist Studies*, Vol. 6, No. 2 (1980), 247–76.

53. Roxanne Dunbar, "Sources of Information," *No More Fun and Games* (February 1969).

54. Sarachild, "The Power of History," 28.

55. Shulamith Firestone, *The Dialectic of Sex: The Case for Feminist Revolution* (New York: Bantam, 1970), 7.

56. Ibid, 5.

57. Ibid., 108.

58. Morgan, *Going Too Far*, 119. Italics added.

59. Sarachild, "The Power of History," 27.

60. Kate Millett, *Sexual Politics* (New York: Avon, 1971). See "Feminist Philosopher," *New York Times*, August 27, 1970.

61. Millett, *Sexual Politics*, 53.

62. Ibid., 473.

63. Kathie Sarachild, "Consciousness-Raising: A Radical Weapon," in Redstockings, *Feminist Revolution*, 146.

64. Gayle Graham Yates, *What Women Want: The Ideas of the Movement* (Cambridge, MA: Harvard University Press, 1975), 77, 94. See Gayle Graham Yates, "Ideologies of Contemporary American Feminism," (Ph.D. dissertation, University of Minnesota, 1973), 124–87.

65. For a broad survey of these issues, see Section 3, "Issues: Consciousness Raising," *Notes from the Second Year* (1970), 76–86.

66. "A Guide to Consciousness-Raising," *Ms.*, July 1972, 18.

67. Carmichael, interview with author, November 10, 1977.

68. Kathryn Clarenbach, interview with author, Washington, DC, October 28, 1977; Marguerite Rawalt, interview with author, Arlington, VA, October 6, 1978; Pauli Murray, interview with author, Alexandria, VA, October 30, 1977. Note that it is the National Organization *for* Women not *of* Women. Interestingly, black feminists seldom grappled with the "man question," since they tended to see black men as natural allies in the larger struggle against racism. See Bell Hooks, *Feminist Theory: From Margin to Center* (Boston: South End Press, 1984), 67–81.

69. See Hole and Levine, *Rebirth of Feminism*, 235–39; Carden, *The New Feminist Movement*, 42–43; Dana Densmore, "Who Is Saying Men Are the Enemy?" KNOW, Inc. pamphlet; Joanna Russ, "The New Misandry: In Defense of Hating Men," KNOW, Inc. reprint (one page); "Women's Liberation Aims to Free Men, Too," *The Washington Post*, June 7, 1970.

70. Cited in Vivian Gornick, "The Next Great Movement in History Is Theirs," *The Village Voice*, November 27, 1969.

71. "Women's Lib: The War on 'Sexism,'" *Newsweek*, March 23, 1970, 73; Gornick, "The Next Great Movement in History Is Theirs."

72. Cited in "Five Women Protest the 'Slavery' of Marriage," *New York Times*, September 24, 1969.

73. Betty Friedan, *It Changed My Life: Writings on the Women's Movement* (New York: Dell, 1977), 152. See Russ, "The New Misandry."

74. "Politics of the Ego: A Manifesto for N.Y. Radical Feminists," *Notes from the Second Year* (1970), 124.

75. Valerie Solanas, "SCUM Manifesto" (mimeographed), Friedan Papers, Schlesinger Library, Cambridge, MA. The "Manifesto" is also available, in part, in Morgan, *Sisterhood Is Powerful*, 577–83, although not in the same grammatical form as the original.

76. Cited in "Valeria Solanis [*sic*] a Heroine to Feminists," *New York Times*, June 14, 1968.

77. Solanas, "SCUM Manifesto."

78. Russ, "The New Misandry."

79. Carroll Smith-Rosenberg, "The Female World of Love and Ritual: Relations Between Women in Nineteenth-Century America," *Signs*, Vol. 1, No. 1 (1975), 1–29, and "The New Woman and the New History," *Feminist Studies*, Vol. 3, No. 1/2 (1975), 185–98. See Elizabeth Janeway on women's special psychosocial unity in *Between Myth and Morning: Women Awakening* (New York: William Morrow, 1974), 16–45.

80. Gerda Lerner, "Placing Women in History: Definitions and Challenges," *Feminist Studies*, Vol. 3, No. 1/2 (1975), 5–14; Jessie Bernard, *The Female World* (New York: Free Press, 1981), 1. The manifestation of a separate female consciousness compared closely with what Robert L. Zangrando defined as a separate psychological consciousness of the black community. Robert L. Zangrando, "Black Outreach: Afro-Americans' Recurring Efforts to Attract Support Abroad," *Phylon*, Vol. 36, No. 4 (1975), 368–77.

81. Charles E. Rosenberg, "Sexuality, Class and Role in 19th-Century America,"

American Quarterly, Vol. 25, No. 2 (1973), 131–53. See Carroll Smith-Rosenberg and Charles Rosenberg, "The Female Animal: Medical and Biological Views of Woman and her Role in Nineteenth-Century America," *Journal of American History*, Vol. 60, No. 2 (1973), 332–56.

82. Morgan, *Going Too Far*, 233–34.

83. Quote, Linda Gordon, "Towards a Radical Feminist History," KNOW, Inc. reprint (three pages). See Sheila Rowbotham, *Hidden from History: Rediscovering Women in History from the 17th Century to the Present* (New York: Vintage, 1974); Ann D. Gordon, Mari Jo Buhle, and Nancy E. Schrom, "Women in American Society: An Historical Contribution," *Radical America*, Vol. 5, No. 4 (1971), 3–67; Gerda Lerner, "New Approaches to the Study of Women in American History," *Journal of Social History*, Vol. 3, No. 1 (1969), 53–62.

84. Shirley McCune and Martha Matthews, "Women's Studies and Teacher Education: Actuality and Potential," *Journal of Teacher Education*, Vol. 26, No. 4 (1975), 340–44; Women's Action Alliance, *Women's Action Almanac: A Complete Resource Guide* (New York: William Morrow, 1979), 336–37.

85. Morgan, *Going Too Far*, 155.

86. Millett, *Sexual Politics*, 83.

87. E. David Cronon, *Black Moses: The Story of Marcus Garvey and the Universal Negro Improvement Association* (Madison: University of Wisconsin Press, 1969), 63, 112–18, 121–24, 157–59; Tony Martin, *Race First: The Ideological and Organizational Struggles of Marcus Garvey and the Universal Negro Improvement Association* (Westport, CT: Greenwood, 1976), 10, 18.

88. H. Rap Brown, *Die Nigger Die!* (New York: Dial, 1969), ix.

89. George Orwell, "Politics and the English Language," in George Orwell, *The Orwell Reader: Fiction, Essays, and Reportage by George Orwell* (New York: Harcourt, Brace, 1956), 364.

90. Varda One, "Manglish," *Everywoman*, November 12, 1971. See Julia P. Stanley, "Gender-Marking in American English: Usage and Reference," in Alleen Pace Nilsen et al., *Sexism in the Language* (Urbana, IL: National Council of Teachers of English, 1977), 43–74.

91. Varda One, "Manglish," *Everywoman*, May 29, 1970.

92. "What's a Ms.?" *Ms.*, Preview Issue (Spring 1972), 4.

93. The Center for a Woman's Own Name, *Booklet for Women Who Wish to Determine Their Own Names after Marriage* (Barrington, IL: Center For a Woman's Own Name, 1974), 7–10; Haig Bosmajian, "Sexism in the Language of Legislatures and Courts," in Nilsen et al., *Sexism in the Language*, 77–104.

94. Varda One, "Manglish," *Everywoman*, July 10, 1970. See Carden, *The New Feminist Movement*, 55.

95. Malcolm X with Alex Haley, *The Autobiography of Malcolm X* (New York: Grove, 1966), 199.

96. "Resolutions of the 1971 Conference, 'Revolution: From the Doll's House to the White House!'" Report of the Fifth Annual Conference of the National Organization for Women (NOW), Los Angeles, California, September 3–6, 1971. National Organization for Women Papers, Schlesinger Library, Cambridge, MA.

97. Charlotte Bunch for The Furies Collective, "Lesbians in Revolt," *The Furies*, January 1972. See Anne Koedt's important article on this subject, "Lesbianism and

Feminism," in *Notes from the Third Year* (1971), 84–89; and Lucia Valeska, "The Future of Female Separatism," *Quest*, Vol. 12, No. 2 (1975), 2–16.

98. Del Martin and Phyllis Lyon, *Lesbian/Woman* (New York: Bantam, 1972), 288–90; Sidney Abbott and Barbara Love, *Sappho Was a Right-On Woman: A Liberated View of Lesbianism* (New York: Stein and Day, 1972), 111; Rita Mae Brown "Coitus Interruptus," *Rat*, February 6, 1970, and her quasi-autobiography, *A Plain Brown Rapper* (Baltimore: Diana, 1976), 86–95; Carden, *The New Feminism Movement*, 68.

99. Clarenbach, interview with author: Rawalt, interview with author; Friedan, *It Changed My Life*, 189, 211–13.

100. Barbara Sinclair Deckard, *The Women's Movement: Political, Socioeconomic, and Psychological Issues* (New York: Harper and Row, 1975), 358.

101. Radicalesbians, "The Woman Identified Woman," *Notes from the Third Year* (1971), 81–84, quote, 83–84, now found in numerous anthologies and feminist press reprints as "The Woman-Identified-Woman." See Diana Davies and Judith Cartisan, "The Lavender Menace," *Everywoman*, June 19, 1970; Sidney Abbott and Barbara Love, "Is Woman's Liberation a Lesbian Plot?" in Gornick and Moran, *Woman in Sexist Society*, 615.

102. "Communal Living" (editorial), *Women: A Journal of Liberation* (Winter 1971), 1.

103. Fritz, *Dreamers and Dealers*, 91; Barbara Deming, "Afterword," in Leah Fritz, *Thinking Like a Woman* (Rifton, NY: WINBooks, 1975), 152–60, quote, 154.

104. "Women's Collective," *Everywoman*, July 31, 1970. *Alternative Newsmagazine*'s "Commune Directory" (1971) lists no other women's communes or collectives through 1971.

105. Sandra Kovach Shahady (participant in Califia), interviews with author, Akron, OH, February 24, 1977; March 2, 1977; March 9, 1977. Information on women's separatist communities is not readily accessible. The communities purposely keep a low profile and are seldom discussed in women's literature. Most information is passed among women orally. In addition, members usually decline to discuss the experiments with women who are not like-minded. It is instructive to note that no women's communes or collectives are listed in Patrick Conover's *The Alternative Culture and Contemporary Communes, Revised: A Partly Annotated Bibliography* (Monticello, IL: Council of Planning Librarians, 1976). Although this study identifies four women's communities, unverifiable information on many others was uncovered by the author. On the lesbian commune formation, see two important articles in *It Ain't Me Babe*, "Separatism Still Makes Sense," April 1971, and "A Weekend in Lesbian Nation," April 1971.

106. Shahady, interview with author, March 2, 1977; *Califia Community* (newsletter), January 17, 1977, Shahady personal papers.

107. Shahady, interview with author, March 9, 1977. Shahady recalled that Califia had not established a permanent site through 1977.

108. *Living with Lesbians* (record album), Shahady personal papers. The author could obtain the record jacket only. Information on another well-known communal experience was obtained from "Sagaris Confrontation and Growth," *Hera* (1975), and "Sagaris" (pamphlet), probably 1975, Shahady personal papers.

109. Lois Gould, "Creating a Women's World," *New York Times Magazine*, January 2, 1977, 11.

110. Cronon, *Black Moses*, 188–95.

111. The Boston Women's Health Book Collective, *Our Bodies, Ourselves: A Book by and for Women* (New York: Simon and Schuster, 1973); Susan Brownmiller, *Against Our Will: Men, Women, and Rape* (New York: Simon and Schuster, 1975); Shere Hite, *The Hite Report: A Nationwide Study on Female Sexuality* (New York: Macmillan, 1976); Adrienne Rich, *Of Woman Born: Motherhood as Experience and Institution* (New York: W. W. Norton, 1976); Anne Kent Rush, *Getting Clear: Body Work for Women* (New York: Random House, 1973).

112. Fritz, *Dreamers and Dealers*, xiii.

113. Nancy Gager, ed., *Women's Rights Almanac* (New York: Harper and Row, 1974); Kathryn Paulsen and Ryan A. Kuhn, eds., *Woman's Almanac: 12 How-To Handbooks in One* (New York: J. B. Lippincott, 1976); Women's Action Alliance, *Women's Action Almanac: A Complete Resource Guide* (New York: William Morrow, 1979); Kirsten Grimstad and Susan Rennie, *The New Woman's Survival Catalog* (New York: Coward, McCann and Geoghegan, 1973).

114. Paulsen and Ryan, *Woman's Almanac*, 610–11.

115. Robin Morgan, *Monster* (New York: Vintage, 1972), 58.

Economic-Oriented Feminism

THE ECONOMIC APPROACH: INTRODUCTION

Within feminism there has been a historical division between the committed proponents of gender analysis and the equally staunch advocates of class analysis. The latter group, which we shall call women socialists, or Marxists, has sought a historical explanation of male/female power relationships solely in terms of economic relations. Other socialists, whom we shall call radical socialist, or Marxist, women, have sought to analyze the male-female power relationship in terms of both economic and biological realities. Women socialists have been those who accepted the basic tenets of classical Marxism about the oppression of women; these doctrinaire, orthodox Marxists embraced a critical framework of analysis which held that female oppression developed as a direct result of the institution of private property and that female emancipation will be achieved only by the abolition of capitalism.

Radical socialist women, on the other hand, have embraced Marxism only to the limits of its feminist insights. Their vision is more comprehensive than that of doctrinaire socialists in that they have targeted for attack not only economic oppression, but biological and caste oppressions as well. As a result, for women socialists the historical thrust has been to incorporate the Woman Question, that is, what woman's sphere should be in an industrial society, within a broader Marxist-oriented ideology. For radical socialist women the drive has been toward achieving a truly gender-egalitarian society by attacking not only capitalism but sexism as well. In many ways both approaches have retained nineteenth-century feminist concerns about the general oppression of women, and both currents of the contemporary movement have been characterized by lower levels of numerical participation and acceptance than the mass-membership legal wing and the cultural-oriented radical wing.

Roots and Development of the Economic-Oriented Approach

The socialist feminist argument first surfaced during the era of Utopian Socialism in the pre–Civil War decades. Many Utopian ventures developed commitments to communitarianism and feminism, instituting domestic reforms like the centralized food preparation facilities and collective kitchens introduced by the Amana Inspirationists. Others presented bold challenges to a vast array of traditional beliefs, including housework, division of labor, dress, sexual norms, marriage and child rearing. Moreover, these early experiments provided examples of women who departed from traditional spheres and entered, by design or by chance, areas of collective feminist reform. For many female participants in these unique experiments, socialism and Christian communism became a basic act of faith, a commitment that has lived on and, in a fundamental sense, has linked generations of women to socialist solutions through contemporary times.

The Shakers, the largest of the pre–Civil War religious perfectionist societies, made one notable attack on the notion of women's parochial spheres. Ann Lee Stanley provided the force behind Shaker experiments, although the society did not peak in membership until well after "Mother Ann's" death. First appearing in Niskeyuna, New York, in the 1770s, the Shaker society had some six thousand members and twenty-five settlements by the mid-nineteenth century. The society, also known as the Millennial Church and as the United Society of Believers, was perhaps most noted by contemporaries for its unconventional religious practices. Its approach toward division of labor and duty was equally unconventional.[1]

In an age of strict convention, the "Shaking Quakers," like subsequent socialist groups, challenged a number of bedrock race and gender norms. Endemic racism, for example, did not dissuade the sect from admitting blacks; notions of women as benefactors of the hearth and children did not deter it from allowing females a full share in community leadership. Although the sect did practice celibacy and certain sex-based divisions of labor, historian Alice Felt Tyler has confirmed that women occupied fully one-half of all community directorships. Mother Ann herself was elevated to a kind of sainthood and often referred to as the "daughter of God" and the "Female Christ."[2]

Among others involved in egalitarian experiments, Frances Wright symbolized an early commitment by women to merge Utopian Socialism with feminism.[3] In philosophical harmony with British socialist Robert Owen, Wright argued that classism, sexism and racism were branches of the same social tree and should thus be addressed through the same strategies. Wright designed her Utopian community at Nashoba, Tennessee (c.1825–1828) to eliminate these kinds of oppressions, which she had observed firsthand in Owen's New Harmony experiment.

Although Wright, like Mother Ann Lee, demonstrated that strong-willed women could pursue their ambitions with what English visitor Frances Trollope described as "religious fanaticism,"[4] the experiment at Nashoba never took root. One reason was its detractors' abhorrence for the commune's practice of sex and race equality, including miscegenation. Yet equally at fault was the Scotswoman herself, who failed to address adequately the critical realities of financing and supporting the attempt. She abandoned the experiment in 1828 and turned her energy to championing such controversial causes as education for women and free love. Through the turn of the century critics used the label "Fanny Wrightists" to deride many avant-garde feminists.[5]

Although the Civil War ended many of the Utopian experiments, Wright's and the Shakers's models had provided early visions of an egalitarian society based on socialist thought. Their examples of leadership added pioneering dimensions to the women's rights cause and eventually would become accepted feminist standards. Though radical for their periods, these examples established models of behavior and criteria for women in the early and mid-nineteenth century that in time would come to represent a clear ideological grafting of socialist and feminist theory.

On a different level, evidence indicates that postbellum women criticized capitalism and class relationships much more consistently than many chroniclers of this era have acknowledged.[6] Specifically, militant suffragists Elizabeth Cady Stanton and Susan B. Anthony openly criticized the evils of labor exploitation and industrial capitalism and thus helped pioneer a new female class consciousness that would reach an ideological crescendo almost exactly one century later. Their feminist paper *The Revolution* reflected working-class perspectives and feminist positions on a variety of social questions, while both women traveled around the country proselytizing for labor reform.[7] This insight was significant since it identified the roots of women's oppression in economic factors in addition to biological and social realities.

This type of feminist critique demonstrably broadened the base of the woman's movement. It established a common thread of interest for women of diverse situations—homemakers, domestic workers, factory workers and even prostitutes. Although these feminist challenges to industrial capital did not produce a universal socialist feminist theory, they did present a lasting feminist analysis of capitalist antagonisms that postulated a clear connection between sex and class.

The belief that women's lives were connected to changes in the economy and the material needs of society surfaced most clearly in women's experience with the Socialist Party of America (SPA). In fact, the SPA itself offered an unprecedented political forum for women who wished to pursue unorthodox feminist solutions. Some women took active roles both within the ranks of socialism and without as auxiliaries to the Party structure. Other women simply proffered socialist-oriented arguments apart from Party contact. All such attacks, consequently, offered early visions of what feminists could do to link ideologically their sex oppression to their economic oppression.

Marxism and Feminism: The Orthodox Line

Although Karl Marx never championed feminism specifically, many twentieth-century feminists have nevertheless accepted his worldview of the Woman Question.[8] That is, they have followed Marx and Frederick Engels on the origin of women's oppression in society and the family, and German Social Democrat August Bebel's subsequent synthesis of that position. Marx viewed the Woman Question tangentially, however, since he simply assumed that like working-class men, women had become victimized by an industrial, class-based society. In essence, Marx and many of his followers subsumed the Woman Question under the larger issue of the worker revolution. Even so, these authors' works have indeed comprised the basic handbooks for those women who have attempted to synthesize radical Marxist and feminist ideology.

In the *Communist Manifesto* (1848), Marx and Engels made one of their rare references to relationships between the social division of labor and the Woman Question by assessing the interconnection between capitalism and woman's domestic role in the family. Their argument held out the family as a bourgeois institution contrived to keep workers in wage bondage. From this reference point they argued that the family itself constituted a specific mode of production—a means of producing and reproducing laborers. The capitalist found the family mode of production advantageous because it guaranteed a perpetual servile class. They must maintain such a system to guarantee that a segment of society would always be waiting to "prostitute" its labor in the economic marketplace. As Marx and Engels stated in the *Communist Manifesto*: "On what foundation is the present family...based? On capital, on private gain."[9] In *The Origin of the Family, Private Property and the State* (1884), a seminal source for modern feminist analysis of the family, Engels presented a full-scale analysis of the interconnection between women's emancipation and the destruction of the family.[10] While Marx had concentrated on the family as an artificial bourgeois contrivance that reduced its members into abstract "objects," Engels expounded more directly on the inherently sexually repressive nature of the family. Hence Engels related women's subjugation not only to family relationships, but more specifically to the capitalist system of private ownership and production.[11]

In *Origin of the Family* Engels used Marx's dialectical materialism to argue that the contemporary family represented one of many repressive institutions arising out of private property relations. At the core of this theory was Engels's notion that the historical passage from matriarchy to patriarchy marked the inauguration of women's oppression and paralleled directly the development of private property.[12] In fact, he theorized, in earliest times when there had existed only community goods, there had been no such thing as a monogamous marriage. The end of communalism came when primitive society introduced private property through the monopolization of the means of production; monogamous marriage appeared when it became necessary to assure the transmission of private property through the dominant male line. Once capitalism overtook a culture the phenomenon of mother-right, or matriarchal rearing of children born into nonmonogamous societies, became obsolete. In what has come to be one of the most repeated tenets of contemporary Marxism on the Woman Question, Engels stated: "The overthrow of mother-right was the *world historical defeat of the female sex*. The man took command in the home also; the woman was degraded and reduced to servitude, she became the slave of his lust and a mere instrument for the production of children.... The establishment of the exclusive supremacy of the man shows its effects first in the patriarchal family, which now emerges as an intermediate form." As a result, Engels surmised, "she is delivered over unconditionally into the power of the husband."[13] Releasing women from this stultifying state, then, was—and is—the Marxist key to female liberation.

Bebel forged similar pioneering links between socialism and feminism. His *Woman Under Socialism* (1883) set standards for Marxist approaches to the Woman Question and largely provided the basis for contemporary socialist thought on the liberation of women.[14] As Engels had postulated, Bebel found the basis of women's oppression in economic dependence. Here the latter went further than Engels by identifying the Woman Question as part of the whole fabric of social problems in the late nineteenth century. He wrote that it "is only one of the aspects of the general Social Question, [yet] it is necessary to treat the so-called Woman Question separately." From this analysis Bebel concluded that women must force a change in their status: "Accordingly, this solution of the Woman Question coincides completely with the solution of the Social Question." And Bebel continued, "*There can be no emancipation of humanity without the social independence and equality of the sexes*."[15] As the American socialist Anita Block noted about Bebel's pronouncements: "For this great service, revealing as it does the large vision and deep understanding of its author, the memory of August Bebel will be forever enshrined in the grateful hearts of all Socialist women."[16] Indeed, by the time of World War I Bebel and Engels had achieved "canonical status" within the Social-Democratic movement.[17]

Bebel therefore bequeathed a critical corpus of theory to contemporary Marxists and feminists. His writings convinced many that women's oppression had grown exponentially after the advent of private property and Christianity. Furthermore, Bebel's argument that women were, in effect, culturally retarded victims and not inherently inferior beings gained wide currency. The German intellectual convinced many socialist feminists that oppression reached from the economic realm into the social sphere and that if women were to gain release from this oppression they must rely on their own faculties. Men would be unlikely converts to women's cause, since males were benefiting directly from the very conditions feminists opposed.[18]

This kind of logic came to represent two important tenets of contemporary socialist feminism: 1) that sexism could not be eliminated without a general social revolution; and 2) that women were fighting the two-pronged problem of capitalist oppression and male oppression—a battle that would require them to look, at least partially, to Marxist ideological strategies for strength and sustenance. Many subsequent feminists came to embrace these theories as the standard line on how females might become masters of their own struggle and destinies. Consequently, the economic position has held a central place in the history of contemporary feminism.

The Orthodox Line Through Two Approaches: The SPA and Leftist Women

Founded in 1901, the Socialist Party of America inherited the approach to the Woman Question that Marx, Engels and Bebel had developed. The SPA was actually not the first to purport a Marxist-based theory of female liberation. As early as 1871 *Woodhull and Claflin's Weekly* published perhaps the first full-length English translation of the *Communist Manifesto*, which it partly imbued with its own militant feminism.[19] Herein lies an important example of how radical women manifested a special propensity to seek solutions in socialist answers. As we shall see, such women as Crystal Eastman kept the feminist/socialist torch burning through the twentieth century, at which time a number of women continued to press the economic line until it took unusually strong root alongside legal- and cultural-oriented feminism. But in 1901, the SPA provided the only viable alternative for women who wished to pursue socialism on a collective basis.

From its inception the SPA accepted the standard Marxist line, and even included women's rights in its platform. Eight women and 120 men attended the founding convention of the SPA in 1901 at which they agreed, at least vocally, that suffrage would be a Socialist cause and that women's participation in the Party would be equal to that of men.[20] Soon founders like Margaret Haile, Corinne Brown and Elizabeth H. Thomas recognized a dichotomy between the symbolic representation of women in the party and the reality of Socialist men's sexist practices, a realization that presaged later women's concerns in the contemporary movement. The formal recognition of women's rights, on the other hand, put the Party in the political vanguard of feminist causes. As historian Mari Jo Buhle has found, women rank-and-file participants in the Socialist movement numbered in the tens of thousands. By 1913 they accounted for possibly 20 percent of SPA membership.[21]

One by-product of organized socialism was that it provided through its feminist discussions a sort of sisterhood among Party women, members of women's auxiliaries and even some non-party women. The sessions' discussions often precipitated new awareness of gender inequities rooted in economic, social and biological differences. In many communities women created discussion groups to study socialism. One such group, the sixty-five–member Woman's Socialist League of Los Angeles (sometimes called Union), appeared in December 1901.[22] In Chicago the SPA created a Ladies' Branch in an attempt to dissuade the formation of similar women's socialist clubs outside formal party structures.[23] Apparently too much female autonomy was not entirely welcomed by the male leadership, which continued to manifest clearly defined concepts of women's proper sphere. Yet initiatives by socialist women continued.

In June 1907 Josephine Conger-Kaneko published *Socialist Woman* in an attempt to encourage a sense of the importance of female socialists as women and not simply as members of the SPA. Conger-Kaneko, a member of the SPA since 1903, started the magazine with non-Party funding as a forum for socialist women and as a means of coordinating news from many of the Ladies' branches. *Socialist Woman* lasted roughly seven years. During that time the publication increased its initial subscription list from 26 to 15,000,with special mass distribution issues numbering as high as 100,000.[24] Somewhat analogous to the spate of radical journals in the 1960s, it reflected a growing network for economic-oriented women and stimulated other women to look in a socialist direction for answers to feminist issues. Hence the magazine served as a harbinger of future developments for women of both economic and noneconomic perspectives.

Party and non-Party members then, and now, offered feminist critiques on class and sex and thereby reinforced a feminist awareness of the socialist argument. Even before the founding of the SPA tracts stating the position of the non-legal-oriented women had begun to appear. Many of these works, such as Frances Willard's speech "Why I am a Socialist," delivered to the National Temperance Convention in 1897, encouraged new feminist arguments. Other statements included May Wood Simons's "Why the Professional Woman Should Be a Socialist," Theresa Malkiel's "To the Union Man's Wife" and "Where Do We Stand on the Woman Question?" Caroline Lowe's "The Teacher and Socialism," Lena Morrow Lewis's "The Socialist Party and Women Suffrage," Kate Richards O'Hare's "Wimin Ain't Got No Kick" and Jessie M. Molle's "The National Convention and the Woman's Movement." Longer, more sophisticated pieces on economic questions included Florence Kelley's translation of Engels's *Condition of the Working Class in England* (1892), Charlotte Perkins Gilman's *Women and Economics* (1898), May Wood Simons's *Woman and the Social Problem* (1899), Vida Scudder's *Socialism and Character* (1912), Kate Richards O'Hare's *Sorrows of Cupid* (1912), Meta Stern Lilienthal's *From Fireside to Factory* (1916) and Theresa Malkiel's *Women and Freedom* (1916).[25]

The pace at which women raised such socialist issues slowed in 1917, when the exigencies of World War I and the hyperpatriotic fervor of the times sidetracked much of the drive for American reform. Nevertheless, women's activity in exploring theoretical and political feminist issues before the war contributed in a lasting way to cementing a female dedication to socialism in both oral and written and individual and organizational forms.

As we saw earlier, the economic approach to both blacks' and women's concerns from the time of World War I through the 1960s manifested itself largely through the Socialist Party structure or through contact with the Communist Party of America. The CP-USA reached out to black Americans in the late 1920s and early 1930s in its southern Black Belt strategies, or in the notion of a separate Black Republic, which promised self-determination for black Americans away from oppressive white society. Still, the Communist appeal made relatively few converts among black Americans.[26]

Many women in the period under discussion saw a hollow ring in communism. Some active socialists, like Freda Kirchwey, eschewed the communist line as being alien to the traditional American consensus. Other women, like Rose Pastor Stokes and Elizabeth Gurley Flynn, found communism quite compatible with their past socialist commitment.[27] Labor attorney Crystal Eastman represented one such leftist woman who sought feminist answers in socialist frameworks.

Eastman disliked organized socialism for a number of reasons, but still argued feminist positions in tandem with socialism, or what was alternately called the "social revolution." Eastman, a long-standing socialist thinker, had by the time of her death in 1928 blended her beliefs in socialism and feminism into one coherent philosophy without taking a strict orthodox Marxist position. She once wrote that a feminist "knows that the whole of woman's slavery is not summed up in the profit system, nor her complete emancipation assured by the downfall of capitalism."[28] Eastman presented a somewhat unique approach to the socialist-feminist question. Just as some socialist feminists in the 1960s and 1970s encountered skepticism and frequently opposition from their sister feminists, so did Eastman as she vigorously pursued an equal commitment to feminism and socialism during the first third of this century. Researcher Blanche Wiesen Cook has noted that Eastman was often the only socialist at feminist meetings.[29] Another parallel between Eastman and her co-socialist-feminists of the 1970s was the fact that she argued the revolutionary concept of "wages for housework," which she called a "motherhood endowment."[30]

Eastman and her sister socialists embraced Marxist viewpoints in a rather tangential manner, that is, Eastman and others have not been totally consumed by the Marxist ideological fires. Rather they wanted first the emancipation of women, then that of workers. On the other hand, there were women who subscribed to doctrinaire Marxism, some of whom pursued their beliefs organizationally through the Communist Party of the United States of America after 1920. It is instructive to note examples of women who worked for equality through that structure.

In her study on American communism, Vivian Gornick has noted that the CP-USA never articulated a clear position on women's rights.[31] As a result, the Party lost touch with the mass of women who sought feminist redress. And in this respect the CP-USA was "out of step" with women, much as it had been with the black masses through the 1960s. Yet there were women among the founding members of the CP-USA and the active party membership thereafter.[32] Gornick's work remains especially useful in tracing the association of such women as Sarah Gordon, Dina Shapira, Selma Gordinsky, Maggie McConnell and Esther Allen with the CP-USA. Of particular note was the fact that almost all these women became disenchanted with the party and moved into other arenas in later life. Their years in the party, as Diane Vinson stated, were only "part of the journey."[33] Jessica Mitford and Peggy Dennis represented two such women.

Mitford related in her autobiography the tale of joining the party in 1943 and ultimately leaving it in 1958.[34] Her story catalogued Mitford's criticism of the Party based on her belief that it was notoriously hierarchical and rigid and that this left no room for women to pursue their personal goals.[35] While Mitford's recollections proved educational and poignant, Dennis's straightforward autobiographical presentation shed even more light on the problem leftist women had within organized Marxism.[36] Dennis stated that she deserted the Party in 1976 after fifty years of membership because of leadership elitism and Party "sexism."[37] Her "Letter of Resignation from the Communist Party, U.S.A."[38] remains one of the most definitive documents on women's discontent with the policies and practices of the CP-USA. In this political statement Dennis provided a litany of complaints against the arrogance of Party leaders and the blatant form of sexism they practiced. In Dennis's words, the CP-USA's "attitudes are rooted in an explicit, deliberate and reprehensible sexism."[39]

These autobiographies were but two accounts of women who could not reconcile their struggles for equal rights with the orthodox Communist organization. Their eventual dissociation from the Party illustrated all too vividly how women often found it difficult to pursue political struggles and independent thought through communist structures. It was, in short, impossible for some women to be both feminist and communist. For this reason organized Communism has played a rather minor role in twentieth-century feminism much as it has in black activism. Let us now turn our attention to the 1960s and 1970s to determine the courses contemporary women pursued in the area of economic analysis and feminist praxis.

Contemporary Economic-Oriented Feminism in Perspective

There is no single contemporary theory governing socialist or Marxist feminism. Rather, contemporary Marxist thought within the context of women's rights has developed along two disparate lines. The older one, an outgrowth of traditional Marxist class doctrine, maintains that women's emancipation from sexism can be achieved only through social revolution and changes in the mode of production. Proponents of this theory argue that women's secondary status in history is rooted in economic determinism and has a distinct relation to production and property in almost all societies. The practitioners of this ideology are committed Marxists, that is to say, Marxists first and feminists second. In contrast with this "feminist Marxist" position are the radical "Marxist feminists" who seek first the liberation of women from male tyranny and second the institution of a new social egalitarianism based on Marxist precepts. Theirs is a vision of women shared by many radical feminists who encourage overturning the "true roots" of oppression—that is, cultural and economic restrictions. Furthermore, since women transcend all economic classes and are even numbered within the ruling elites, the Marxist-feminist theory of subjugation emphasizes caste or gender oppression as well as class oppression. This has made it relatively easy for some radical cultural feminists, as Zillah Eisenstein and Batya Weinbaum have pointed out, to draw upon the perspectives of Marxist feminism.[40]

Radical Marxian feminism remains eclectic and flexible in its approach. Its advocates agree with their sister feminist Marxists that the origin of female oppression is buried deep in Western culture and ethos, but they dismiss the orthodox line of Engels and Bebel that attributes sexism solely to the rise of private property and its contingent family labor patterns.[41] Radical Marxist feminists argue that a socialist-based society is indeed necessary, but that it cannot by itself answer the needs of women who have suffered centuries of submissive role-typing over which they have no control. They cite contemporary Russia, frequently as sexist in its social patterns as any Western nation, as a case in point.

Modern radical Marxist feminism in its earliest stages came to distrust older socialist structures. Certainly, as already witnessed, a historical awareness of the gap between the Socialist Party's rhetoric and its actions in regard to women's rights played a significant role in dissuading feminists from easily accepting organized socialism as a vehicle for fulfilling their goals. The radicals' experiences in the male-dominated Left, mentioned earlier, also provided reason for distrusting organized socialism.[42] But a more basic uneasiness with socialism was rooted in the belief of radical Marxist feminists that doctrinaire socialists had relegated the Woman Question to a peripheral status. And since the issue of women's rights remained outside the mainstream of organized socialist ideology, it seemed obvious to feminist leaders that they were being courted by Marxists simply to increase membership rolls. Radical Marxist feminists further felt that Socialist and Communist Party workers were tepid in their approach to feminism, an approach that simply and universally applied Marxist dogma to myriad gender issues.

For their part feminist Marxists harbored certain doubts about their counterparts. They were particularly uncomfortable with the predominant middle-class orientation and "bourgeois mentality" of contemporary feminism. The orthodox socialists found further fault with the flexible nature of radical Marxist feminism, a feature they interpreted as being more self-serving than truly useful to all peoples exploited by capitalism. Finally, traditional socialists were disturbed by many radical feminist tactics. They feared that a considerable number of radicals were exploring and adopting forms of ideological and cultural protest fundamentally different from time-honored Marxist dialectical materialism. Nonetheless, both women Marxists and radical Marxist women, as we have seen, looked to nineteenth-century theorists, primarily Marx, Engels and Bebel, for fundamental political inspiration.

Some Contemporary Devotees of Marx, Engels and Bebel

Many modern feminists have found the theories of Marx, Engels and Bebel on women's oppression and emancipation structurally sound but functionally flawed.[43] While women socialists continued to ape the basic Marxist thesis on the Woman Question, radical Marxist feminists opted to point out the inconsistencies in the orthodox line, for instance, how the *Communist Manifesto* ignored the question of women's role in a noncapitalist society. In a similar vein orthodox Marxism failed to discuss new sexual relationships after the overthrow of private property and the family had occurred. Such issues simply were left for future deliberation and resolution after the all-encompassing social revolution.

Feminist critics argued most forcefully that Marx and Engels failed to identify and take into account the unique problems of gender. In this case they simply applied wholesale the tenets of economic determinism to the Woman Question and subsequently ignored the biological, social and cultural imperatives of oppression. Their solutions to this issue were specious at best. This fact led some contemporary feminists to conclude that Marxists have looked at the Woman Question in impractical terms.

There has yet remained, even for its detractors, a positive side to Marx and Engels's approach to the Woman Question. Marx and Engels had, after all, correctly identified women as an oppressed group and had subsequently attempted to address women's problems through empirical and dialectical analyses. Marx and Engels themselves rejected sexual stereotyping and were meticulously careful not to mythologize the female historical record. They endorsed women's liberation cells within the European socialist movement; Marx personally proposed a resolution to the General Council to encourage "working women's branches" within the First International in 1871.[44] By so launching a political inquiry into the nature of women's oppression, Marx, Engels and Bebel brought this issue to the critical attention of future generations.

Evelyn Reed, one such contemporary theorist, qualifies as an important and articulate spokesperson for the orthodox Marxist approach to feminist solutions. Many feminist Marxists have accepted her theories, as has the ubiquitous Socialist Workers Party/Young Socialist Alliance (SWP/YSA). The Socialist Workers Party traces its roots to 1937–1938, when a Trotskyist faction of some one thousand partisans was expelled from the Socialist Party. The ousted socialists organized the SWP in the belief that the CP-USA and the SPA had strayed from genuine Marxism and the true principles of the Russian Revolution. The SWP in its earliest days stressed youth membership and organization, much as the SWP/YSA of the 1970s did.[45] Although Reed and the SWP/YSA have argued forcefully for women's rights and a destruction of such notions as women's proper place, the ideological character of their arguments usually reflected the earlier worldview of Marx, Engels and Bebel as well as other seminal socialist arguments. While the female members of organized socialism have acquiesced to this orthodox approach, radical/cultural feminists generally have not.

In 1969 Reed published *Problems of Women's Liberation: A Marxist Approach*, a compendium of her speeches and papers on the evolution of and solution to female oppression.[46] Like her ideological forbears, Reed saw women's subjugation as a historical phenomenon linked to the introduction of an economy based on private-property ownership; she held that the only solution was the inclusion of feminism as an "integral force" in the world socialist revolution. In Reed's words, "Marx and Engels, and their disciples ... taught that the oppression and degradation inflicted on women today could not be separated from the exploitation of the working masses by the capitalist profiteers. Therefore, women could secure full control over their lives and reshape their destinies only as an integral force in the world socialist revolution."[47]

Reed preached the destruction of the nuclear family, which she identified as the crux of women's problems.[48] She pointed out that women producers in the family were engaged in nonproductive economic labor while they were simultaneously forced to live stultifying and unfulfilling lives. Woman in her family role "is of course, socially speaking, a 'nobody,' the 'second sex,' while the men who are foremost in economic, political, and intellectual life are the superior sex," Reed stated.[49] Embellishing earlier socialist theories with anthropological evidence, she expanded the orthodox position that women had functioned fully and usefully in precapitalist communal societies in which parentage per se was unimportant since children were raised by all adults. "Children were not possessed like other articles of private property."[50]

Reed based her evidence almost wholly on classical Marxism and on Robert Briffault's *The Mothers* (1927), an update of J. J. Bachofen's pioneering *Das Mutterrecht* (1861).[51] These works purported to be early scientific evidence that women held predominant positions in ancient societies. Reed and her socialist disciples have argued that the downfall of the system they described came with the advent of private property. At that time the system gave way to class society based on the primacy of the male-centered family.[52] In short, when men re-

placed women as the principal producers, they relegated women to servile positions within the home and village. Reed reasoned (and subsequently others
have held) that "the disintegration of... communal society began some six to
eight thousand years ago with the introduction of large-scale agriculture and
stock raising," at which stage "the old sprawling tribal commune began to
break down: first into separate clans, then into separate farm families often
called 'extended families,' and finally into the individual family which we call
the 'nuclear family.' It is in the course of this process that the father-family
completely displaced the clan as the basic unit of society."[53]

Accordingly, feminist Marxists like Reed and her followers have argued that
it was the system of family economic patterns and not biology, as de Beauvoir,
for example, had argued, that relegated women to subservient positions. The
significant impact of Reed's pronouncements upon recent feminist socialist
theory has established her as one of the preeminent contemporary proponents
of the orthodox Marxist line on the Woman Question. Her ideas have been as-
similated by many contemporary women Marxists and continue to permeate
socialist literature. The Socialist Workers Party's platform on women's rights,
for instance, has closely paralleled Reed's contemporary Marxist line.

Feminism and Socialism (1975), a collection of feminist Marxist essays
edited by former SWP presidential candidate Linda Jenness, presented "the
socialist position on the character of women's oppression and on the strategy
and tactics for winning our [women socialists'] full liberation."[54] Like Reed,
Jenness attempted to link women's oppression directly to the rise of male-
dominated families. Jenness and Reed based their conclusions almost uniformly on the orthodox line that we have traced: change the economic system,
and the relationship between the sexes will change, too. In *Feminism and
Socialism*, Jenness outlined this argument: "The achievement of full liberation
for women, however, will require the elimination of the social and material
basis for that oppression; it will require a fundamental change in the social
structure of American society; that is, it will require a socialist revolution."[55]

Even though the essays in her book ran the gamut of contemporary thought
on the need for women's liberation, none really offered a new Marxist synthesis on the resolution of the problem of women's subjugation. As Jenness's position demonstrated, proponents of feminist socialism often have simply
reworded orthodox Marxist thought to fit their particular situations. As a result
the SWP's line on women's rights has sometimes reflected a lack of understanding about women's historical oppression and the true complexities of gender-
based discrimination. This has led SWP proponents to pursue women's liberation in a rather tangential manner, not entirely unlike the approach to the
Woman Question taken by other socialist movements in the past and the historical approach to the Negro Question taken by similar economic-oriented organizations.

Black feminists, too, have accepted the older Marxist analysis of emancipation as they offered their own analyses and solutions to the black female's

unique and often inferior positions in the social fabric and in the labor force. Unlike black radical Marxist feminists, as Angela Davis's research and that of others have demonstrated, these orthodox women have chosen to couch the questions of race and sex within the conventional Marxist line rather than to pursue them as separate issues.[56] In terms of ideology black feminist Marxists have subordinated their particular problems to the greater cause of the class struggle. In "Black Women and the Struggle for Liberation," black SWP member Maxine Williams articulated many of the injustices black women faced, and concluded that none could be eliminated without a socialist revolution.[57] Her argument bore striking similarity to Bebel's nineteenth-century thesis that women must work through socialism to control their own destinies. Williams wrote further of the "necessity of [black] women building our own movement," yet she maintained her call for black women to organize solely under the socialist umbrella.[58] Her work has demonstrated how traditional Marxism had expropriated within the revolutionary proletariat struggle issues of race and sex oppression and appealed to a small number of black women.

In reality the question of the black woman's struggle occupied a very small niche in feminist Marxist doctrine. The subject was addressed neither often nor authoritatively. Through the 1970s black feminists continued to be divided most visibly on the issue of whether their oppression was race- or sex-based. As a result, like the black feminist Combahee River Collective, for example, they often failed to identify a single oppressor, as some white women had done in their analysis of world capitalism.[59] Myrna Hill, a self-styled "Black revolutionary nationalist socialist feminist," epitomized this tendency. In her black women's manifesto, "Feminism and Black Nationalism," she stated that "feminists who are revolutionary Marxists, like myself, hold that all women are potential allies, but that those—like Black women—who suffer most from this system will lead the fight to liberate us all."[60] Hill was not bothered by the fact that Marxists throughout the twentieth century had condemned autonomous black nationalism as anathema to the unity of the working-class struggle.[61] More will be said about black Marxist feminists in the following section on radical socialist feminists.

By the 1970s many economic-oriented feminists argued that orthodox socialism could not, or would not, speak to their needs. Their experiences in the civil rights and Left led radical feminists, in particular, to search for solutions along lines specifically attuned to the cultural imperatives of women. Charnie Guettel, Sheila Rowbotham and Juliet Mitchell stood out among the feminists who sought a new socialist self-awareness in the women's movement and laid the theoretical groundwork for subsequent discussions among varying segments of contemporary feminism.

Efforts to Connect Feminism to Radical Social Revolution: Guettel, Mitchell and Rowbotham

In her slim volume *Marxism and Feminism*, radical feminist Charnie Guettel set out to re-examine feminism from "the tradition of bourgeois liberalism" and to provide the beginnings of a new Marxism that spoke specifically to the needs of women.[62] In the first section of her book Guettel attempted to debunk classical liberalism as a metaphor aimed at the liberal wing of the contemporary "bourgeois" movement. Specifically, she labeled John Stuart Mill a utopian socialist whose *On the Subjection of Women* (1869) simply manifested a "be kind to animals" approach toward women. Guettel herself argued that an end to sex contradictions was predicated on "the resolution of [all] class contradictions."[63] Like Frances Wright and Charlotte Perkins Gilman, earlier feminists who argued that women were becoming the slaves of domestic chores, Guettel found that woman's role of housekeeper was capitalism's main evil. Wives and mothers, she argued, were oppressed not only as victims of wage capitalism, but also as homemakers and child rearers. In order for women to achieve total liberation, they must be freed from the restrictive, nonproductive labor of the household. The question of who would assume domestic responsibilities under a system like that proposed by Guettel had been addressed by many earlier advocates of feminist change. Wright and Gilman in their time had urged the creation of kitchenless apartments and the implementation of other collectivist solutions. Members of the Shaker community, in fact, practiced certain divisions of labor designed to free women from traditionally prescribed chores. Guettel proposed: "And for this socialism is necessary. The kinds of changes necessary to liberate women from the female 'monopoly' of childrearing would necessarily be so far-reaching and unprofitable for capitalism, that the workers would need the ownership of the means of production simply to make them possible."[64]

Offering variations of Guettel's ideas, other Marxist feminists suggested that women's housework could become economically productive labor. Such theorists held that women working in the home and raising children should receive financial remuneration, preferably from the state. The idea was not new to contemporary feminism. As noted earlier, many women had attacked the institution of "kitchen slavery." Crystal Eastman in the early twentieth century presented one of the more articulate positions in defense of pay (in the form of government subsidies) for household labor—what today is termed the "wages for housework" thesis. Eastman, both socialist and long-standing feminist, theorized that women had low esteem primarily because of their unpaid, inferior position in the home. At the same time Eastman had set forth not only a theory on women as unpaid labor, but a related political theory on dependency and inferiority.[65] Radical Margaret Benston in 1969 mirrored this very argument in a broadside, "The Political Economy of Women's Liberation," a theme that radical Betsy Warrior and others also seized upon and developed. Accordingly, a number of contemporary feminists, radical and Marxist alike, have capitalized on the notion that remuneration for housework would generate increased dignity and freedom for women.[66]

Two Marxist feminists, Mariarosa Dalla Costa and Selma James, presented a lasting analysis of this in *The Power of Women and the Subversion of the Community* by arguing that women's domestic labor was indeed socially and economically productive.[67] Dalla Costa and James reasoned that as members of the proletariat, wives and mothers deserved just compensation for their work. By so arguing they went well beyond the orthodox Marxist line, which held that women in the home were not part of social and economic production. James summed up the position: "When previously so-called Marxists said that the capitalist family did not produce for capitalism, was not part of social production, it followed that they repudiated women's potential social power. Or rather, presuming that women at home could not have social power, they could not see that women at home produced."[68] Like Guettel, Dalla Costa and James represented an ideologically maturing approach by contemporary Marxist women toward reassessing and redistributing the burdens of housework and family labor, which has fallen almost exclusively to females in Western societies.

In the widely read *Woman's Estate* (1973), Juliet Mitchell articulated similar attacks on the traditional Marxist approach to the Woman Question. Many contemporary radical feminists have found her theme, that women "should ask the feminist questions, but try to come up with some Marxist answers," particularly felicitous.[69] Mitchell's theories singularly benefited those who sought a new economic synthesis within feminist perspectives. Indeed, her ideas have grown to characterize the thoughts and arguments of a deep channel of contemporary radical feminism.

Mitchell identified the family as the main obstacle to women's emancipation, but went further than the others in her arguments by analyzing family oppressions in terms of both the structural and ideological needs of women. She theorized that the historical impasse between feminism and Marxism had developed because of the abstract nature of Marxist analysis of women's oppression. Yet Mitchell accepted the feminist Marxist position that "until there is a revolution in production, the . . . situation will prescribe women's situation within the world of men."[70] Her conclusions were based almost solely on an analysis and critique of late nineteenth-century and recent twentieth-century orthodox Marxist thought on this issue, as has been traced in this study. For these theorists, she argued, "the liberation of women remains a normative ideal, an adjunct to socialist theory, not structurally integrated into it."[71] Mitchell did point out, as did other Marxists, that liberation from the family was critically important to women. But even more essential, as she and others have maintained, was the total liberation of women in all areas: "Past socialist theory has failed to differentiate woman's condition into separate structures. . . . To do this will mean rejecting the idea that woman's condition can be deduced derivatively from the economy (Engels), or equated symbolically with society (early Marx). Rather, it must be seen as a *specific* structure, which is a unity of different elements."[72]

Mitchell's argument, then, centered on her holistic interpretation of the position of women within the capitalist mode of production and labor designation. That position encompassed four perspectives: (1) production, (2) sexuality, (3) reproduction, and (4) socialization. Under capitalism these four elements combined into a unit, the family, which defined the "woman's world," as nonfamily production defined "man's world." Mitchell postulated that this practice underscored definitions of women as "natural beings" (a.k.a., proper spheres) in charge of conventionally defined domestic functions, especially child rearing. These structural relationships led men and women to perceive differently their roles in society. Sex role differentiation, Mitchell felt, sprang from the division of labor within and outside the family.

> Any emancipation movement must still concentrate on the economic element—the entry of women fully into public industry and *the right to earn a living wage*. The error of the old socialists was to see the other elements as reducible to the economic; hence the call for the entry of women into production was accompanied by the purely abstract slogan of the abolition of the family. Economic demands must be accompanied by coherent policies for the other . . . elements; policies which at particular junctures may take over the primary role in immediate action.
>
> Economically, the most elementary demand is not the right to work or receive equal pay for work—the two traditional demands—but *the right to equal work itself.*[73]

Mitchell's work on the subject of women, the family and unsubsidized housework in no small way reflected a clear stream of earlier feminist writers like Gilman and Eastman. Her synthesis of past and present ideologies offered a particularly good blueprint for contemporary radical women who sought to take feminist theory and practice beyond the confines of socialist argument and practice.

Sheila Rowbotham, whose works received wide acclaim in the 1970s, represents one such theorist. She suggested in particular that women's role was to analyze and instigate the sex revolution—social as well as economic—because conventional Marxist analysis primarily sought, and would always seek, the labor revolution. Rowbotham's disclosures came most forcefully in *Women, Resistance and Revolution* (1974) and *Woman's Consciousness, Man's World* (1973) in which she examined the specious theme of total liberation for women under socialism.[74] In these widely cited works Rowbotham discussed in turn the differentiation between the family and the industrial mode of production and their roles in shaping the contrasting consciousness of women and men—a consciousness dictating the behavior of women in all aspects of labor and production. By analyzing the interaction between feminist and revolutionary thought, including that of contemporary socialist nations, Rowbotham, like Mitchell, concluded that "the liberation of women has remained marginal in Marxist theory." Why? Because "there were many questions they [the early Marxists] left open and they took some ideas for granted which appear incredible now."[75]

Women, Resistance and Revolution examined the ideologies of past revolutions from the French to the Russian and Chinese experiences. Rowbotham found that the major upheavals consistently, and perhaps deliberately, had

failed to incorporate a program of women's total liberation into their subsequent societies. Some, like the Russian Revolution, paid lip service to feminism. But after an initial spate of women's rights reforms, the Soviets
regressed to their prerevolution masculine ethos in an attempt to restabilize
the worker's family. Even Mao's efforts on behalf of women fell woefully
short of feminist ideals. In China, as in the Soviet Union, women still per-
formed the double duties of paid laborers and home managers. Rowbotham
and many of her followers concluded from these occurrences that women
would do well to concentrate on Marxist programs only insofar as they were
designed to achieve their own liberation: "Women's liberation implies that
if the revolutionary movement is to involve women, not as supporters or
attendants only, but as equals, then the scope of production must be seen in
a wider sense and cover also the production undertaken by women in the
family and the production of self through sexuality."[76]

In *Woman's Consciousness, Man's World* Rowbotham expanded her theory
and called for a socialist-feminist revolution. In this widely read study she
linked the full implication of gender identity and oppression to a women's
general "lack of wage militancy."[77] In short, the standardization of sex roles
drove a wedge between women and men that transcended even their common enemy, capitalism. Rowbotham suggested that after the social revolution
society "will still express the viewpoint of sections which [were] the stronger
within capitalism, most obviously men, for example."[78]

In the final analysis, Rowbotham—like a wide range of radical Marxist
feminists—saw women's role in the traditional family as one of producer-
servant. Although her arguments were more detailed than those of Guettel
and Mitchell, her conclusions were markedly similar. The three feminists
agreed on the need to form a woman-centered movement that must not be
allowed to be subsumed within the socialist revolution under the banner of
Marxist ideology. Rowbotham epitomized this position when she stated that
feminism and Marxism "cohabit in the same space somewhat uneasily. Each
sits snorting at the other and using words which are strange and foreign to
the other. Each is huffy and jealous about its own autonomy. They are at once
incompatible and in real need of one another."[79] Such conclusions clearly
lent new definitions to contemporary Marxism/feminism and reflected an
uneasy working relationship.

Woman-Centered Socialism: The Radical/Cultural Approach

Authors like Guettel, Mitchell and Rowbotham contributed to the development of an important body of contemporary socialist-feminist theory. Almost simultaneously their restatement of feminist priorities turned the tide
of the socialist-oriented position towards a distinctly radical approach, both
in praxis and in decentralization. The different priorities but similar commitments evidenced in the approach of radical women took a new turn in

the works of such radical authors as Shulamith Firestone and Kate Millett, who themselves built upon earlier radical feminist theory. A significant feminist synthesis of class and caste evolved that reflected a new awareness of the need for a total feminist theory of economic and social liberation, rather than a unified theoretical approach to what came to be seen as the disparate elements of the total problem.

In recent times radical feminists, seeking redefinition of women and the family, have invoked both anti- and pro-Marxist arguments. Members of such radical organizations as Redstockings and New York Radical Feminists drew their inspiration from both Marxism and radical black analyses of one group's inferior place in capitalist society. Roxanne Dunbar, in "Female Liberation as the Basis for Social Revolution," gave insight to this position: "The present female liberation movement, like the movements for black liberation...has begun to identify strongly with Marxist class analysis. And like other movements, we have taken the basic tools of Marxist analysis (dialectical and historical materialism) and expanded the understanding of the process of change."[80] Such feminists reasoned that America does have a class system in the traditional Marxist sense, but that the classes themselves are transcended by a castelike status that developed from the unique problems of race and sex. Radical feminists maintained further that women, especially, comprised a caste since their unique problems and oppressions arose in every economic and social strata.[81] Because women spanned the entire range of class strata from the proletariat to the ruling class, women suffered more widespread caste-generated injustice. As a result, radical feminists, like radical blacks, argued that no meaningful change in American society could be achieved until both class and caste oppressions were eliminated. Radical Marxist feminists subsequently have paralleled somewhat the thesis among radical Marxist blacks (e.g., the Black Panthers) that an economic and social revolution is the necessary instrument for the elimination of these dual oppressions.

Since the contemporary women's movement differed significantly in the degree of dedication to and practice of orthodox determinism, ideological clashes occurred almost predictably between factions. Radicals were particularly careful to repulse the attempted takeover of their organizations from within by feminist Marxists. The SWP/YSA women presented just such a threat by pursuing an infiltration tactic, a method used in past years by other Marxist groups, most notably the CP-USA in the 1920s in an attempt to "bore from within" black civil rights organizations and other reformist groups. The CP-USA itself abandoned the principle in the late 1920s and 1930s, choosing rather to emphasize initially a self-determination policy for blacks and later a "united front" approach against international oppression. The Party, however, never seemed to come to grips with either black or feminist theory and policy and, as noted earlier in this study, actually manifested its own brand of sexism, which tended to drive what few women loyalists there were from Party affiliation. Women's antipathy for the CP-USA characterized Party-feminist relationships throughout the modern era. The fact that the CP-USA argued strongly against the proposed federal Equal Rights Amendment by asserting that the ERA issue was sidetracking women and men from the more important "workers' struggle" further highlighted and exacerbated the rift.[82]

Besides recognizing the Left's male leadership as sexist, radical Marxist feminists often criticized the Left and organizational socialism in general for restricting gender questions to the fringe of their programs. Even Linda Jenness, a feminist spokesperson for the Socialist Workers Party, admonished feminists in 1976, "We need a party whose only reason for existence is to make the socialist revolution."[83] Consequently, the radical Marxist feminist rejection of the approach of the SWP and other socialist organizations represented as much a difference in basic politics and structural priorities as a difference in organizational philosophy.

Such a dichotomy between the ideological critique of and the capitulation to orthodox Marxism was represented by Seattle Radical Women (RW) in its attempt to take the economic thrust in a direction separate from the SWP and similar organizations. RW represented a model of how some united feminists saw a need for socialist solutions based on the seminal works but also recognized the insights and deficiencies inherent in socialist ideology regarding feminism. Like other such groups that sprang up in the 1970s, RW attempted to construct a systematic theory that avoided the weaknesses of orthodoxy and capitalized on Marxism's useful insights. But by so doing the group and similar feminists have argued for a feminist transformation much more sweeping than that of dialectical materialism. The results of such arguments were reflected in the growth and sophistication of feminist theory in the 1970s. For this reason it becomes instructive to look at the history of RW itself.

Seattle Radical Women appeared in 1967 as an outgrowth of a "Free University" course. Its founders had been active in the Left and the SWP for years while gradually developing a new political consciousness that moved them toward Marxist feminism.[84] Radical Women stated in its "Manifesto" that "the oppression of women is a first-priority political, legal, and economic question ... [A]nd we are accordingly destined to play a vanguard part in the general movement for revolutionary social change."[85] Its statement went on to confirm that RW, most of whose members had belonged to some type of leftist-socialist group at one time, considered itself feminist first and Marxist second, while simultaneously maintaining that "Feminism—women's rights—is inseparable from socialism."[86]

By interpreting women's position in the nuclear family as one of social producer, RW's position on this subject closely paralleled the arguments of Engels and his twentieth-century disciple Evelyn Reed.[87] Yet RW went beyond their economic theories of causality by declaring that women's oppression resulted just as much from the culturally oppressive acts of a male-dominated society. As stated in its "Manifesto," "We are oppressed as a sex and for our sexuality...and triply oppressed as minority women workers....[W]e must simultaneously address ourselves to the social and material source of sexism: the capitalist form of production and distribution of products, characterized by intrinsic class, race, sex, ethnic and caste struggles."[88]

As an "oppressed sex," members defined themselves as an unequal group within a group, much as militants like James Foreman and Stokely Carmichael had done regarding black life in predominantly white society. The approach of radical Marxist blacks, it will be recalled, centered on the notion of dual oppressions in the form of class and race. This new scientific socialism of Carmichael and others grew in large part from the class and race synthesis of African nationalist Kwame Nkrumah. Marxist blacks maintained that socialist revolution must result in the "total destruction of the racist capitalist system."[89] Of course the key word "racist" symbolized not only the determination of black people to lead in the socialist struggle for power and equality, but also certain blacks' distrust of doctrinaire socialism, which spoke neither authoritatively nor consistently to the problems of the black masses.

What this implies is that groups like Seattle Radical Women reflected a strikingly analogous attempt to synthesize sex and class into a more appropriate revolutionary ideology. This particular group and others continued through the 1970s to rail against "the capitalist form of production" and the fact that all women were "oppressed as a sex."[90] In short, a revolution not prefaced by the word sex (or feminist) held little sway for women in groups like RW, whose theories set it apart from the traditions of doctrinaire organized socialism. In fact, RW itself took special precautions to remain outside the sphere of organized socialism. Only a few years after RW's inception, the SWP/YSA made a concerted effort to infiltrate and reorganize the group under the sole banner of socialism. RW denounced the attempted infiltration as an "opportunist political program of the SWP/YSA." Thereafter, RW did welcome new members who shared its vision of a socialist-feminist revolution, but put so many stipulations on SWP/YSA participation that apparently no one of that bent bothered to apply.[91]

As the decade of the 1970s unfolded, women like those in RW began to challenge fundamental concepts of females as producer both within and without the family on an increasingly sustained basis. The proliferation of literature on the subject offered one indicator of this expansion. Many women began to look to the standard work of Simone de Beauvoir and to recent original works for socialist feminist answers. In rejecting the orthodox Socialist line, radical socialist feminists turned to those theorists who demanded that the family and its female producers be analyzed in a more sophisticated and systematic manner than orthodox Marxists had done. Women's production, sexuality, reproduction and child rearing came under special critical review.

New Radical Socialist Feminist Expectations in the 1970s: De Beauvoir,
Firestone and Millett

It is widely agreed that Simone de Beauvoir provided one of the most
influential statements in the Western world on the cause and nature of wom-
en's historical oppression and largely pioneered the modern radical sex-
economic analysis. That is not to say that all contemporary arguments on the
subject sprang from her works, but her theories on the failure of classical
socialism to provide for women's unique needs continue to be considered
and revered in a wide spectrum of feminist literature. Among her other goals,
de Beauvoir set out to expose socialism's ambiguities with respect to the
Woman Question. Contemporary feminists have been quick to adopt her
reinterpretation of Engels's position on the family and her analysis of the
contradictions between classical Marxism and feminism. However, de Beauvoir came to accept Bebel's theory on women and the proletariat fight, even
though her acceptance was veiled in existentialist terminology. De Beauvoir
disclosed her feelings on this subject in the introduction of *The Second Sex*:

> The parallel drawn by Bebel between women and the proletariat is valid in that
> neither ever formed a minority or a separate collective unit of mankind. And instead
> of a single historical event it is in both cases a historical development that explains
> their status as a class and accounts for the membership of *particular individuals* in
> that class. But proletarians have not always existed, whereas there have always been
> women. They are women in virtue of their anatomy and physiology. Throughout
> history they have always been subordinated to men, and hence their dependency is
> not the result of a historical event or a social change—it was not something that
> *occurred.*[92]

For de Beauvoir, then, the "division of the sexes is a biological fact, not
an event in human history."[93] In *The Second Sex* she explained that women
were defined by men and were therefore cast in an inferior role, but she
also believed that existing socialist theory did not provide for a full analysis
of women's oppression. The germ of de Beauvoir's analysis was her belief
that women needed a political theory to overcome their oppression. Thus,
a large part of her study sought a socialist orientation which would "describe
how woman undergoes her apprenticeship, how she experiences her situation, in what kind of universe she is confined, what modes of escape are
vouchsafed her."[94] De Beauvoir's approach both drew upon classical Marxist
methodology yet differed from it. Many of her conclusions presaged similar
radical Marxist feminist analyses in more recent times.

Shulamith Firestone shared de Beauvoir's criticisms of nineteenth-century
Marxist methodology but rejected other important features of de Beauvoir's
arguments, including her existentialist framework. In what evolved into one
of radical feminism's handbooks on this subject, Firestone sought in *The
Dialectic of Sex* (1970) to carry Marxist feminist theory beyond orthodox

Marxism by broadening significantly de Beauvoir's concept of biological and psychoanalytic views of historical materialism: "I have attempted to take the class analysis one step further to its roots in the biological division of the sexes. We have not thrown out the insights of the socialists; on the contrary, radical feminism can enlarge their analysis, granting it an even deeper basis in objective conditions and thereby explaining many of its insolubles."[95]

Firestone asserted that all forms of historical and contemporary oppression sprang from the original biological subjugation of women. She postulated that the "natural reproductive difference between the sexes led directly to the first division of labor at the origins of class, as well as furnishing the paradigm of caste (discrimination based on biological characteristics)."[96] Sex, class and caste remained for Firestone primarily natural phenomena—reactionary forces that could be changed only by altering nature itself. But Firestone's analysis did not include a clear explanation of how alternatives in "natural" biological functions would alleviate the evils of racism in tandem with the evils of sexism. Even here, as orthodox Marxists had been prone to do, Firestone dealt only tangentially with the race issue. Traditional Marxists themselves viewed the radicals' argument as antithetical to their cause, since it implied that a sex and caste revolution could be attained without a general proletarian revolution. Even though Firestone's theories did not attract a wide range of feminists, she nonetheless did have a major impact on radical/cultural feminism and socialist feminism as one of their most cited figures.

Although differing from Firestone in methodology and temperament, the equally popular Kate Millett had similar visions of a new socialist order rooted in the destruction of familial relationships and a new revolutionary unfettering of women in order that they might pursue total liberation. Millett, who specialized in literary and social criticism, defined oppression as a consequence of the "white patriarchy's" psychological oppression of blacks and women— Millett used "patriarchy" to describe a power-structure relationship whereby one group is controlled by another in terms strikingly similar to Thompson's and Wirth's generally accepted models of "minority status."[97] In *Sexual Politics* (1971), Millett argued that cultural differences imposed by white males on blacks and women led to their "castelike" status. She stated that the crux of the feminist Marxist shortcomings was "that beyond declaring that the compulsive family must go, Marxist theory had failed to supply a sufficient ideological base for a sexual revolution, and was remarkably naive as to the historical and psychological strength of patriarchy."[98]

Millett also theorized that all oppressed groups were subject to degradation by white males, who practiced a universal social "caste of virility." To illustrate her point and her awareness of collateral oppression, Millett drew a race and sex analogy: "A black doctor or lawyer has higher social status than a poor white sharecropper. But race, itself a caste system which subsumes class, persuades the latter citizen that he belongs to a higher order of life, just as it oppresses the black professional in spirit, whatever his material success may be. In much the same manner, a truck driver or butcher has always his 'manhood' to fall back upon. Should this final vanity be offended, he may contemplate more violent methods."[99]

This brand of contemporary radical feminism called primarily for cultural *and* social revolution based on Engels's theory of family dissolution and the development of a new feminist-based socialism. It countermanded organized socialism and orthodox Marxist doctrine by postulating that social revolution should be led by a coalition of radical women rather than by the largely male-controlled proletariat. Millett's revolutionary coalition would be composed of all those who rejected the dominant white male's program of violence and virility. As Millett stated, "A cultural revolution, which, while it must necessarily involve the political and economic reorganization traditionally implied by the term revolution, must go far beyond this as well."[100] Moreover, Millett's arguments further convinced many radical feminists that the failure of the Soviet experiment to eradicate sexism was proof to women that economic reforms alone could not reverse centuries of traditional, gender-based oppression.[101]

Despite their limitations, the existence of such economic-determinist tracts brought together a wide cross-section of women who believed they had the opportunity to learn from and to reach out to important class-based analyses. As Rosalyn Baxandall pointed out in *Beyond the Fragments: Feminism and the Making of Socialism*, this approach has been "presented as an alternative to . . . Marxism. . . . Sisterhood is seen as the model for socialism with a human face."[102] Without this opportunity feminists would have continued to pursue traditional theoretical frameworks based on reformist and caste arguments, but perhaps not, at least in a purely theoretical sense, class ones. As noted in another relevant work, The Furies's *Class and Feminism*, economic analysis was a way "to understand class as a political mechanism for maintaining not only capitalism but also patriarchy and white supremacy. More simply, class, sexism and racism."[103]

The works of de Beauvoir, Firestone and Millett perhaps best articulated the common ground of radical socialist feminist dedication to expanding Marxist theoretical systems. They and many others—again, precise numbers are elusive—came to argue that orthodox Marxism was wanting as an ideological vehicle of liberation for women. They thus maintained that the whole existing social and economic structure, particularly the family, must be socially and economically revolutionized. By so doing they placed socialism within the broader context of the radical feminist struggle. That is to say, from a historical perspective radical socialist women, like cultural-oriented women, moved feminist theories away from legal goals and commitments toward a new and profound woman-centered perspective. On this subject, Catherine A. MacKinnon reminds us of a salient point: "As marxist [sic] method is dialectical materialism, feminist method is consciousness raising."[104] Indeed, the growing body of radical feminist literature in the late 1960s and early

1970s reflected an ideological wedding of these very themes, especially in the popular periodicals such as *It Ain't Me Babe, No More Fun and Games, Off Our Backs, The Outpost* and *Tooth and Nail.*

This leads us to the conclusion that radical socialist feminism and radical cultural feminism have shared a unique commitment to developing ideological constructs beyond those of the legal feminist movement. At the heart of radical Marxist feminism is the conviction that oppression is not ultimately biological in nature, but rather is "man-made," and as such can and must be rectified by human intervention. Meanwhile, the belief that male dominance would disappear concurrently with social revolution—as in those theories espoused by feminist Marxists—failed to take into consideration the range of cultural-based injustice that women have faced. In a large sense, then, Marxism/feminism represented a feminist ideological realignment, based upon notions of both cultural and economic oppression, against legal-oriented feminism, which continued in the midst of this unfolding ideological maelstrom to seek primarily changes in laws only. Certainly the goals, patterns of behaviors and critical analyses of older organizational movements were, therefore, not demonstrably different from a large segment of the contemporary black movement, for example, the Black Panthers and Stokely Carmichael's All-Afrikan People's Revolutionary Party.

To recapitulate briefly, organizational women felt that the lack of political and civil rights for women could be addressed by a total integration of women into a male-dominated society. Their concept of "equality of opportunity" would be achieved through educational and legal priorities. The radicals, on the other hand, sensed a more virulent form of sex victimization than legal women perceived; radicals saw the answer to sexist society in women's cultural unity and at times even withdrawal from male-dominated structures. The very norms of that society were reprehensible to many radicals and served to encourage them to reject the legalists' goal of total integration. Consequently, lesbian separatism became justified and necessary. Marxist feminists, many of whom had radical/cultural leanings or backgrounds other than legal/reform orientations argued that a male-female power relationship included important economic determinants as well as biological realities. All the feminist analyses—legal, cultural and economic—exhibited a multidimensional character of historical feminism and demonstrated women's determination on many protest levels to come to grips with oppression through their own energy and ingenuity.

SUMMARY

In the 1960s and 1970s the socialist feminist wheel generally returned to the position of economic theory and dedication that it had manifested in various forms since the Utopian Socialism of the pre–Civil War era. In that era contemporary socialist-inclined women largely adopted complex approaches to class and caste oppression that went beyond orthodox Marxist solutions to the Woman Question. To quote Batya Weinbaum, "Like a Marxist, I am looking for a material basis; but, like a feminist, I am looking for what is going on underneath the problems identified by Marxism as well."[105] Radical socialist feminists, often in tandem with cultural-oriented feminists, as opposed to the doctrinaire and homogeneous feminist Marxists, have sought a fresh theoretical synthesis of sex and class oppression. Orthodox women Marxists, on the other hand, like male Marxists, have been quick to criticize that approach. As one wrote, nonorganizational socialist feminism, "isolated from theoretical and practical links to the class struggle, eventually will lead 'middle-class' women back to the psychiatrist's couch or to some form of collective therapy.... [I]t will unwittingly contribute to division and political paralysis within the working-class movement and will further the maintenance of the oppression and economic exploitation of working-class women."[106]

We can therefore conclude that radical Marxian feminism was not pure economic determinism, but rather an ideological wedding of concerns about sex and class much akin to Nkrumah's synthesis of race and class concerns. Both black scientific socialists and socialist feminists traced the roots of their oppression to economic class doctrine; both groups sought to blend Marxist theory with historical race and gender theories of oppression. Neither blacks nor women have found it generally expedient to pursue their goals within the mainstream of contemporary socialism. Both largely repudiated organized socialism for an approach that stressed group solidarity and those tenets of Marxism that could be reconciled with cultural as well as economic revolution. What emerged among radical socialist blacks and radical Marxist feminists in recent times, then, was a hybrid model of Marxism applicable in cultural and economic terms to the special forms of oppression facing African peoples and women.

In other words, blacks and Marxist women show similarities in their eclectic determination to merge theory and action. This has led to revisionist approaches scornful of, as well as scorned by, more traditional, established socialist groups. The fact that certain black and women Marxists have felt it necessary to abandon the path of orthodoxy is an indication of their appraisal of historical realities and their perceptions of male and white leadership, both within and beyond Marxist conventions.

NOTES

1. Alice Felt Tyler, *Freedom's Ferment: Phases of American Social History from the Colonial Period to the Outbreak of the Civil War* (New York: Harper and Brothers, 1944), 140–65; Nardi Reeder Campion, *Ann the Word: The Life of Mother Ann Lee, Founder of the Shakers* (Boston: Little, Brown, 1976), 63–80. C. Lane estimated the population of the various Shaker communities at about six thousand in "A Day with the Shakers," *The Dial*, October 1843, 168, see 165–73. See Mari Jo Buhle, "Feminism

and Socialism in the United States, 1820–1920" (Ph.D. dissertation, University of Wisconsin, 1974), 1–2.

2. Tyler, *Freedom's Ferment*, 149–65; H. L. Eads, *Shaker Sermons: Scripto-Rationale* (Shakers, NY: The Shaker Manifesto, 1884), 83; Arthur F. Joy, *The Queen of the Shakers* (Minneapolis: T. S. Denison, 1960), 49; The United Society, with the Approbation of the Ministry, *A Summary View of the Millennial Church, or United Society of Believers, Commonly Called Shakers* (Albany, NY: C. Van Benthuysen, 1848), 65–70.

3. Buhle, "Feminism and Socialism," 2; Tyler, *Freedom's Ferment*, 206–11.

4. Frances Trollope, *Domestic Manners of the Americans*, Donald Smalley, ed. (New York: Alfred A. Knopf, 1949 [1832]), 27–28, n.4.

5. Edd Winfield Parks, *Nashoba* (New York: Twayne, 1963), 36–326; Richard Stiller, *Commune on the Frontier: The Story of Frances Wright* (New York: Thomas Y. Crowell, 1972), 106–13, 123–35; *Margaret Lane, Frances Wright and the "Great Experiment"* (Totowa, NJ: Rowman and Littlefield, 1972), 1–46; A.J.G. Perkins and Theresa Wolfson, *Frances Wright, Free Enquirer: The Study of Temperament* (New York: Harper and Brothers, 1939), 123–207; William Randall Waterman, *Frances Wright* (New York: Columbia University Press, 1924), 92–160; Tyler, *Freedom's Ferment*, 206–11; Buhle, "Feminism and Socialism," 2–5; Eleanor Flexner, *Century of Struggle: The Woman's Rights Movement in the United States* (New York: Atheneum, 1974), 27.

6. Ellen DuBois, "The Nineteenth-Century Woman Suffrage Movement and the Analysis of Women's Oppression," in Zillah R. Eisenstein, ed., *Capitalist Patriarchy and the Case for Socialist Feminism* (New York: Monthly Review, 1979), 137–50; Mary Oppenheimer, "The Suffrage Movement and the Socialist Party," *New Review*, Vol. 3 (1915), 358–61; Vida Scudder, "Women and Socialism," *New Review*, Vol. 3 (1915), 454–70.

7. DuBois, "The Nineteenth-Century Woman Suffrage Movement," 140, 145; Ellen DuBois, "On Labor and Free Love: Two Unpublished Speeches of Elizabeth Cady Stanton," *Signs*, Vol. 1, No. 1 (1975), 257–68; Israel Kugler, "The Trade Union Career of Susan B. Anthony," *Labor History*, Vol. 2, No. 1 (1961), 90–100.

8. See Marilyn J. Boxer and Jean H. Quataert, "The Class and Sex Connection: An Introduction," in Marilyn J. Boxer and Jean H. Quataert, eds., *Socialist Women: European Socialist Feminism in the Nineteenth and Early Twentieth Centuries* (New York: Elsevier, 1978), 1–18.

9. Karl Marx and Frederick Engels, *Manifesto of the Communist Party* (commonly known as the *Communist Manifesto*), in *Karl Marx and Frederick Engels: Selected Works* (Moscow: Progress, 1970), 49. See Hal Draper, "Marx and Engels on Women's Liberation," in Roberta Salper, ed., *Female Liberation: History and Current Politics* (New York: Alfred A. Knopf, 1972), 83–107; Paul Lafargue, "The Woman Question," trans. Charles H. Kerr, *International Socialist Review*, Vol. 5 (March 1905), 547–59.

10. Frederick Engels, *The Origin of the Family, Private Property and the State* (New York: International, 1942, [1884]). See Kathleen Gough, "The Origin of the Family," in Jo Freeman, ed., *Women: A Feminist Perspective* (Palo Alto, CA: Mayfield, 1979), 83–105.

11. See chapter 3, "Dialectical Disturbances," in Sheila Rowbotham, *Women, Resistance and Revolution: A History of Women and Revolution in the Modern World* (New York: Vintage, 1974), 59–77.

12. Engels, *Origin of the Family*, 25–74. One can compose a general index of the

cultural standards of matriarchal and patriarchal systems by using the historical and current literature. This would include:

Matriarchal	Patriarchal
(1) Permissive attitude toward sex	(1) Restrictive attitude toward sex
(2) Freedom for women	(2) Limitations of freedom for women
(3) Women accorded high status	(3) Women seen as inferior, sinful
(4) Welfare more valued than chastity	(4) Chastity more valued than welfare
(5) Deep fear of incest	(5) Deep fear of homosexuality
(6) Sex differences minimized	(6) Sex differences maximized
(7) Mother-religion	(7) Father-religion
(8) Communal ownership	(8) Primogeniture

13. Engels, *Origin of the Family*, 50–51.

14. August Bebel, *Woman Under Socialism*, trans. Daniel De Leon (New York: Labor News, 1904 [1883]); Mari Jo Buhle, *Women and American Socialism, 1870–1920* (Urbana: University of Illinois Press, 1981), 41.

15. Bebel, *Women Under Socialism*, 1–6, quotes, 1, 5 and 6.

16. "Woman's Sphere," *New York Call*, August 31, 1913.

17. Buhle, *Women and American Socialism*, 41; George Lichtheim, *Marxism: An Historical and Critical Study* (London: Routledge and Kegan Paul, 1961), 222–43, quote, 241.

18. This, of course, is a variation of the Marxist principle that a group in power will never relinquish that power voluntarily.

19. Buhle, "Feminism and Socialism," 40.

20. See Buhle, *Women and American Socialism*, 105–7, and Buhle, "Women and the Socialist Party, 1901–1914," in Edith Hoshino Altbach, ed., *From Feminism to Liberation* (Cambridge, MA: Schenkman, 1971), 65–86, esp. 66–68; Bruce Dancis, "Socialism and Women in the United States, 1900–1917," *Socialist Revolution*, Vol. 27 (January–March 1976), 99–100; Margaret S. Marsh, *Anarchist Women, 1870–1920* (Philadelphia: Temple University Press, 1981), 160–66; Meredith Tax, *The Rising of the Women: Feminist Solidarity and Class Conflict, 1880–1917* (New York: Monthly Review, 1980), 164–201.

21. Buhle, *Women and American Socialism*, xvi, and Buhle, "Feminism and Socialism," 109. See Dancis, "Socialism and Women," 125; Jessie M. Molle, "The National Convention and the Woman's Movement," *International Socialist Review*, Vol. 9 (1908), 688–90; Theresa Malkiel, "Where Do We Stand on the Woman Question?" *International Socialist Review*, Vol. 10 (1909), 158–63; Sally M. Miller, "Women in the Party Bureaucracy: Subservient Functionaries," in Sally M. Miller, ed., *Flawed Liberation: Socialism and Feminism* (Westport, CT: Greenwood, 1981), 13–35; Mari Jo Buhle, "Socialist Woman, Progressive Woman, Coming Nation," in Joseph R. Conlin, ed., *The American Radical Press, 1880–1960*, Vol. 2 (Westport, CT: Greenwood, 1974), 442–49.

22. Buhle, "Feminism and Socialism," 114–15.

23. Dancis, "Socialism and Women," 105; Buhle, *Women and American Socialism*, 134.

24. Dancis, "Socialism and Women," 108–9; Buhle, *Women and American Socialism*, 148, 156.

25. Buhle, "Feminism and Socialism," 97–98, 205–8; Malkiel, "Where Do We Stand on the Woman Question," 159–62; Molle, "The National Convention and the Woman's Movement," 688–90. The longer works are held in the Library of Congress. Note that later editions of Vida Scudder's *Socialism and Character* are sometimes listed as *Socialism and Spiritual Progress*, and that May Wood Simon's *Woman and the Social Problem* (Chicago: Charles H. Kerr, 1899) is also found as an extended pamphlet.

26. See Brunetta R. Wolfman, "The Communist Party, Always Out of Step," in Raymond L. Hall, ed., *Black Separatism and Social Reality: Rhetoric and Reason* (New York: Pergamon, 1977), 109–14; and the more comprehensive view of Wilson Record, *The Negro and the Communist Party* (Chapel Hill: University of North Carolina Press, 1951), 54–183.

27. Freda Kirchwey, "The Pan-American Conference of Women," *The Nation*, May 10, 1922, 565; "Freda Kirchwey, 82, Dies: Long Editor of *The Nation*," *New York Times*, January 4, 1976; "Rose Stokes Dies after Operation," *New York Times*, June 21, 1933; Elizabeth Gurley Flynn, *The Rebel Girl: An Autobiography, My First Life, 1906–1926* (New York: International, 1955), 280, and "Editor's Note," same work, 9–11; Flynn, *I Speak My Own Piece: Autobiography of "The Rebel Girl"* (New York: Masses and Mainstream, 1955), 11; Rosalyn Baxandall, "Elizabeth Gurley Flynn: The Early Years," *Radical America*, Vol. 8, No. 1 (1975), 97–115; Robert Shaffer, "Women and the Communist Party, USA, 1930–1940," *Socialist Review*, Vol. 45 (May–June 1979), 73–118.

28. Cited in Blanche Wiesen Cook, ed., *Crystal Eastman on Women and Revolution* (New York: Oxford University Press, 1978), 23, see 1–36.

29. Ibid.

30. Crystal Eastman, "Now We Can Begin," *The Liberator* (December 1920).

31. Vivian Gornick, *The Romance of American Communism* (New York: Basic, 1977), 10–27, see 231–34, 256–65; Robert Shaffer, "Women and the Communist Party," 73–118.

32. Gornick, *American Communism*, 30–31.

33. Ibid., 227–34.

34. Jessica Mitford, *A Fine Old Conflict* (London: Michael Joseph, 1977), esp. 59–69, 202–20.

35. Ibid.

36. Peggy Dennis, *The Autobiography of an American Communist: A Personal View of a Political Life, 1925–1975* (Westport, CT: Lawrence Hill, 1977).

37. Ibid., quote, 294, see 289–96.

38. Peggy Dennis, "Letter of Resignation from the Communist Party, U.S.A.," in ibid., 289–96.

39. Ibid., 294.

40. Zillah R. Eisenstein, "Developing a Theory of Capitalist Patriarchy and Socialist Feminism," in Eisenstein, *Capitalist Patriarchy*, 5–40; Batya Weinbaum, *The Curious Courtship of Women's Liberation and Socialism* (Boston: South End, 1978), 20–32, 56–65.

41. Joyce Cowley, "Women Who Won the Right to Vote," *Fourth International* (Spring 1955); George Novack, "Revolutionary Dynamics of Women's Liberation," *The Militant*, October 17, 1969; Mary-Alice Waters, "Feminism and the Marxist Movement," *International Socialist Review* (October 1972); Linda Jenness, "Feminism and Social-

ism," *International Socialist Review* (March and May 1976); Cindy Jaquith, "What Strategy for Women?" *International Socialist Review* (March 1977).

42. See, for example, "The Berkeley-Oakland Women's Union Statement," in Eisenstein, *Capitalist Patriarchy*, 355–61.

43. Catharine A. MacKinnon, "Feminism, Marxism, Method, and the State: An Agenda for Theory," in Nannerl O. Keohane, Michelle Z. Rosaldo, and Barbara C. Gelpi, eds., *Feminist Theory: A Critique of Ideology* (Chicago: University of Chicago Press, 1982), 1–30; Mary O'Brien, "Feminist Theory and Dialectical Logic," in Keohane, Rosaldo, and Gelpi, *Feminist Theory*, 99–112.

44. Hal Draper, "Marx and Engels on Women's Liberation," 102. One must further take into account Marx's condemnation of the militantly antifeminist Proudhonists of the French-speaking nations. See Karl Marx, *The First International and After: Political Writings*, Vol. 3, ed. David Fernbach (Middlesex, England: Penguin, 1974), 16, 16–17, n.20.

45. Daniel Bell, *Marxian Socialism in the United States* (Princeton, NJ: Princeton University Press, 1967), 176, and Bell, "The Background and Development of Marxian Socialism in the United States," in Donald Drew Egbert and Stow Persons, eds., *Socialism and American Life*, Vol. 1 (Princeton, NJ: Princeton University Press, 1952), 213–405, esp. 388; James P. Cannon, *The History of American Trotskyism: Report of a Participant* (New York: Pioneer, 1944), 1–2, 254–55. On SWP/YSA and feminism, see Jo Freeman, *The Politics of Women's Liberation: A Case Study of an Emerging Social Movement and Its Relation to the Policy Process* (New York: David McKay, 1975), 129–34.

46. See Evelyn Reed's "Foreword" and "Note to the Fifth Edition," in Reed, *Problems of Women's Liberation: A Marxist Approach* (New York: Pathfinder, 1976 [1969]), 7–11.

47. Ibid., 9.

48. Ibid., 12–27.

49. Ibid., 18.

50. Evelyn Reed, "In Defense of Engels on the Matriarchy," *The Militant*, March 5, 1971; quote, Reed, *Problems of Women's Liberation*, 18.

51. Robert Briffault, *The Mothers: A Study of the Origins of Sentiments and Institutions*, 3 vols. (New York: Macmillan, 1927), esp. Vol. 1, 85–116, 268–432; J. J. Bachofen, *Das Mutterrecht: Eine Untersuchung über die Gynaikokratie der alten Welt nach ihrer religiösen und rechtlüchen Natur* (Stuttgart: Verlag von Krais and Hoffman, 1861). Bachofen's theory on matrilineal descent was counterbalanced by Henry Maine's classical anthropological study, published also in 1861, arguing the thesis of patrilineal descent. Henry James Sumner Maine, *Ancient Law: Its Connection with the Early History of Society and Its Relation to Modern Ideas* (London: John Murray, 1885 [1861]), 113–70.

52. There is a continuing argument over the original nature of marriage. The controversy centers around the theses of Robert Briffault, who maintained that a mother-right, promiscuous communal society predated monogamous marriage, and Edward Westermarck, who argued that the matriarchal, promiscuous communal society never existed and that monogamous marriage was a primeval institution rooted in the ethos of human society. Briffault, *The Mothers*, Vol. 1, 614–781, and Vol. 2, 2–96; Edward Westermarck, *A Short History of Marriage* (New York: Macmillan, 1926),

1–30, 229–50, and Westermarck, *The History of Human Marriage*, 3 vols. (London: Macmillan, 1891 [1844]), Vol. 1, 8–24.

53. Reed, *Problems of Women's Liberation*, 23.

54. Linda Jenness, ed., *Feminism and Socialism* (New York: Pathfinder, 1975), 5.

55. Ibid., 6.

56. Angela Y. Davis, *Women, Race and Class* (New York: Random House, 1981), 149–71, 222–44; Willie Mae Reid, "Black Women's Struggle for Equality," (Pathfinder, pamphlet, 1976); The Combahee River Collective, "A Black Feminist Statement," in Eisenstein, *Capitalist Patriarchy*, 362–372.

57. Maxine Williams, "Black Women and the Struggle for Liberation," *The Militant*, July 3, 1970. See Pamela Newman, "Take a Good Look at Our Problems," *The Militant*, October 30, 1970.

58. Williams, "Black Women and the Struggle for Liberation."

59. Combahee River Collective, "A Black Feminist Statement."

60. Myrna Hill, "Feminism and Black Nationalism" (mimeographed), n.d., Vertical File, Schlesinger Library, Cambridge, MA.

61. In addition to the discussion of this issue in this study, see the historical narrative of Mark Naison, "Marxism and Black Radicalism in America: Notes on a Long (and Continuing) Journey," *Radical America*, Vol. 5, No. 3 (1971), 3–25.

62. Charnie Guettel, *Marxism and Feminism* (Toronto: The Women's Press, 1974), 1.

63. Ibid., 6, quote, 50.

64. Ibid., 59.

65. Crystal Eastman, "Now We Can Begin," *The Liberator*, December 1920.

66. Margaret Benston, "The Political Economy of Women's Liberation," New England Free Press reprint, probably 1972, author's personal papers; Robin Morgan, *Going Too Far: The Personal Chronicle of a Feminist* (New York: Vintage, 1978), 196, n.4; Betsy Warrior, "Battered Lives," KNOW, Inc. reprint, probably 1970, author's personal papers.

67. Mariarosa Dalla Costa and Selma James, *The Power of Women and the Subversion of the Community* (London: Falling Wall, 1975), esp. "Introduction," 5–20, and 21–23, 49–51, 57–79; Mariarosa Dalla Costa, "Women and the Subversion of the Community," *Radical America*, Vol. 6, No. 1 (1972), 67–102.

68. Selma James, "Women and the Subversion of the Community: Introduction to the English Translation," *Radical America*, Vol. 6, No. 1 (1972), 64. The arguments on women and production in the home are summarized by Lise Vogel, "The Earthly Family," *Radical America*, Vol. 7, Nos. 4 and 5 (1973), 9–50.

69. Juliet Mitchell, *Woman's Estate* (New York: Vintage, 1973), 99. Many of Mitchell's arguments in this study are based on her earlier "Women: The Longest Revolution," *New Left Review*, No. 40 (November–December 1966), 11–37.

70. Mitchell, *Woman's Estate*, 99.

71. Ibid., 81.

72. Ibid., 100.

73. Ibid., 148–49.

74. Rowbotham, *Women, Resistance and Revolution*, and Rowbotham, *Woman's Consciousness, Man's World* (Baltimore: Penguin, 1973).

75. Rowbotham, *Women, Resistance and Revolution*, 76.

76. Ibid., 246.

77. Rowbotham, *Woman's Consciousness, Man's World*, 94.

78. Ibid., 125.

79. Rowbotham, *Women, Resistance and Revolution*, 246.

80. Roxanne Dunbar, "Female Liberation as the Basis for Social Revolution," *Notes from the Second Year* (1970), 51.

81. Jo Freeman provides insight on this subject in "The Legal Basis of the Sexual Caste System," *Valparaiso Law Review*, Vol. 5, No. 2 (1971), 203–36, esp. through her discussion of caste, 204–10.

82. Maren Lockwood Carden, *The New Feminist Movement* (New York: Russell Sage Foundation, 1974), 88–89; Judith Hole and Ellen Levine, *Rebirth of Feminism* (New York: Quadrangle, 1971), 163–65, on the SWP/YSA question; Carmen Ristorucci, "Why We Oppose the ERA," *Political Affairs*, Vol. 55, No. 3 (1976), 8–17, for the CP-USA's position on the federal Equal Rights Amendment. On the question of the CP-USA and black Americans, see Wilson Record, *Race and Radicalism: The NAACP and the Communist Party in Conflict* (Ithaca, NY: Cornell University Press, 1964), 93–95; Record, *The Negro and the Communist Party*, 120–83; and Record, "New Steps in the United Front," *Communist*, Vol. 24 (November 1935), 1005; Walter White, "The Negro and the Communists," *Harper's Magazine*, Vol. 164, December 1931, 62–72.

83. Linda Jenness, "Socialism and the Fight for Women's Rights," Pathfinder pamphlet, 1976.

84. Letter, Melba Windoffer (corresponding secretary for RW) to Joan Jordan, n.d., Jordan Papers, Social Action Collection, State Historical Society of Wisconsin, Madison, WI (hereafter cited as SAC, SHSW); Radical Women, "Revolutionary Socialist Feminists"(mimeographed), March 20, 1974, Vertical File, Schlesinger Library. Much information about Radical Women's programs and praxis was derived from Cindy Gipple, *The Women's Movement and the Class Struggle* (Seattle: Radical Women Publications, pamphlet, 1972), and Clara Fraser, *The Emancipation of Women* (Seattle: Radical Women Publications, pamphlet, n.d.), both in the University of Washington Libraries, Seattle. See Freeman, *The Politics of Women's Liberation*, 133.

85. Radical Women, "Radical Women Manifesto: Theory, Program and Structure" (mimeographed), April 1973, Vertical File, Schlesinger Library.

86. Gipple, *The Women's Movement and the Class Struggle*, 4.

87. See ibid.

88. Radical Women, "Radical Women Manifesto."

89. Stokely Carmichael, interview with author, Akron, OH, November 10, 1977.

90. Radical Women, "Radical Women Manifesto."

91. "Letter from Seattle," *Ain't I A Woman*, February 19, 1971.

92. Simone de Beauvoir, *The Second Sex*, trans. and ed. H. M. Parshley (New York: Vintage, 1974 [1952]), xxi.

93. Ibid., 3–41, quote, xxiii.

94. Ibid., xxxv.

95. Shulamith Firestone, *The Dialectic of Sex: The Case for Feminist Revolution* (New York: Bantam, 1970), 12; see Jane Ursel, "The Nature and Origin of Women's Oppression: Marxism and Feminism," *Contemporary Crisis*, Vol. 1, No. 1 (1977), 23–36.

96. Firestone, *Dialectic of Sex*, 9.

97. Kate Millett, *Sexual Politics* (New York: Avon, 1971), 43–87.

98. Ibid., 231.

99. Ibid., 59.

100. Ibid., 473.

101. Ibid., 229–30.

102. Rosalyn Baxandall, "Introduction to the U.S. Edition," in Sheila Rowbotham, Lynne Segal, and Hilary Wainwright, *Beyond the Fragments: Feminism and the Making of Socialism* (Boston: Alyson, 1981), ix.

103. Charlotte Bunch and Nancy Myron, eds., *Class and Feminism: A Collection of Essays from The Furies* (Baltimore: Diana, 1974), 7.

104. MacKinnon, "Feminism, Marxism, Method, and the State," 29.

105. Weinbaum, *Curious Courtship*, 14.

106. Martha E. Gimenez, "Marxism and Feminism," *Frontiers*, Vol. 1, No. 1 (1975), 76.

Epilogue

By reviewing closely the women's movement of the 1960s and 1970s this study has demonstrated that it resembles the history of black civil rights protest in having experienced three distinct ideological currents: legal, cultural and economic. We entered into this dialogue in order to determine if there were common ideological grounds where influences could be demonstrated and differences could be mutually illuminated. Although continuities and discontinuities between blacks and women indeed have been traced through these currents, the analogies are neither perfect nor universal. Clearly blacks and women throughout American history have eclectically defined the myriad kinds of legal and psychological oppression afflicting them, but both groups have sought just as clearly to resist or overturn oppression through various self-directed actions that have resulted in movements evolving like biological organisms. It is our final contention that such movements to a degree are and have been responsive and vulnerable to external forces and extant models. Both groups did, in fact, rebel against those forces that restricted them to "minority status," "proper spheres" and "proper roles." Consequently, despite similarities in protest ideologies, the energy, leadership and direction of each movement sprang largely from within.

The development of race and sex protest in the 1960s and 1970s illustrated that blacks and women were particularly determined to press for social change by drawing upon intragroup strengths and goals. Meanwhile, numerous other protests, such as those against the war in Southeast Asia and arbitrary authority in general, offered only marginal appeal to blacks and women, who felt that white male protesters were driven by values and priorities fundamentally different from their own—particularly based on perceived evidence that white males had abandoned civil rights and ignored feminism.

Race and sex protests often seemed to white males worlds away from the other rebellions that characterized the era under study. As blacks and women became more sensitive to these issues, they were forced into new modes of self-examination and protest goals and commitments. They adopted or resurrected beliefs that only a racially proud civil rights movement could hope to shatter centuries of racism, and only a culturally oriented feminist movement could hope to alter centuries of sexism. Today the historical fight against racism and sexism still challenges the American social consensus, while other movements such as the antiwar and student protests have largely receded. The history of black and women's protests leading up to the era under review was uniquely important, then, since it demonstrated how three models of race and sex protests that are deeply rooted in America's past recurred in modern times.

Contemporary black activism traces its historical reference points largely to the 1920s. In the post–World War I decade race pride and spirit reached a crescendo that manifested itself in the mass movement of Marcus Garvey and the literary achievements of the Harlem Renaissance. Working primarily through the NAACP, Afro-Americans increased their efforts to dismantle the "color line" in the years that marked the Renaissance. With the changing wartime milieu of the early 1940s, some blacks departed from the time-honored legal lobbying tactics of the NAACP to experiment with more dramatic actions—namely, the nonviolent, direct-action and mass-protest strategies of A. Philip Randolph and the Congress of Racial Equality. With the Supreme Court's sweeping school desegregation decision in the mid–1950s, many blacks felt that at long last the legal crusade of the NAACP had reached fruition. But it quickly became apparent to all concerned that the federal government's reluctance to enforce *Brown* and similar decisions would continue white America's policy of promises unfulfilled. Through the middle and late 1950s de facto segregation became increasingly common. Renewed feelings of social injustice permeated black America. New protests flared. The intransigent South, particularly, became the focal point of determined black activism.

Beginning with the Montgomery, Alabama, bus boycott in 1955, black struggles for equality mushroomed. Innovative organizations exhibited new protest commitments and spawned new personal leadership, for instance, that of the charismatic Dr. Martin Luther King, Jr., who became an internationally recognized civil rights figure. King exercised his leadership primarily through the Southern Christian Leadership Conference until the early 1960s, at which time other more youthful and impatient voices catapulted the civil rights movement into new phases. The Student Nonviolent Coordinating Committee and the Congress of Racial Equality utilized reactivated techniques that employed conflict methods of protest in place of the NAACP's legal consensus model and used such rallying cries as "Jail with no bail" to stretch King's nonviolent approach to its limits. But in the face of these new militant chal-

lenges, the NAACP showed no willingness to relinquish its traditional organizational leadership in the quest for social equality. It continued to press
vigorously for legislation and precedent-setting court decisions and to furnish
legal counsel and financial backing for a wide range of national and grass-
roots actions.

Accordingly, into the mid–1960s black protest goals were aimed for the
most part not at overturning the fundamental mechanisms of racist society,
but rather at altering its legal basis. As a result, despite decades of struggles
and apparent successes, most Afro-Americans remained economically, edu-
cationally and politically marginal to the dominant white society in terms of
its most relevant indicators. Since black Americans had shown clearly that
they were hardly reconciled to their second-class status, it was predictable
that a new militancy would sweep civil rights. The new thrust appeared as
the Black Power movement, which marked an important crossroad in the
transition from legal-oriented to cultural-oriented protest.

Black Power generated fresh momentum in the movement by challenging
forcefully and dramatically King's philosophy of "turning the other cheek."
The new "young Turks" were weary of being beaten and vilified during
peaceful marches and innocent prayer vigils, rendered economically and
politically impotent in their communities and denied their cultural heritage.
For them it was clear that too often civil rights initiatives had served merely
to comfort guilt-ridden white liberals rather than to address the imperatives
of black life in America. In short, Black Power prophesied a restated strategy
for black protest predicated on the concepts of self-defense, self-definition
and self-determination. Stokely Carmichael and Charles V. Hamilton echoed
this goal in *Black Power*: "Our basic need is to reclaim our history and our
identity from what must be called cultural terrorism, from the depredation
of self-justifying white guilt. We shall have to struggle for the right to create
our own terms through which to define ourselves and our relationship to
the society, and to have these terms recognized."[1]

For blacks this new focus, but old theme, called for cultural introspection
as well as increased militancy and departures from past legal-oriented coalition policies. At first whites involved with the Black Power movement were
expected to defer to black leadership; later they were forced to withdraw
completely from the movement. Whites were discounted as extraneous cultural baggage. The thrust of Black Power soon turned to an old stream of
nationalistic militancy that in no small way reflected earlier approaches—
especially that of Marcus Garvey, the Nation of Islam and Malcolm X.

Black Power profoundly influenced the nature and direction of protest
thought in contemporary America by offering action models to those who
wished to challenge traditional assumptions of the proper place of American
subgroups. It taught that both values and laws were at stake. Society needed
structural and social change as well as legal change. By attacking a whole
range of institutional inequalities, Black Power helped to crystallize much of

the protest thought of the late 1960s and 1970s that came to characterize the more militant wings of other cultural-oriented movements, in particular radical women in the feminist cause.

By the 1970s Afro-Americans expressed their determination to overthrow the shackles of American racism in other ways, including a restated economic thrust. There had always been a small number of black Marxists, some of whom had become prominent in the Communist Party of the United States of America, but most of whom generally appeared only on the fringes of black protest. In the late 1960s and early 1970s a Marxist ideology resurfaced under the aegis of radical militant groups like the Black Panthers and the new advocates of black scientific socialism, principally Stokely Carmichael. Black scientific socialism rested on the twin pillars of anticapitalism and pro-Pan-Africanism as articulated by the nationalist Kwame Nkrumah of Ghana, and later of Guinea. It was, in effect, an attempt to reconcile race and Marxist precepts within the context of new attacks on the centrifugal pulls of the black diaspora and the cultural and economic perplexities of neocolonialism. Practitioners of the new hybrid socialism argued that racism and capitalism were inexorably fused and therefore must be confronted simultaneously— their panacea called for revolution in both social and economic spheres.

Like Black Power advocates and black Marxists, some women held radical perceptions of the underlying social, economic and political problems of America. Moreover, similar to blacks, there always had been women who pursued self-defined goals in defiance of a white male patriarchy. Anne Hutchinson certainly fit that pattern, as did Susan B. Anthony and Elizabeth Cady Stanton. Women like the freethinker Victoria Woodhull, or avant-garde feminists like Charlotte Perkins Gilman, Emma Goldman, Elizabeth Gurley Flynn, Kate Richards O'Hare and Alice Paul, surely offered lasting models to those who were not content to remain within prescribed roles or to adopt traditional patterns of organizational reform. Indeed, these women assaulted some of the most deeply rooted cultural assumptions underlying the social and economic landscape of this nation. In other words, both blacks and women had activists and theorists who historically had fashioned challenges to long-standing cultural definitions of place and role. And, as we have seen, such women often moved with fluidity from one strategy to another as their protest horizons and commitments grew.

After the implementation of the Nineteenth Amendment in 1920 many of those protest boundaries became especially clouded as feminism largely slipped back into legal-oriented organizational modes. Dorothy Johnson, in a study based on data from the period, found that during the interwar years women focused their reform efforts almost solely on professional, social welfare and peace issues.[2] Yet the record also shows just as clearly that women shared with blacks heightened concern for the economic instabilities amplified by the Great Depression. As a reserve army of "dispensable" laborers,

both groups suffered exacerbated unemployment and underemployment during the 1930s.

World War II brought new hope to both blacks and women as millions answered their country's call to assist the war effort. The war years therefore should have been distinguished from the earlier decades by the unprecedented extent of black and female integration into the paid labor force. After the war, nonetheless, military demobilization and the priorities of private-sector consumerism meant that both groups faced the retrenchment of wartime gains. In retrospect, the Depression and World War II only underscored the historical frustrations of blacks and women. The heightened expectations of blacks and women during wartime gave way later to disenchantment and even cynicism among certain groups. Women, especially, were forced back into traditional labor patterns. While the war whetted their desires for employment outside the home and broadened avenues of self-fulfillment, the basic path assigned to women after the conflict led to what Betty Friedan identified as a "feminine mystique" role.[3] And indeed there was great cultural pressure for women to conform once more to extragroup definitions of prescribed "place." Despite any inner ambitions that women might have harbored, little dramatic feminist progress took place between the war and the early 1960s.

The transition decade of the 1960s ushered in a period of turmoil and crisis that would forever put an end to any illusions about a pax Americana in terms of blacks' and women's acceptance of and adherence to traditional and extraneous ideals of their "proper place." The social and political discontent of the era gave rise to fresh protests that questioned persistent race and gender inequities, the legitimacy of authority, the privileges of leadership, and the American involvement in Vietnam. A sense of urgency breathed new life into the fires of agitation and served to reinvigorate quiescent protests, especially those of blacks and women. Given the exigencies of the 1960s, the decade marked a true watershed in the history of mass activism in the United States. In that respect this study is an observation of historical intersections and discontinuities not only between blacks and women, but also between women and a broad range of contemporary protest ideologies. This new protest milieu led in no small way to a resurgence of historical feminism as women began to see themselves as an oppressed group and began to respond as one by drawing on their own rich protest history and by agitating both collectively and individually for structural change. Although this so-called third wave of feminism followed closely on the heels of similar dramatic black initiatives and victories, it would be naive to assume that civil rights alone had spawned this latest women's liberation thrust.

While civil rights in the early 1960s created a new confidence that certain protest ideologies could produce change, there were equally important woman-oriented events occurring simultaneously that served to revive fem-

inism. In retrospect President Kennedy's Commission on the Status of Women lent momentum to this reawakening, as did other 1963 events, like the Commission's *Report*, the publication of Betty Friedan's *Feminine Mystique* and the passage of the Equal Pay Act. All of these developments had a profound impact on raising women's consciousness of their status as a historically disadvantaged and unfulfilled group. Moreover, the legislative battle leading to Title VII of the 1964 Civil Rights Act—and the ensuing lack of federal initiative in pressing for strict enforcement of sex redress under that measure—led many women to mobilize ideologically for a new struggle. Similarly, a sense of unfulfillment and denial of their own potential encouraged a whole new generation of feminists to speak out against the covert and overt sexist practices of the civil rights movement and the Left. These developments combined to create a renewed interest among women in their collective identity, their public prospects and their private aspirations.

By the late 1960s the women's movement had once again, as in the earlier suffrage era, reached massive national dimensions. Women vigorously asserted their self-interest as they organized to lobby, to agitate and to create new cultural awareness and standards regarding the inequities of their position in society in general and in "progressive" protest structures in particular. This new women's initiative manifested itself in clear streams of historical ideological strategies.

As an extension of the earlier legal lobbying model of the suffragists, the National Organization for Women represented one such current. Its founders stressed women's legal rights and actively petitioned federal and state governments for meaningful actions in this area. NOW was to be, in its organizers' view, "a militant civil rights group." Indeed, NOW even touted itself publicly as an "NAACP for women," although the similarity of terminology reflected perhaps the only bridge between the two organizations.[4] On a conceptual level, the analogy of black and female discrimination remained prominent in the minds of NOW members at both the national and local levels, as witnessed, for example, by the Pittsburgh Chapter's "Notice to Job Seekers," which drew a parallel between race and sex discrimination in want ads.[5] By the 1970s NOW shared the national spotlight with other feminist legal-minded groups like the Women's Equity Action League and the National Women's Political Caucus, while the legal thrust of contemporary feminism itself became symbolized in the frenetic drive for a federal Equal Rights Amendment.

Radical women in the 1960s and 1970s, on the other hand, came to reject the legal branch in favor of the historical caste/class analysis of women's oppression. Radicals were determined to attack both the myriad institutions which discriminated against women and the ingrained cultural biases that sustained those institutions. Spurred to a rite of passage by the harsh realities of personal and group experiences as women, many young female radicals took the organizing skills and ideological lessons acquired from the civil rights and leftist movements and put them to use for feminist purposes. They defined their primary goal as one of total liberation. They clearly adopted

certain feminist ideologies from the past in striving to a$~$
particularly in cultural and economic realms. Black Pow$~$
and black scientific socialism were very much in the p$~$
as radical feminism grew. The principal ideological tactic$~$
feminism paralleled in compelling ways the strategies an$~$
nationalism, with its revolutionary perspectives on cultura$~$
agitation and immediacy. Radical women, like radical blacl$~$
fore, became the real ideological shock troops on the protest front as they
forcefully and dramatically repudiated the notion that removal of legal and
political shackles would solely create a truly egalitarian social mosaic.

In this pursuit of nonconsensus goals, radical women, like radical blacks,
adopted no-compromise politics and confrontation tactics as they placed
needs, not rights, at the center of their worldview. Some radicals even chose
to reject the dominant heterosexual living patterns in favor of alternative
arrangements. No single group or organization dominated the radical movement. Rather it was primarily ad hoc in nature, made up of independent
liberation "cells." Together these comprised a militant, radical community
in which like-minded individuals interacted; their communication network
ran the gamut from word-of-mouth to underground papers and manifestos
to sophisticated national publications. These protesters largely thought of
themselves as revolutionary ideological insurgents; they were, in fact, self-
proclaimed revolutionary feminists. A short passage from the classic "WITCH
Manifesto" reminds us of this: "Whatever is repressive, solely male-oriented,
greedy, puritanical, authoritarian—those are your targets. Your weapons are
. . . your own boundless beautiful imagination. Your power comes from your-
self as a woman, and it is activated by working in concert with your sisters."[6]

Radical ideology and tactics increasingly attracted supporters and sympa-
thizers from other protest groups and even from women not previously
supportive of feminism. By 1970 radicals had created numerous organizations
that exhibited considerable diversity in size, resources and continuity. While
groups like Redstockings, New York Radical Women and The Feminists represented the more visible element of the cultural wing of the movement, in
actuality less conspicuous local groups and individuals comprised the movement's true rank-and-file. There never appeared a radical organization of truly
national proportions that would have matched the scope and program of
SNCC and CORE in the black movement. Yet radical women were moved by
the ambiguities and ironies of existence and failed protest ideology not unlike
that expressed by black Americans.

This leads us to the conclusion that the structure, style and rhetoric of
black radicalism and radical feminism bore certain striking similarities, particularly with regard to a restated nationalistic mood. Perhaps the best comparison can be made by citing the parallels between the terms "Black Power"
and "Brotherhood" on the one hand and "Sisterhood is Powerful" and "Sisterhood" on the other. Both spoke to the radicals' revolutionary commitment
to achieving independent group power and solidarity among their respective

stituencies. Both rejected stereotypes such as "Sambo" and "femininity." The key to a liberation from myths, radicals argued, lay in "telling it like it is" and consciousness raising. In both cases local rap sessions and contact groups provided renewed energy and ideological insights for the movements. As participants talked about their experiences both in and out of the protest arena, they became aware of the fact that they shared common grievances and visions of a more equitable (i.e., a more perfect) future linked with cultural imperatives of self-determination.

A certain comparison may be drawn, as well, between black and feminist attempts to recover and reconstruct their past. New approaches influencing the methodology and interpretation of history came into vogue, resting on the assumption that blacks and women were distinct groups whose behavior in the present and past had been overtly and covertly manipulated by white supremacist males. Radicals led the crusade to illustrate how historical scholarship had subsumed their unique characteristics and collective accomplishments under the prescriptive roles assigned to nonwhite and nonmale groups. Since history traditionally had been written from a white male perspective, that approach had become the only significant measure of the past. Clearly such radical perceptions represented a crucial turning point. Positions stated in such tracts as H. Rap Brown's *Die Nigger Die!* and "Redstockings Manifesto" addressed this central theme of radical ideology: what is a group's identity and who defines it?[7] Ultimately efforts to deal with that issue produced the many black studies and women's studies curricular innovations and the numerous black cultural centers and women's centers on college campuses and in communities across the nation.

Assaults upon white male dominance and appeals to cultural autonomy attracted considerable public attention as blacks and women documented their historically marginal status in American life. Black Pride practitioners provided one measure of this as they sought to discard all white cultural baggage in favor of traditions and symbols associated with a new Pan-Africanism, or what Carmichael and Hamilton argued was "*our* image of ourselves."[8] Similarly, the new feminist analysis emphasized rejection of white male images of femininity. The Atlantic City protest of 1968 was the first event to focus the nation's attention on this matter. Later assaults like the WITCH bridal fair actions in New York and San Francisco further underscored these beliefs. In short order authors like Shulamith Firestone and Kate Millett articulated influential ideological restatements of women's cultural identity (i.e., theories of cultural oppression); Millett's theory on psychosexual imperialism especially won wide currency in the radical community. In the postscript to *Sexual Politics*, Millett stated: "The enormous social change involved in a sexual revolution is basically a matter of altered consciousness, the exposure and elimination of social and psychological realities underlining political and cultural structures. We are speaking, then, of a cultural revolution."[9]

Another converging point between the two movements under review is that much of the radicals' cultural thrust resulted in new or restated separatist thought and ventures. As in the case of black militancy, a fine line existed between outright physical separation and what some social historians have termed mental autonomy expressions of cultural consciousness.[10] Some women, to be specific, did as blacks had done, and adopted a personal or collective vision manifested in an outlook, an attitude, a value orientation or a perception of shared female identity—a variation on what feminist Simone de Beauvoir had referred to in existentialist terms as a recognition of "the Other."[11] In addition, there appeared certain women who severed past affiliations with men to establish alternative all-female living arrangements and allegiances. While militant black groups like the Republic of New Africa had advocated and exhibited similar attitudinal and behavioral patterns, women did so with greater difficulty, in part because of their more random distribution throughout the population across class, ethnic, religious, racial and regional lines, and in part because they lacked control of any geographically definable territory (such as an all-black neighborhood or an independent African or Caribbean nation-state that blacks could turn to for identity). Accordingly, separatist commitments by women were harder to achieve and, in demonstrable ways, were more creative endeavors. Some took the form of women's health care and self-help experiments, while others took shape— often under lesbian inspiration—in such physically autonomous endeavors as the Califia community, Olivia Records and Daughters, Inc. publishing house. Women who became practitioners of separatism, or what we might call psychological and cultural nationalism, often demonstrated most starkly the radicals' ideological dedication to intragroup strength, purpose and solidarity.

Meanwhile orthodox Marxists rejected most forms of radical feminism for fear that those in the cultural camp had adopted ideologies linked more to feminist perspectives than to time-honored economic determinism. As we have witnessed, the complex approaches to Marxism that radical blacks and feminists adopted represented a primary dedication to a fusing of race and gender protest strategies. Still, a general synthesis of sex and class did appear to characterize a good deal of the feminist movement, though it was never large or powerful enough to challenge or displace such mainstream feminist groups as NOW, WEAL and the NWPC. Shulamith Firestone outlined one such position in *The Dialectic of Sex* as follows: "I have attempted to take the class analysis one step further to its roots in the biological division of the sexes. We have not thrown out the insights of the socialists; on the contrary, radical feminism can enlarge their analysis, granting it an even deeper basis in objective conditions and thereby explaining many of its insolubles."[12]

Firestone's biological-economic theories of female oppression complemented and overlapped the similar conclusions of Simone de Beauvoir, Kate

Millett, Sheila Rowbotham, Charnie Guettel, Juliet Mitchell and Roxanne Dunbar, whose writings had in common two important hypotheses: (1) there could be no meaningful class and caste liberation without a social revolution and (2) there could be no meaningful social revolution without accompanying liberation in the realm of sex relations. Feminist Marxists scorned radical Marxist feminists for what the former perceived was feminism's lack of true commitment to the working-class struggle and dialectical materialism. For their part, radical socialist feminists feared that the Marxist view of economic oppression historically had sacrificed women's cultural imperatives. In the end, each faction remained implacably suspicious of the other's priorities and intentions. As Sheila Rowbotham noted, the two factions "cohabit in the same space somewhat uneasily. Each sits snorting at the other and using words which are strange and foreign to the other. Each is huffy and jealous about its own autonomy. They are at once incompatible and in real need of one another." Rowbotham provided further valuable insight into the complexity of the situation: "As a feminist and a Marxist I carry their contradictions within me and it is tempting to opt for one or the other in an effort to produce a tidy resolution of the commotion generated by the antagonism between them. But to do that would mean evading the social reality which gives rise to the antagonism. It would mean relying on pre-packaged formulas which come slickly off the tongue and then melt as soon as they are exposed to the light of day."[13]

RECAPITULATION

What emerges from the foregoing is the theme that the 1960s and 1970s represented a pivotal era when measured against the experiences of the historical women's movement, but one that was not necessarily spawned from black civil rights nor divorced from earlier feminist commitments to ideological battles. In this sense the women's movement from its inception through contemporary times has been one of commitment and rededication to self-defined goals. We have examined ideologically the emergence of the new feminism against the backdrop of another powerful social movement, the black crusade, rather than against the entire spectrum of active protest movements in those two decades. We have found that the resurgence of feminism in this era coincided with the great momentum of black civil rights and reflected certain intersections with it as well as divergences from it. We have concluded from the evidence at hand that contemporary feminism paralleled and reflected the nature of black civil rights, but neither grew from civil rights nor reflected a mere ideological extension of it. For contemporary women, political strategy might have been partly historical and partly borrowed, but spiritual empowerment came entirely from within.

A combination of elements in addition to civil rights converged in the 1960s to give rise to contemporary feminism. In major part women's own history helped define the ideological thrust and quicken pace of the new feminism. Furthermore, women of the 1960s and 1970s learned the techniques of modern protest thought and action from a number of historical and contemporary sources. A massive protest milieu that included civil rights, pacifism, the student movement and the New Left, among others, produced two overlapping generations of alumnae who joined other women to form, lead and validate their own self-defined and self-directed eclectic movement.

The effect of civil rights on contemporary feminism, in brief, may best be described as historically coincidental. That is to say, civil rights certainly set a mood for liberation and offered viable protest models, but it neither constructed nor offered formal ideological bridges between the two movements. Rather, the two protest phenomena pursued independent courses designed to nudge, or force, the American system into social responsiveness. Clearly, activists in both movements followed legal, cultural and economic strategies, none of which were mutually exclusive categories of protests. Many combined one or more of these approaches in an attempt to procure legal and economic redress, self-definition and self-determination. There were, of course, numerous instances of people and groups shifting from one strategy to another to meet the changing protest exigencies as conditions and priorities seemed to require. Yet each of the movements posed its own questions and designed its own blueprints for action. The fact remains that both movements have worked and are working for individual and group survival. Both have pursued ideological courses designed to create a more egalitarian, cooperative society in which the quality of the human spirit is measured by standards of personal dignity, potential and performance rather than by arbitrary culturally imposed criteria of proper place and role.

NOTES

1. Stokely Carmichael and Charles V. Hamilton, *Black Power: The Politics of Liberation in America* (New York: Vintage, 1967), 34–35.

2. Dorothy Elizabeth Johnson, "Organized Women and National Legislation, 1920–1941" (Ph.D. dissertation, Western Reserve University, 1960), 502–28.

3. Betty Friedan, *The Feminine Mystique* (New York: Dell, 1963), 11–94. See William O'Neill, *Everyone Was Brave: A History of Feminism in America* (Chicago: Quadrangle, 1971), 332; William Henry Chafe, *The American Woman: Her Changing Social, Economic, and Political Roles, 1920–1970* (New York: Oxford University Press, 1972), 199–225.

4. Betty Friedan, "How NOW Began" (mimeographed), Friedan Papers (partly restricted), Schlesinger Library, Cambridge, MA.

5. *NOW Hear This* (NOW newsletter), October 1969.

6. Women's International Terrorist Conspiracy from Hell, "The WITCH Manifesto" (mimeographed), Vertical File, Schlesinger Library.

7. H. Rap Brown, *Die Nigger Die!* (New York: Dial, 1969); "Redstockings Manifesto," Vertical File, Schlesinger Library.

8. Carmichael and Hamilton, *Black Power*, 37.

9. Kate Millett, *Sexual Politics* (New York: Avon, 1971), 473.

10. Robert L. Zangrando, "From Civil Rights to Black Liberation: The Unsettled 1960's," *Current History*, Vol. 57, No. 339 (1969), 281–86, 299; Gerda Lerner, "Placing Women in History: Definitions and Challenges," *Feminist Studies*, Vol. 3, No. 1/2 (1975), 5–14.

11. Simone de Beauvoir, *The Second Sex*, trans. and ed. H. M. Parshley (New York: Vintage, 1974 [1952]), xix.

12. Shulamith Firestone, *The Dialectic of Sex: The Case for Feminist Revolution* (New York: Bantam, 1970), 12.

13. Sheila Rowbotham, *Women, Resistance and Revolution: A History of Women and Revolution in the Modern World* (New York: Vintage, 1974), 246.

Selected Bibliography

PRIMARY SOURCES

Manuscripts and Related Data

Kimble, Lodovic, B. Personal Papers, Nashville, TN:
    Collection on the All-Afrikan People's Revolutionary Party
KNOW, Inc. Library, Pittsburgh, PA:
    KNOW, Inc. Business and Private Papers
Library of Congress, Washington, DC:
    National Association for the Advancement of Colored People Papers
    National Urban League Papers
Moorland-Spingarn Research Center, Howard University, Washington, DC:
    Ralph J. Bunche Oral History Collection, Taped Interviews

    Marion Barry Interview, 1967.

    Julian Bond Interview, 1968.

    Lester B. Granger Interview, 1968.

    David Hillard Interview on "Face the Nation," December 28, 1968.

    Charles E. McDew Interview, 1967.

    John Morsell Interview, 1967.

    Rosa Parks Interview, 1967.

    Bobby Seale Interview, 1968.

National Women's Education Fund, Washington, DC:
    National Office Files

National Women's Political Caucus, Washington, DC:
  National Office Files
Schlesinger Library on the History of Women in America, Cambridge, MA:

  Betty Friedan Papers

  National Organization for Women Papers

  Bernice Sandler Papers

  Vertical File on Contemporary Feminism

  Women's Equity Action League Papers

Shahady, Sandra Kovach. Personal Papers, Akron, OH:
  Collection on Feminist Separatist Ventures
Social Action Collection, State Historical Society of Wisconsin, Madison, WI:

  Ella Baker Papers

  Ann and Carl Braden Papers

  Congress of Racial Equality Papers

  Mimi Feingold Papers

  Aviva Futorian Papers

  Fannie Lou Hamer Papers

  Lillian Hamwee Papers

  Sandra Dugan Hard Papers

  Joan Jordan Papers

  Linda Seese Papers

  Third National Black Power Conference Papers

Women's Center. University of Pittsburgh, PA:
  Collection on Pittsburgh Area NOW

Unbound Sources

Benston, Margaret. "The Political Economy of Women's Liberation." New England Free
        Press reprint, probably 1972.
Carmichael, Stokely. Speech to the "May 4 Memorial Rally." Kent State University,
        Kent, OH, May 4, 1977.
Densmore, Dana. "Who is Saying Men are the Enemy?" KNOW, Inc. pamphlet.
ERAmerica, National Office, Washington, DC: Various pamphlets and literature.
Freeman, Jo. "The Women's Liberation Movement: Its Origins, Structure and Ideas."
        KNOW, Inc., reprint, n.d.
Gordon, Linda. "Towards a Radical Feminist History." KNOW, Inc. reprint.
KNOW News. September 1975. KNOW, Inc. Library (partly restricted), Pittsburgh, PA.
Jenness, Linda. "Socialism and the Fight for Women's Rights." Pathfinder pamphlet,
        1976.
New York Radical Women. *Notes from the First Year.* 1968.

New York Radical Feminists. *Notes from the Second Year*. 1970.

————. *Notes from the Third Year*. 1971.

"Nkrumaism [*sic*]: The Ideology of the All-Afrikan People's Revolutionary Party." Mimeographed. Author's personal papers.

Norton, Eleanor Holmes. Interview, "The MacNeil/Lehrer News Hour." Corporation for Public Broadcasting, P.B.S., February 12, 1988.

"Pan-Afrikanism: Why Afrikans World-Wide Must Support It." Mimeographed, n.d. Author's personal papers.

Reid, Willie Mae. "Black Women's Struggle for Equality." Pathfinder pamphlet, 1976.

"Resolutions of the 1971 Conference, 'Revolution: From the Doll's House to the White House!' Report of the Fifth Annual Conference of the National Organization for Women (NOW), Los Angeles, California, September 3–6, 1971." NOW Papers, Schlesinger Library.

Russ, Joanna. "The New Misandry: In Defense of Hating Men." KNOW, Inc. reprint.

Schlesinger Library on the History of Women In America. Cambridge, MA:

Hill, Myrna. "Feminism and Black Nationalism." Mimeographed, n.d.

New York Radical Women. "Principles." Mimeographed, probably 1967.

Radical Women. "Radical Women Manifesto: Theory, Programs and Structure." Mimeographed, April 1973.

————. "Revolutionary Socialist Feminists." Mimeographed.

"Redstockings." Mimeographed, 1970.

Redstockings. "Redstockings Manifesto." Mimeographed, 1969.

Women's International Terrorist Conspiracy from Hell. "The WITCH Manifesto." Mimeographed, probably 1968.

Solanas, Valerie. "SCUM Manifesto." Mimeographed. Friedan Papers.

University of Washington Libraries, Seattle, WA:

Fraser, Clara, *The Emancipation of Women*. Pamphlet. Seattle, WA: Radical Women Publications, n.d.

Gipple, Cindy. *The Women's Movement and the Class Struggle*. Pamphlet. Seattle, WA: Radical Women Publications, 1972.

Warrior, Betsy. "Battered Lives." KNOW, Inc. reprint, probably 1970.

Interviews with Author

Elizabeth Boyer. Cleveland, OH, August 11, 1977.

Stokely Carmichael. Akron, OH, October 8, 1976; November 10, 1977.

Kathryn Clarenbach. Washington, DC, October 28, 1977.

Catherine East. Arlington, VA, October 1, 1978.

Lodovic B. Kimble. Nashville, TN, June 3, 1988.

Lizabeth Moody. Cleveland, OH, November 17, 1977.

Pauli Murray. Alexandria, VA, October 30, 1977; September 22, 1978.

Eleanor Holmes Norton. Washington, DC, October 30, 1978.

Esther Peterson. Washington, DC, October 27, 1978.

Marguerite Rawalt. Arlington, VA, October 6, 1978.

Flo Scardenia. Pittsburgh, PA, February 22, 1977.

Sandra Kovach Shahady. Akron, OH, February 24, 1977; March 2, 1977; March 9, 1977.
Betsey Wright. Washington, DC, September 18, 1978.

U.S. Government Documents

American Women: Report of the President's Commission on the Status of Women.
    Washington, DC: Government Printing Office, 1963.
American Women, 1963–1968: Report of the Interdepartmental Committee on the
    Status of Women. Washington, DC: Government Printing Office, 1968.
Chisholm, Shirley. Speech to the Conference on Women's Employment. Hearings
    before the Special Subcommittee on Education of the Committee on Education
    and Labor, House, 91st Cong., 2d sess. Washington, DC: Government Printing
    Office, 1970.
Code of Federal Regulations, 1961–1970 (1962–1971).
Congressional Record (1983).
Equal Employment Opportunity Commission. *Equal Employment Opportunity, Report*
    No. 1: Job Patterns for Minorities and Women in Private Industry, 1966.
    Washington, DC: Government Printing Office, 1967.
————. *1st Annual Report.* Washington, DC: Government Printing Office, 1967.
Interdepartmental Committee on the Status of Women and the Citizens' Advisory
    Council on the Status of Women. *Targets for Action: The Report of the Third*
    National Conference of Commissions on the Status of Women. Washington,
    DC: Government Printing Office, 1966.
National Commission on the Observance of International Women's Year. *The Spirit*
    of Houston: The First National Women's Conference. Washington, DC: Gov-
    ernment Printing Office, 1978.
————. *To Form a More Perfect Union: Justice for American Women.* Washington,
    DC: Government Printing Office, 1976.
Report on Progress in 1965 on the Status of Women: Second Annual Report of
    Interdepartmental Committee and Citizens' Advisory Council on the Status of
    Women, December 31, 1965. Washington, DC: Government Printing Office,
    1965.
U.S. Statutes at Large, 1963–1964 (1964–1965).
U.S. Bureau of the Census. *U.S. Census of Population: 1960, Subject Reports, Nativity*
    *and Parentage.*Washington, DC: Government Printing Office, 1965.
U.S. Civil Service Commission. *Federal Employment of Women.* Washington, DC:
    Government Printing Office, 1966.
U.S. Commission on Civil Rights. *Federal Civil Rights Enforcement Effort.* Washington,
    DC: Government Printing Office, 1971–1975.
————. *Social Indicators of Equality for Minorities and Women.* Washington, DC:
    Government Printing Office, 1978.
————. *Statement on the Equal Rights Amendment.* Washington, DC: Government
    Printing Office, 1978.
————. *Women's Rights in the United States of America.* Washington, DC: Government
    Printing Office, 1979.

U.S. Congress, House. "House Joint Resolution Proposing an Amendment to the Constitution of the United States Relative to Equal Rights for Men and Women." H. J. Res. 1, 98th Cong. 1st sess., January 3, 1983. *Congressional Record,* Vol. 129, No. 1 (1983), 46.

U.S. Department of Commerce, Bureau of the Census. "USA Statistics in Brief, 1975: A Statistical Abstract Supplement." Pamphlet, 1975.

U.S. Department of Labor. *Directory of National and International Labor Unions in the United States, 1965: Listing of National and International Unions, State Labor Organizations, Developments Since 1963, Structure and Membership.* Washington, DC: Government Printing Office, 1966.

U.S. Department of Labor, Women's Bureau. "Fact Sheets on Trends in the Educational Attainment of Women." 1967.

―――. "Fact Sheet on the Earnings Gap." 1971.

―――. *1975 Handbook on Women Workers,* Bulletin 297.

―――. *Time of Change: 1983 Handbook on Women Workers.* Washington, DC: Government Printing Office, n.d.

Newspapers and Periodicals Consulted

Ain't I A Woman

Alternative Newsmagazine

Atlanta Journal and Constitution

The Black Worker

Chicago Bee

Communist

Delta Democratic Times (Greenville, MS)

Detroit News

Equal Rights

Everywoman

Fourth International

The Furies

Hera

International Socialist Review

It Ain't Me Babe

The Killer Dyke

Leviathan

The Liberator

The Militant

National NOW Times

National Observer

Newsday

New York Call

New York Review of Books

New York Times

New York Times Magazine

No More Fun and Games

NOW Act

NOW Hear This

Off Our Backs

Philadelphia Inquirer

Pittsburgh Courier

Pittsburgh Press

The Plain Dealer (Cleveland)

Rat

Richmond Afro-American

The Seed

Socialist Revolution

Social Revolution

Today (Brevard County, FL)

USA Today

The Village Voice

Voice of the Women's Liberation Movement

The Washington Post	Women's Studies Abstract
The Washington Star	*Women's Studies Newsletter*
Women: A Journal of Liberation	*Woodhull and Claflin's Weekly*
Women's Political Times	

Bound Sources

Atkinson, Ti-Grace. *Amazon Odyssey*. New York: Links, 1974.

Beauvoir, Simone de. *The Second Sex*. Trans. and ed. H. M. Parshley. New York: Vintage, 1974 [1952].

Bebel, August. *Woman Under Socialism*. Trans. Daniel De Leon. New York: Labor News, 1904 [1883].

Brown, H. Rap *Die Nigger Die!* New York: Dial, 1969.

Carmichael, Stokely, and Hamilton, Charles V. *Black Power: The Politics of Liberation in America*. New York: Vintage, 1967.

Cleaver, Eldridge. *Soul on Ice*. New York: Delta, 1968.

Cook, Blanche Wiesen, ed. *Crystal Eastman on Women and Revolution*. New York: Oxford University Press, 1978.

Dalla Costa, Mariarosa, and James, Selma. *The Power of Women and the Subversion of the Community*. London: Falling Wall, 1975.

Dennis, Peggy. *The Autobiography of an American Communist: A Personal View of a Political Life, 1925–1975*. Westport, CT: Lawrence Hill, 1977.

Engels, Frederick. *The Origin of the Family, Private Property and the State*. New York: International, 1942 [1884].

Firestone, Shulamith. *The Dialectic of Sex: The Case for Feminist Revolution*. New York: Bantam, 1970.

Flynn, Elizabeth Gurley. *I Speak My Own Piece: Autobiography of "The Rebel Girl."* New York: Masses and Mainstream, 1955.

———. *The Rebel Girl: An Autobiography, My First Life, 1906–1926*. New York: International, 1955.

Friedan, Betty. *It Changed My Life: Writings on the Women's Movement*. New York: Dell, 1977.

———. *The Feminine Mystique*. New York: Dell, 1963.

Fritz, Leah. *Dreamers and Dealers: An Intimate Appraisal of the Women's Movement*. Boston: Beacon, 1979.

Guettel, Charnie. *Marxism and Feminism*. Toronto: The Women's Press, 1974.

Jenness, Linda, ed. *Feminism and Socialism*. New York: Pathfinder, 1975.

King, Martin Luther, Jr. *Stride Toward Freedom: The Montgomery Story*. New York: Harper and Row, 1958.

———. *Where Do We Go from Here: Chaos or Community?* New York: Bantam, 1968.

Millett, Kate. *Sexual Politics*. New York: Avon, 1971.

Mitchell, Juliet. *Woman's Estate*. New York: Vintage, 1973.

Mitford, Jessica. *A Fine Old Conflict*. London: Michael Joseph, 1977.

Morgan, Robin. *Going Too Far: The Personal Chronicle of a Feminist*. New York: Vintage, 1978.

———, ed. *Sisterhood Is Powerful: An Anthology of Writings from the Women's Liberation Movement*. New York: Vintage, 1970.

Newton, Huey P. *Revolutionary Suicide*. New York: Harcourt Brace Jovanovich, 1973.

Reed, Evelyn. *Problems of Women's Liberation: A Marxist Approach*. New York: Pathfinder, 1976.

Rowbotham, Sheila. *Women's Consciousness, Man's World*. Baltimore: Penguin, 1973.

———. *Women, Resistance and Revolution: A History of Women and Revolution in the Modern World*. New York: Vintage, 1974.

Sellers, Cleveland. *The River of No Return: The Autobiography of a Black Militant and the Life and Death of SNCC*. New York: William Morrow, 1973.

Shulman, Alix Kates, ed. *Red Emma Speaks: Selected Writings and Speeches by Emma Goldman*. New York: Random House, 1972.

Stanton, Elizabeth Cady; Anthony, Susan B.; and Gage, Matilda Joslyn, eds. *History of Woman Suffrage*. Vol. 1 and Vol. 2. New York: Arno and the New York Times, 1969.

X, Malcolm, with Haley, Alex. *The Autobiography of Malcolm X*. New York: Grove, 1966.

Articles

Carmichael, Stokely. "Marxism-Leninism and Nkrumahism." *The Black Scholar*. Vol. 4, No. 5 (1973), 41–43.

Dalla Costa, Mariarosa. "Women and the Subversion of the Community." *Radical America*. Vol. 6, No. 1 (1972), 67–102.

Dennis, Peggy. "Letter of Resignation from the Communist Party, U.S.A." In Peggy Dennis, *The Autobiography of an American Communist: A Personal View of a Political Life, 1925–1975*. Westport, CT: Lawrence Hill, 1977, 289–96.

Dixon, Marlene. "On Women's Liberation: Where Are We Going?" *Radical America*. Vol. 4, No. 2 (1970), 26–35.

Dunbar, Roxanne. "Female Liberation as the Basis for Social Revolution." *Notes from the Second Year* (1970), 48–54.

"The Feminists: A Political Organization to Annihilate Sex Roles." *Notes from the Second Year* (1970), 114–18.

Forman, James. "Control, Conflict and Change: The Underlying Concepts of the Black Manifesto." In Robert S. Lecky and H. Elliott Wright, eds., *Black Manifesto: Religion, Racism, and Reparations*. New York: Sheed and Ward, 1969, 34–51.

———. "The Black Manifesto." In Floyd B. Barbour, ed., *The Black Seventies*. Boston: Porter Sargent, 1970, 296–308.

Hanish, Carol. "A Critique of the Miss America Protest." *Notes from the Second Year* (1970), 86–88.

———. "The Liberal Takeover of Women's Liberation." In Redstockings of the Women's Liberation Movement, ed., *Feminist Revolution: An Abridged Edition with Additional Writings*. New York: Random House, 1978, 163–67.

Hayden, Casey, and King, Mary. "Sex and Caste: A Kind of Memo from Casey Hayden and Mary King to a Number of Other Women in the Peace and Freedom Movements." *Liberation* (April 1966), 35–36.

"Ideological Statement by Congress of African People." *Pan-African Journal*. Vol. 4, No. 1 (1971), 1–7.

"Issues: Consciousness Raising." *Notes from the Second Year*. Section 3 (1970), 76–86.

James, Selma. "Women and the Subversion of the Community: Introduction to the English Translation." *Radical America*. Vol. 6, No. 1 (1972), 62–67.

Koedt, Anne. "Lesbianism and Feminism." *Notes from the Third Year* (1971), 84–89.

———. "Women and the Radical Movement." *Notes from the First Year* (1968), n.p.

Leon, Barbara. "Separate to Integrate." In Redstockings of the Women's Liberation Movement, ed., *Feminist Revolution: An Abridged Edition with Additional Writings*. New York: Random House, 1978, 152–57.

Minnis, Jack. "The Mississippi Freedom Democratic Party: A New Declaration of Independence." *Freedomways*. Vol. 5, No. 2 (1965), 264–78.

Mitchell, Juliet. "Women: The Longest Revolution." *New Left Review*. No. 40 (November–December 1966), 11–37.

National Black Feminist Organization. "Statement of Purpose." In Ella Lasky, ed., *Humanness: An Exploration into the Mythologies about Women and Men*. Borough of Manhattan: Community College of CUNY, 1975, 410.

One, Varda. "Manglish." *Everywoman*, May 29, 1970; July 10, 1970; November 12, 1971.

"The Opportunity Presidential Poll." *Opportunity*. Vol. 10 (May 1932), 141.

"Politics of the Ego: A Manifesto for N.Y. Radical Feminists." *Notes from the Second Year* (1970), 124–26.

Radicalesbians. "The Woman Identified Woman." *Notes from the Third Year* (1971), 81–84.

"Redstockings Manifesto." *Notes from the Second Year* (1970), 112–13.

Ristorucci, Carmen. "Why We Oppose the ERA." *Political Affairs*. Vol. 55, No. 3 (1975), 8–17.

"The Roosevelt Record." *The Crisis*. Vol. 47 (November 1940), 343.

Sarachild, Kathie. "Consciousness-Raising: A Radical Weapon." In Redstockings of the Women's Liberation Movement, ed., *Feminist Revolution: An Abridged Edition with Additional Writings*. New York: Random House, 1978, 144–50.

———. "The Power of History." In Redstockings of the Women's Liberation Movement, ed., *Feminist Revolution: An Abridged Edition with Additional Writings*. New York: Random House, 1978, 13–43.

White, Walter. "The Negro and the Communists." *Harper's Magazine*. Vol. 164, December 1931, 62–72.

"Witch." In Robin Morgan, ed., *Sisterhood Is Powerful: An Anthology of Writings from the Women's Liberation Movement*. New York: Vintage, 1970, 603–21.

"The Woman Wage Earner: Her Situation Today." *Women's Bureau Bulletin*. No. 172 (1939), 48.

Supreme Court Cases

Arizona Governing Committee for Tax Deferred Annuity and Deferred Compensation Plans, etc., et al., Petitioners v. *Nathalie Norris etc., No. 82–52. The United States Law Week*, Vol. 51, No. 50, Extra Edition No. 6 (1983), 5243–53.

Bellotti, Attorney General of Massachusetts v. *Baird*. 428 U.S. 132 (1979).

Brown et al. v. *Board of Education of Topeka, Shawnee County, Kan. et al.* 347, U.S. 483 (1954).

Califano v. *Goldfarb*. 430 U.S. 199 (1977).

City of Akron v. *Akron Center for Reproductive Health, Inc., Nos. 81–746 and 81–1172. The United States Law Week*, Vol. 51, No. 48 (1983), 4762–83.

City of Los Angeles, Department of Water and Power v. *Manhart.* 435 U.S. 702 (1978).

Doe v. *Bolton, Attorney General of Georgia.* 410 U.S. 179 (1973).

Frontiero v. *Richardson, Secretary of Defense.* 411 U.S. 677 (1973).

Harris v. *McRae.* 448 U.S. 297 (1980).

Griswold v. *Connecticut.* 381 U.S. 479 (1965).

Harris v. *McRae. No. 79–1268. The United States Law Week.* Vol. 48, No. 50 (1980), 4941–60.

Mitchell v. *United States et al.* 313 U.S. 577 (1941).

Nashville Gas Co. v. *Satty.* 434 U.S. 136 (1977).

Planned Parenthood of Central Missouri v. *Danforth, Attorney General of Missouri.* 428 U.S. 52 (1976).

Regents of the University of California v. *Bakke.* 438 U.S. 265 (1978).

Roe v. *Wade, District Attorney of Dallas County.* 410 U.S. 113 (1973).

Smith v. *Allwright, Election Judge et al.* 321 U.S. 649 (1944).

Taylor v. *Louisiana.* 419 U.S. 522 (1975).

United Steel Workers of America v. *Weber.* 443 U.S. 193 (1979).

GENERAL WORKS

Books

Carden, Maren Lockwood. *The New Feminist Movement.* New York: Russell Sage Foundation, 1974.

Chafe, William Henry. *The American Woman: Her Changing Social, Economic, and Political Roles, 1920–1970.* New York: Oxford University Press, 1972.

———. *Women and Equality: Changing Patterns in American Culture.* New York: Oxford University Press, 1977.

Deckard, Barbara Sinclair. *The Women's Movement: Political, Socioeconomic, and Psychological Issues.* New York: Harper and Row, 1975.

Flexner, Eleanor. *Century of Struggle: The Woman's Rights Movement in the United States.* New York: Atheneum, 1974.

Freeman, Jo. *The Politics of Women's Liberation: A Case Study of an Emerging Social Movement and Its Relation to the Policy Process.* New York: David McKay, 1975.

Hole, Judith, and Levine, Ellen. *Rebirth of Feminism.* New York: Quadrangle, 1971.

Kraditor, Aileen S. *The Ideas of the Woman Suffrage Movement, 1890–1920.* New York: Columbia University Press, 1965.

———, ed. *Up From the Pedestal: Selected Writings in the History of American Feminism.* Chicago: Quadrangle, 1968.

O'Neill, William L. *Everyone Was Brave: A History of Feminism in America.* Chicago: Quadrangle, 1971.

Rothman, Sheila M. *Woman's Proper Place: A History of Changing Ideals and Practices, 1970 to the Present.* New York: Basic, 1978.

Sochen, June. *Movers and Shakers: American Women Thinkers and Activists, 1900–1970.* New York: Quadrangle, 1973.

Yates, Gayle Graham. *What Women Want: The Ideas of the Movement.* Cambridge, MA: Harvard University Press, 1975.

Articles

Freeman, Jo. "The Origins of the Women's Liberation Movement." *American Journal of Sociology*. Vol. 78, No. 4 (1973), 792–811.

Hacker, Helen Mayer. "Women as a Minority Group." *Social Forces*. Vol. 30, No. 1 (1951), 60–69.

Lerner, Gerda. "New Approaches to the Study of Women in American History." *Journal of Social History*. Vol. 3, No. 1(1969), 53–62.

———. "Placing Women in History: Definitions and Challenges." *Feminist Studies*. Vol. 3, No. 1/2 (1975), 5–14.

"The New Woman and the New History." *Feminist Studies*. Vol. 3, No. 1/2 (1975), 185–98.

Riley, Glenda Gates. "The Subtle Subversion: Changes in the Traditional Image of the American Woman." *The Historian*. Vol. 32, No. 2 (1970), 210–27.

Welter, Barbara. "The Cult of True Womanhood, 1820–1860." *American Quarterly*. Vol. 18, No. 2 (1966), 151–74.

Zangrando, Robert L. "From Civil Rights to Black Liberation: The Unsettled 1960's." *Current History*. Vol. 57, No. 339 (1969), 281–86, 299.

LEGAL-ORIENTED WORKS

Books

DuBois, Ellen Carol. *Feminism and Suffrage: The Emergence of an Independent Women's Movement in America, 1848–1869*. Ithaca, NY: Cornell University Press, 1978.

Finch, Minnie. *The NAACP: Its Fight for Justice*. Metuchen, NJ: Scarecrow, 1981.

Kellogg, Charles Flint. *NAACP: A History of the National Association for the Advancement of Colored People*. Vol. 1: *1909–1920*. Baltimore: Johns Hopkins Press, 1967.

Kessler-Harris, Alice. *Out to Work: A History of Wage-Earning Women in the United States*. New York: Oxford University Press, 1982.

———. *Women Have Always Worked: A Historical Overview*. Old Westbury, NY: The Feminist Press, 1981.

Lemons, J. Stanley. *The Woman Citizen: Social Feminism in the 1920s*. Urbana: University of Illinois Press, 1973.

Weiss, Nancy J. *The National Urban League, 1910–1940*. New York: Oxford University Press, 1974.

Zangrando, Robert L. *The NAACP Crusade Against Lynching, 1909–1950*. Philadelphia: Temple University Press, 1980.

Articles

Brown, Wendy. "Reproductive Freedom and the Right to Privacy: A Paradox for Feminists." In Irene Diamond, ed., *Families, Politics, and Public Policy: A Feminist Dialogue on Women and the State*. New York: Longman, 1983, 322–38.

Freeman, Jo. "The Legal Basis of the Sexual Caste System." *Valparaiso Law Review*. Vol. 5, No. 2 (1971), 203–36.

Glen, Kristin Booth. "Abortion in the Courts: A Laywoman's Historical Guide to the New Disaster Area." *Feminist Studies*. Vol. 4, No. 1 (1978), 1–26.

Harrison, Cynthia E. "A 'New Frontier' for Women: The Public Policy of the Kennedy Administration." *Journal of American History*. Vol. 67, No. 3 (1980), 630–46.

Murray, Pauli. "The Liberation of Black Women." In Mary Lou Thompson ed., *Voices of the New Feminism*. Boston: Beacon, 1970, 87–102.

Sexton, Patricia Cayo. "Workers (Female) Arise!: On Founding the Coalition of Labor Union Women." *Dissent*. Vol. 21, No. 3 (1974), 380–95.

Zangrando, Robert L. "The Direction of the March." *Negro History Bulletin*. Vol. 27, No. 3 (1963), 60–64.

———. "The NAACP and a Federal Antilynching Bill, 1934–1940." *The Journal of Negro History*. Vol. 50, No. 2 (1965), 106–17.

CULTURAL/RADICAL-ORIENTED WORKS

Books

Bracey, John H., Jr., Meier, August, and Rudwick, Elliott, eds. *Black Nationalism in America*. Indianapolis: Bobbs-Merrill, 1970.

Brownmiller, Susan. *Against Our Will: Men, Women, and Rape*. New York: Simon and Schuster, 1975.

Cronon, E. David. *Black Moses: The Story of Marcus Garvey and the Universal Negro Improvement Association*. Madison: University of Wisconsin Press, 1969.

Davis, Angela Y. *Women, Race and Class*. New York: Vintage, 1983.

Evans, Sara. *Personal Politics: The Roots of Women's Liberation in the Civil Rights Movement and the New Left*. New York: Vintage, 1979.

Hall, Raymond L. *Black Separatism in the United States*. Hanover, NJ: University Press of New England, 1978.

Irwin, Inez Haynes. *The Story of the Woman's Party*. New York: Harcourt, Brace, 1921.

———. *Up Hill with Banners Flying*. Penobscot, ME: Traversity, 1964.

Kinzer, Nora Scott. *Put Down and Ripped Off: The American Woman and the Beauty Cult*. New York: Thomas Y. Crowell, 1977.

Marsh, Margaret S. *Anarchist Women, 1870–1920*. Philadelphia: Temple University Press, 1981.

Meier, August, and Rudwick, Elliott. *CORE: A Study in the Civil Rights Movement, 1942–1968*. New York: Oxford University Press, 1973.

Nkrumah, Kwame. *Neo-Colonialism: The Last Stage of Imperialism*. New York: International, 1965.

Vincent, Theodore G. *Black Power and the Garvey Movement*. Berkeley, CA: Ramparts, 1971.

Zinn, Howard. *SNCC: The New Abolitionists*. Boston: Beacon, 1965.

Articles

Abbott, Sidney, and Love, Barbara. "Is Women's Liberation a Lesbian Plot?" In Vivian Gornick and Barbara K. Moran, eds., *Woman in Sexist Society: Studies in Power and Powerlessness*. New York: Mentor, 1971, 601–21.

"Consciousness Raising." In Anne Koedt, Ellen Levine and Anita Rapone, eds., *Radical Feminism*. New York: Quadrangle, 1973, 280–81.

Cook, Blanche Wiesen. "Female Support Networks and Political Activism: Lillian Wald, Crystal Eastman, Emma Goldman." *Crysalis*. No. 3 (Fall 1977), 43–61.

Hanish, Carol. "The Liberal Takeover of Women's Liberation." In Redstockings of the Women's Liberation Movement, ed., *Feminist Revolution: An Abridged Edition with Additional Writings*. New York: Random House, 1978, 163–67.

Hayler, Barbara. "Abortion." *Signs*. Vol. 5, No. 2 (1979), 307–23.

Koedt, Anne. "Women and the Radical Movement." *Notes from the First Year*, 1968.

Lewis, Diane K. "A Response to Inequality: Black Women, Racism, and Sexism." *Signs*. Vol. 3, No. 2 (1977), 339–61.

Marsh, Margaret S. "The Anarchist-Feminist Response to the 'Woman Question' in Late Nineteenth-Century America." *American Quarterly*. Vol. 30, No. 4 (1978), 533–47.

Piercy, Marge. "The Grand Coolie Dam." *Leviathan*, October–November 1969.

Shulman, Alix Kates. "Sex and Power: Sexual Basis of Radical Feminism." *Signs*. Vol. 5, No. 4 (1980), 590–604.

Smith-Rosenberg, Carroll. "The Female World of Love and Ritual: Relations Between Women in Nineteenth-Century America." *Signs*. Vol. 1, No. 1 (1975), 1–29.

Stimpson, Catharine. " 'Thy Neighbor's Wife, Thy Neighbor's Servants': Woman's Liberation and Black Civil Rights." In Vivian Gornick and Barbara K. Moran, eds., *Woman in Sexist Society: Studies in Power and Powerlessness*. New York: Mentor, 1972, 622–57.

Valeska, Lucia. "The Future of Female Separatism." *Quest*. Vol. 12, No. 2 (1975), 2–16.

ECONOMIC-ORIENTED WORKS

Books

Buhle, Mari Jo. *Women and American Socialism, 1870–1920*. Urbana: University of Illinois Press, 1981.

Johnson, Olive M. *Woman and the Socialist Movement*. New York: Socialist Labor Party, 1919.

Padmore, George. *Pan-Africanism or Communism*. Garden City, NY: Doubleday, 1971.

Record, Wilson. *Race and Radicalism: The NAACP and the Communist Party in Conflict*. Ithaca, NY: Cornell University Press, 1964.

———. *The Negro and the Communist Party*. Chapel Hill: University of North Carolina Press, 1951.

Rowbotham, Sheila. *Hidden from History: Rediscovering Women in History from the 17th Century to the Present*. New York: Vintage, 1974.

Tax, Meredith. *The Rising of the Women: Feminist Solidarity and Class Conflict, 1880–1917*. New York: Monthly Review, 1980.

Weinbaum, Batya. *The Curious Courtship of Women's Liberation and Socialism*. Boston: South End, 1978.

Women's Liberation and the Socialist Revolution. New York: Pathfinder, 1979.

Articles

Buhle, Mari Jo. "Women and the Socialist Party, 1901–1914." In Edith Hoshino Altbach, ed., *From Feminism to Liberation*. Cambridge, MA: Schenkman, 1971, 65–86.

Dancis, Bruce. "Socialism and Women in the United States, 1900–1917." *Socialist Revolution*, Vol. 27 (January–March 1976), 81–114.

Dill, Bonnie Thornton. "The Dialectics of Black Womanhood." *Signs*. Vol. 4, No. 3 (1979), 543–55.

Eisenstein, Zillah. "Developing a Theory of Capitalist Patriarchy and Socialist Feminism." In Zillah R. Eisenstein, ed., *Capitalist Patriarchy and the Case for Socialist Feminism*. New York: Monthly Review, 1979, 5–40.

Gimenez, Martha E. "Marxism and Feminism." *Frontiers*. Vol. 1, No. 1 (1975), 61–79.

MacKinnon, Catharine, A. "Feminism, Marxism, Method, and the State: An Agenda for Theory." In Nannerl O. Keohane, Michelle Z. Rosaldo and Barbara C. Gelpi, eds., *Feminist Theory: A Critique of Ideology*. Chicago: University of Chicago Press, 1982, 1–30.

Miller, Sally M. "Women in the Party Bureaucracy: Subservient Functionaries." In Sally M. Miller, ed., *Flawed Liberation: Socialism and Feminism*. Westport, CT: Greenwood, 1981, 13–35.

Mitchell, Juliet. "Women: The Longest Revolution." *New Left Review*. No. 40 (November–December 1966), 11–37.

Mouledous, Joseph C. "From Browderism to Peaceful Co-Existence: An Analysis of Developments in the Communist Position on the American Negro." *Phylon*. Vol. 25, No. 1 (1964), 79–90.

Naison, Mark. "Marxism and Black Radicalism in America: Notes on a Long (and Continuing) Journey." *Radical America*. Vol. 5, No. 3 (1971), 3–25.

Record, Wilson C. "The Development of the Communist Position on the Negro Question in the United States." *Phylon*. Vol. 19, No. 3 (1958), 306–26.

Ursel, Jane. "The Nature and Origin of Women's Oppression: Marxism and Feminism." *Contemporary Crisis*. Vol. 1, No. 1 (1977), 23–36.

Wolfman, Brunetta R. "The Communist Party, Always Out of Step." In Raymond L. Hall, ed., *Black Separatism and Social Reality: Rhetoric and Reason*. New York: Pergamon, 1977, 109–14.

DISSERTATIONS

Buhle, Mari Jo. "Feminism and Socialism in the United States, 1820–1920." Ph.D. dissertation, University of Wisconsin, 1974.

Carson, Clayborne, Jr. "Toward Freedom and Community: The Evolution of Ideas in the Student Nonviolent Coordinating Committee, 1960–1966." Ph.D. dissertation, University of California, Los Angeles, 1975.

Evans, Sara Margaret. "Personal Politics: The Roots of Women's Liberation in the Civil Rights Movement and the New Left." Ph.D. dissertation, University of North Carolina, 1976.

Gilman, Stuart C. "An Analysis of American Black Political Thought in the 1960s from a Marxist Perspective: The Phenomenological Approach." Ph.D. dissertation, Miami University, Oxford, OH, 1974.

Johnson, Dorothy Elizabeth. "Organized Women and National Legislation, 1920–1941."
    Ph.D. dissertation, Western Reserve University, 1960.
Jones, Clinton P. "Black Power: An Analysis of Select Strategies for the Implementation
    of Concept." Ph.D. dissertation, Claremont Graduate School, 1971.
Kifer, Allen. "The Negro Under the New Deal, 1933–1941." Ph.D. dissertation, Uni-
    versity of Wisconsin, 1961.
Rothschild, Mary Aickin. "Northern Volunteers and the Southern 'Freedom Summers,'
    1964–1965: A Social History." Ph.D. dissertation, University of Washington, 1974.
Yates, Gayle Graham. "Ideologies of Contemporary American Feminism." Ph.D. dis-
    sertation, University of Minnesota, 1973.
Zimmerman, Loretta Ellen. "Alice Paul and the National Woman's Party, 1912–1920."
    Ph.D. dissertation, Tulane University, 1964.

Index

About the Author

IRVIN D. SOLOMON, who has taught extensively at both the undergraduate and graduate levels, holds a Ph.D. with concentrations in Afro-American history and the history of women in America. Currently, Solomon teaches honors history and Third World studies courses at Edison Community College in Fort Myers, Florida.